· SERMONS ON ·

WOMEN OF THE
NEW TESTAMENT

· SERMONS ON ·
WOMEN OF THE NEW TESTAMENT

C.H. Spurgeon

HENDRICKSON
PUBLISHERS

Sermons on Women of the New Testament

© 2016 Hendrickson Publishers Marketing, LLC
P. O. Box 3473
Peabody, Massachusetts 01961-3473

ISBN 978-1-61970-811-2

Originally published by Hendrickson Publishers in *Sermons on Women of the Bible.*

Printed in the United States of America

Cover photo of Charles Haddon (C. H.) Spurgeon by Herbert Rose Barraud is used by permission of the University of Minnesota Libraries, Special Collections and Rare Books.

Contents

Preface

Charles Haddon Spurgeon
1834–1892

Ask most people today who Charles Haddon Spurgeon was, and you might be surprised at the answers. Most know he was a preacher, others remember that he was Baptist, and others go so far as to remember that he lived in England during the nineteenth century. All of this is true, yet Charles Haddon Spurgeon was so much more.

Born into a family of Congregationalists in 1834, Spurgeon's father and grandfather were both Independent preachers. These designations seem benign today, but in the mid-nineteenth century, they describe a family committed to a Nonconformist path—meaning they did not conform to the established Church of England. Spurgeon grew up in a rural village, a village virtually cut off from the Industrial Revolution rolling over most of England.

Spurgeon became a Christian at a Primitive Methodist meeting in 1850 at age sixteen. He soon became a Baptist (to the sorrow of his mother) and almost immediately began to preach. Considered a preaching prodigy—"a boy wonder of the fens"—Spurgeon attracted huge audiences and garnered a reputation that reached throughout the countryside and into London. As a result of his great success, Spurgeon was invited to preach at the New Park Street Chapel in London in 1854, when he was just nineteen. When he first preached at the church, they were unable to fill even two hundred seats. Within the year, Spurgeon filled the twelve-hundred-seat church to overflowing. He soon began preaching in larger and larger venues, outgrowing each, until finally in 1861 the Metropolitan Tabernacle was completed, which seated six thousand persons. This would be Spurgeon's home base for the rest of his career, until his death in 1892 at age fifty-seven.

Spurgeon married Susannah Thompson in 1856 and soon they had twin sons, Charles and Thomas, who would later follow him in his work. Spurgeon opened Pastors' College, a training school for preachers, which trained over nine hundred preachers during his lifetime. He also opened orphanages for underprivileged boys and girls, providing education to each of the orphans. And with Susannah, he developed a program to publish and distribute Christian literature. He is said to have preached to over ten million people in his forty years of ministry. His sermons sold over twenty-five thousand copies each week and were translated into twenty languages. He was utterly committed to spreading the gospel through preaching and through the written word.

During Spurgeon's lifetime, the Industrial Revolution transformed England from a rural, agricultural society to an urban, industrial society, with all the attendant difficulties and horrors of a society in major transition. The people displaced by these sweeping changes—factory workers and shopkeepers—became Spurgeon's congregation. From a small village himself and transplanted to a large and inhospitable city, he was a common man and understood innately the spiritual needs of the common people. He was a communicator who made the gospel so relevant, who spoke so brilliantly to people's deepest needs, that listeners welcomed his message.

Keep in mind that Spurgeon preached in the days before microphones or speakers; in other words, he preached without benefit of amplifier systems. Once he preached to a crowd of over twenty-three thousand people without mechanical amplification of any sort. He himself was the electrifying presence on the platform: he did not stand and simply read a stilted sermon. Spurgeon used an outline, developing his themes extemporaneously, and speaking "in common language to common people." His sermons were filled with stories and poetry, drama and emotion. He was larger than life, always in motion, striding back and forth across the stage. He gestured broadly, acted out stories, used humor, and painted word pictures. For Spurgeon, preaching was about communicating the truth of God, and he would use any gift at his disposal to accomplish this.

Spurgeon's preaching was anchored in his spiritual life, a life rich in prayer and the study of Scripture. He was not tempted by fashion, be it theological, social, or political. Scripture was the cornerstone of Spurgeon's life and his preaching. He was an expositional preacher mostly, exploring a passage of Scripture for its meaning both within the text as well as in the lives of each member of his congregation. To Spurgeon, Scripture was alive and specifically relevant to people's lives, whatever their social status, economic situation, or time in which they lived.

One has a sense that Spurgeon embraced God's revelation completely: God's revelation through Jesus Christ, through Scripture, and through his own prayer and study. For him, revelation was not a finished act: God still reveals himself, if one made oneself available. Some recognize Spurgeon for the mystic he was, one who was willing and eager to explore the mysteries of God, able to live with those bits of truth that do not conform to a particular system of theology, perfectly comfortable with saying, "This I know, and this I don't know—yet will I trust."

Each of the sermons in this collection was preached at a different time in Spurgeon's career and each has distinct characteristics. These sermons are not a series, as they were not created or intended to be sequential, nor have they been homogenized or edited to sound as though they are all of a kind. Instead, they reflect the preacher himself, allowing the voice of this remarkable man to ring clearly as he guides the reader into a particular account, a particular event—to experience, with Spurgeon, God's particular revelation.

As you read, *listen*. These words were meant to be heard, not merely read. Listen carefully and you will hear the cadences of this remarkable preaching, the echoes of God's timeless truth traveling across the years. And above all, enjoy Spurgeon's enthusiasm, his fire, his devotion, his zeal to recognize and respond to God's timeless invitation to engage the Creator himself.

The Mother of Jesus: Mary's Song

Delivered on Sunday morning, December 25, 1864, at the Metropolitan Tabernacle, Newington. No. 606.

And Mary said, "My soul doth magnify the Lord, and my spirit hath rejoiced in God my Savior."—LUKE 1:46–47

Mary was on a visit when she expressed her joy in the language of this noble song. It were well if all our social intercourse were as useful to our hearts as this visit was to Mary. "Iron sharpeneth iron; so a man sharpeneth the countenance of his friend"; Mary, full of faith, goes to see Elizabeth, who is also full of holy confidence, and the two are not long together before their faith mounts to full assurance, and their full assurance bursts forth in a torrent of sacred praise. This praise aroused their slumbering powers, and instead of two ordinary village women, we see before us two prophetesses and poetesses, upon whom the Spirit of God abundantly rested. When we meet with our kinsfolk and acquaintance, let it be our prayer to God that our communion may be not only pleasant, but profitable; that we may not merely pass away time and spend a pleasant hour, but may advance a day's march nearer heaven, and acquire greater fitness for our eternal rest.

Observe, this morning, the sacred joy of Mary that you may imitate it. This is a season when all men expect us to be joyous. We compliment each other with the desire that we may have a "Merry Christmas." Some Christians who are a little squeamish, do not like the word *merry*. It is a right good old Saxon word, having the joy of childhood and the mirth of manhood in it, it brings before one's mind the old song of the waits, and the midnight peal of bells, the holly and the blazing log. I love it for its place in that most tender of all parables, where it is written, that, when the long-lost prodigal returned to his father safe and sound, "They began to be merry." This is the season when we are expected to be happy; and my heart's desire is that, in the highest and best sense, you who are believers may be "merry." Mary's heart was merry within her; but here was the mark of her joy, it was all holy merriment, it was every drop of it sacred mirth. It was not such merriment as worldlings will revel in today and tomorrow, but such merriment as the angels have around the throne, where they sing, "Glory to God in the highest," while we sing, "On earth peace, goodwill toward men." Such merry hearts have a continual feast. I want you, children of the bride chamber, to possess today and tomorrow, yes, all your days, the high and consecrated bliss of Mary, that you may not only read her words, but use them for yourselves, ever experiencing their meaning: "My soul doth magnify the Lord, and my spirit hath rejoiced in God my Savior."

Observe, first, that she sings; second, she sings sweetly; third, shall she sing alone?

I. First observe, that Mary sings.

Her subject is a Savior; she hails the incarnate God. The long-expected Messiah is about to appear. He for whom prophets and princes waited long is now about to come, to be born of the Virgin of Nazareth. Truly there was never a subject of sweeter song than this—the stooping down of Godhead to the feebleness of manhood. When God manifested his power in the works of his hands, the morning stars sang together, and the sons of God shouted for joy; but when God manifests himself, what music shall suffice for the grand psalm of adoring wonder? When wisdom and power are seen, these are but attributes; but in the incarnation it is the divine person which is revealed wrapped in a veil of our inferior clay: well might Mary sing, when earth and heaven even now are wondering at the condescending grace.

Worthy of peerless music is the fact that "the Word was made flesh and dwelt among us." There is no longer a great gulf fixed between God and his people; the humanity of Christ has bridged it over. We can no more think that God sits on high, indifferent to the wants and woes of men, for God has visited us and come down to the lowliness of our estate. No longer need we bemoan that we can never participate in the moral glory and purity of God, for if God in glory can come down to his sinful creature, it is certainly less difficult to bear that creature, blood washed and purified, up that starry way, that the redeemed one may sit down forever on his throne. Let us dream no longer in somber sadness that we cannot draw near to God so that he will really hear our prayer and pity our necessities, seeing that Jesus has become bone of our bone and flesh of our flesh, born a babe as we are born, living a man as we must live, bearing the same infirmities and sorrows, and bowing his head to the same death. Oh, can we not come with boldness by this new and living way, and have access to the throne of the heavenly grace, when Jesus meets us as Emmanuel, God with us? Angels sang, they scarcely knew why. Could they understand why God had become man? They must have known that herein was a mystery of condescension; but all the loving consequences which the incarnation involved even their acute minds could scarcely have guessed; but we see the whole, and comprehend the grand design most fully. The manger of Bethlehem was big with glory; in the incarnation was wrapped up all the blessedness by which a soul, snatched from the depths of sin, is lifted up to the heights of glory. Shall not our clearer knowledge lead us to heights of song which angelic guesses could not reach? Shall the lips of cherubs move to flaming sonnets, and shall we who are redeemed by the blood of the incarnate God be treacherously and ungratefully silent!

> *Did archangels sing thy coming?*
> *Did the shepherds learn their lays?*
> *Shame would cover me, ungrateful,*
> *Should my tongue refuse to praise.*

This, however, was not the full subject of her holy hymn. Her peculiar delight was not that there was a Savior to be born, but that *he was to be born of her.* Blessed among women was she, and highly favored of the Lord; but we can enjoy the same favor; no, we must enjoy it, or the coming of a Savior will be of no avail to us. Christ on Calvary, I know, takes away the sin of his people; but none have ever known the virtue of Christ upon the cross, unless they have the Lord Jesus formed in them as the hope of glory. The stress of the Virgin's canticle is laid upon God's special grace to her. Those little words, the personal pronouns, tell us that it was truly a personal affair with her. "My soul doth magnify the Lord, and my spirit hath rejoiced in God my Savior." The Savior was peculiarly, and in a special sense, hers. She sang no "Christ for all"; but *"Christ for me"* was her glad subject. Beloved, is Christ Jesus in your heart? Once you looked at him from a distance, and that look cured you of all spiritual diseases, but are you now living upon him, receiving him into your very vitals as your spiritual meat and drink? In holy fellowship you have oftentimes fed upon his flesh and been made to drink of his blood; you have been buried with him in baptism unto death; you have yielded yourselves a sacrifice to him, and you have taken him to be a sacrifice for you; you can sing of him as the spouse did, "His left hand is under my head, and his right hand doth embrace me. . . . My beloved is mine, and I am his: he feedeth among the lilies." This is a happy style of living, and all short of this poor slavish work. Oh! you can never know the joy of Mary unless Christ becomes truly and really yours; but oh! when he is yours, yours within, reigning in your heart, yours controlling all your passions, yours changing your nature, subduing your corruptions, inspiring you with hallowed emotions; yours within, a joy unspeakable and full of glory—oh! then you *can* sing, you *must* sing, who can restrain your tongue? If all the scoffers and mockers upon earth should bid you hold your peace, you must sing; for your spirit must rejoice in God your Savior.

We should miss much instruction if we overlooked the fact that the choice poem before us is *a hymn of faith*. As yet there was no Savior born, nor, as far we can judge, had the Virgin any evidence such as carnal sense requires to make her believe that a Savior would be born of her. "How can this thing be?" was a question which might very naturally have suspended her song until it received an answer convincing to flesh and blood; but no such answer had been given. She knew that with God all things are possible, she had his promise delivered by an angel, and this was enough for her: on the strength of the Word which came forth from God, her heart leaped with pleasure and her tongue glorified his name. When I consider what it is which she believed, and how unhesitatingly she received the Word, I am ready to give her, as a woman, a place almost as high as that which Abraham occupied as a man; and if I dare not call her the mother of the faithful, at least let her have due honor as one of the most excellent of the mothers in Israel. The benediction of Elizabeth, Mary right well deserved, "Blessed is she that believeth." To her, the "substance of things hoped for" was her faith, and that was also her "evidence of things not seen"; she knew, by the revelation of God, that she was to bear the promised Seed who should bruise the serpent's head; but other proof she had none.

This day there are those among us who have little or no conscious enjoyment of the Savior's presence; they walk in darkness and see no light; they are groaning over inbred sin, and mourning because corruptions prevail; let them now trust in the Lord, and remember that if they believe on the Son of God, Christ Jesus is within them; and by faith they may right gloriously chant the hallelujah of adoring love. What—though the sun gleam not forth today, the clouds and mists have not quenched his light; and though the Sun of righteousness shine not on you at this instant, yet he keeps his place in yonder skies, and knows no variableness, neither shadow of a turning. If with all your digging, the well spring not up, yet there abides a constant fullness in that deep, which crouches beneath in the heart and purpose of a God of love. What—if like David, you are much cast down, yet like him do you say unto your soul, "Hope thou in God, for I shall yet praise him for the help of his countenance." Be glad then with Mary's joy: it is the joy of a Savior completely hers, but evidenced to be so, not by sense, but by faith. Faith has its music as well as sense, but it is of a diviner sort: if the viands on the table make men sing and dance, feastings of a more refined and ethereal nature can fill believers with a hallowed plenitude of delight.

Still listening to the favored Virgin's canticle, let me observe that her lowliness does not make her stay her song; no, it imports a sweeter note into it. "For he hath regarded the low estate of his handmaiden." Beloved friend, you are feeling more intensely than ever the depth of your natural depravity, you are humbled under a sense of your many failings, you are so dead and earthbound even in this house of prayer, that you cannot rise to God; you are heavy and sad, while our Christmas carols have been ringing in your ears; you feel yourself to be today so useless to the church of God, so insignificant, so utterly unworthy, that your unbelief whispers, "Surely, surely, you have nothing to sing for." Come, my brother, come my sister, imitate this blessed Virgin of Nazareth, and turn that very lowliness and meanness which you so painfully feel, into another reason for unceasing praise; daughters of Zion, sweetly say in your hymns of love, "He hath regarded the low estate of his handmaiden." The less worthy I am of his favors, the more sweetly will I sing of his grace. What if I be the most insignificant of all his chosen; then will I praise him who with eyes of love has sought me out, and set his love upon me. "I thank thee, O Father, Lord of heaven and earth, that while thou hast hid these things from the wise and prudent, thou hast revealed them unto babes: even so, Father; for so it seemed good in thy sight." I am sure, dear friends, the remembrance that there is a Savior, and that this Savior is yours, must make you sing; and if you set side by side with it the thought that you were once sinful, unclean, vile, hateful, and an enemy to God, then your notes will take yet a loftier flight, and mount to the third heaven, to teach the golden harps the praise of God.

It is right well worthy of notice, that *the greatness of the promised blessing* did not give the sweet songstress an argument for suspending her thankful strain. When I meditate upon the great goodness of God in loving his people before the earth was, in laying down his life for us, in pleading our cause before the eternal throne, in providing a paradise of rest for us forever, the black thought has troubled me, "Surely this is too high a privilege for such an insect of a day as this poor creature, man." Mary did not look at this matter unbelievingly; although she appreciated the greatness of the favor, she did but rejoice the more heartily on that account. "For he that is mighty hath done to me great things." Come, soul, it is a great thing to be a child of God, but your God does great wonders, therefore be not staggered through unbelief, but triumph in your adoption, great mercy though it be. Oh! it is a mighty mercy, higher than the mountains, to be chosen of God from all eternity, but it is true that even so are his redeemed chosen, and therefore you sing of it. It is a deep and unspeakable blessing to be redeemed with the precious blood of Christ, but you are so redeemed beyond all question. Therefore doubt not, but shout aloud for gladness of heart. It is a rapturous thought, that you shall dwell above, and wear the crown, and wave the palm branch forever; let no mistrust interrupt the melody of your psalm of expectation, but—

> Loud to the praise of love divine,
> Bid every string awake.

What a fullness of truth is there in these few words: "He that is mighty hath done to me great things." It is a text from which a glorified spirit in heaven might preach an endless sermon. I pray you, lay hold upon the thoughts which I have in this poor way suggested to you, and try to reach where Mary stood in holy exultation. The grace is great, but so is its Giver; the love is infinite, but so is the heart from which it wells up; the blessedness is unspeakable, but so is the divine wisdom which planned it from of old. Let our hearts take up the Virgin's Magnificat, and praise the Lord right joyously at this hour.

Still further, for we have not exhausted the strain, *the holiness of God has sometimes damped the ardor of the believer's joy*; but not so in Mary's case. She exults in it: "And holy is his name." She weaves even that bright attribute into her song. Holy Lord! when I forget my Savior, the thought of thy purity makes me shudder; standing where Moses stood upon the holy mountain of thy law, I do exceedingly fear and quake. To me, conscious of my guilt, no thunder could be more dreadful than the seraph's hymn of "Holy! holy! holy! Lord God of Sabaoth." What is thy holiness but a consuming fire which must utterly destroy me—a sinner? If the heavens are not pure in thy sight and thou chargeth thine angels with folly, how much less then can thou bear with vain, rebellious man, that is born of woman? How can man be pure, and how can thine eyes look upon him without consuming him quickly in thine anger? But, O thou holy One of Israel, when my spirit can stand on Calvary and see thy holiness vindicate itself in the wounds of the man who was born at Bethlehem, then my spirit rejoices in that glorious holiness which was once her terror. Did the thrice holy God stoop down to man and take man's flesh? Then is there hope indeed! Did a holy God bear the sentence which his own law pronounced on man? Does that holy God incarnate now spread his wounded hands and plead for me? Then, my soul, the holiness of God shall be a consolation to thee. Living waters from this sacred well I draw; and I will add to all my notes of joy this one, "and holy is his name." He hath sworn by his holiness, and he will not lie; he will keep his covenant with his anointed and his seed forever.

When we take to ourselves the wings of eagles, and mount toward heaven in holy praise, the prospect widens beneath us; even so as Mary poises herself upon the poetic wing, she looks down the long aisles of the past, and beholds the mighty acts of Jehovah in the ages long back. Mark how her strain gathers majesty; it is rather the sustained flight of the eagle-winged Ezekiel, than the flutter of the timid dove of Nazareth. She sings, "His mercy is on them that fear him from generation to generation." She looks beyond the captivity, to the days of the kings, to Solomon, to David, along through the Judges into the wilderness, across the Red Sea to Jacob, to Isaac, to Abraham, and onward, till, pausing at the gate of Eden, she hears the sound of the promise, "The seed of the woman shall bruise the serpent's head." How magnificently she sums up the book of the wars of the Lord, and rehearses the triumphs of Jehovah, "He hath shewed strength with his arm; he hath scattered the proud in the imagination of their hearts." How delightfully is mercy intermingled with judgment in the next canto of her psalm: "He hath put down the mighty from their seats, and exalted them of low degree. He hath filled the hungry with good things; and the rich he hath sent empty away."

My brethren and sisters, let us, too, sing of the past, glorious in faithfulness, fearful in judgment, teeming with wonders. Our own lives shall furnish us with a hymn of adoration. Let us speak of the things which we have made touching the King. We were hungry, and he filled us with good things; we crouched upon the dunghill with the beggar, and he has enthroned us among princes; we have been tossed with tempest, but with the eternal Pilot at the helm, we have known no fear of shipwreck; we have been cast into the burning fiery furnace, but the presence of the Son of man has quenched the violence of the flames. Tell out, O daughters of music, the long tale of the mercy of the Lord to his people in the generations long departed. Many waters could not quench his love, neither could the floods drown it; persecution, famine, nakedness, peril, sword—none of these have separated the saints from the love of God which is in Christ our Lord. The saints beneath the wing of the most High have been ever safe; when most molested by the enemy, they have dwelled in perfect peace: "God is their refuge and strength, a very present help in trouble." Plowing at times the bloodred wave, the ship of the church has never swerved from her predestined path of progress. Every tempest has favored her: the hurricane which sought her ruin has been made to bear her the more swiftly onward. Her flag has braved these eighteen hundred years the battle and the breeze, and she fears not what may yet be before her. But lo! she nears the haven; the day is dawning when she shall bid farewell to storms; the waves already grow calm beneath her; the long-promised rest is near at hand; her Jesus himself meets her, walking upon the waters; she shall enter into her eternal haven, and all who are on board shall, with their Captain, sing of joy, and triumph, and victory through him who hath loved her and been her deliverer.

When Mary thus tuned her heart to glory in her God for his wonders in the past, she particularly dwelled upon the note of election. The highest note in the scale of my praise is reached when my soul sings, "I love him because he first loved me." Well does Kent put it—

> A monument of grace,
> A sinner saved by blood;
> The streams of love I trace,
> Up to the fountain, God;
> And in his mighty breast I see,
> Eternal thoughts of love to me.

We can scarcely fly higher than the source of love in the mount of God. Mary has the doctrine of election in her song: "He hath put down the mighty from their seats, and exalted them of low degree. He hath filled the hungry with good things; and the rich he hath sent empty away." Here is distinguishing grace, discriminating regard; here are some suffered to perish; here are others, the least deserving and the most obscure, made the special objects of divine affection. Do not be afraid to dwell upon this high doctrine, beloved in the Lord. Let me assure you that when your mind is most heavy and depressed, you will find this to be a bottle of richest cordial. Those who doubt these doctrines, or who cast them into the cold shade, miss the richest clusters of Eshcol; they lose the "wines on the lees well refined"; "the fat things full of marrow"; but you who by reason of years have had your senses exercised to discern between good and evil, you know that there is no honey like this, no sweetness comparable to it. If the honey in Jonathan's wood, when but touched enlightened the eyes to see, this is honey that will enlighten your heart to love and learn the mysteries of the kingdom of God. Eat, and fear not a surfeit; live upon this choice dainty, and fear not that you shall grow weary of it, for the more you know, the more you will want to know; the more your soul is filled, the more you will desire to have your mind enlarged, that you may comprehend more and more the eternal, everlasting, discriminating love of God.

But one more remark upon this point. You perceive she does not finish her song till she has reached the covenant. When you mount as high as election, tarry on its sister mount, the covenant of grace. In the last verse of her song, she sings, "As he spake to our fathers, to Abraham, and to his seed forever." To her, that was the covenant; to us who have clearer light, the ancient covenant made in the council chamber of eternity is the subject of the great-est delight. The covenant with Abraham was in its best sense only a minor copy of that gracious covenant made with Jesus, the everlasting Father of the faithful, before the blue heavens were stretched abroad. Covenant engage-ments are the softest pillows for an aching head; covenant engagements with the surety, Christ Jesus, are the best props for a trembling spirit.

> *His oath, his covenant, his blood,*
> *Support me in the raging flood;*
> *When every earthly prop gives way,*
> *This still is all my strength and stay.*

If Christ did swear to bring me to glory, and if the Father swore that he would give me to the Son to be a part of the infinite reward for the travail of his soul; then, my soul, till God himself shall be unfaithful, till Christ shall cease to be the truth, till God's eternal council shall become a lie, and the red roll of his election shall be consumed with fire, you are safe. Rest you, then, in perfect peace, come what will; take your harp from the willows, and never let your fingers cease to sweep it to strains of richest harmony. Oh, for grace from first to last to join the Virgin in her song.

II. Second, *she sings sweetly.*

She praises her God right *heartily.* Observe how she plunges into the midst of the subject. There is no preface, but "My soul doth magnify the Lord, and my spirit hath rejoiced in God my Savior." When some people sing, they appear to be afraid of being heard. Our poet puts it—

> *With all my powers of heart and tongue*
> *I'll praise my Maker in my song;*
> *Angels shall hear the notes I raise,*
> *Approve the song, and join the praise.*

I am afraid angels frequently do not hear those poor, feeble, dying whis-perings, which often drop from our lips merely by force of custom. Mary is all heart; evidently her soul is on fire; while she muses, the fire burns; then she speaks with her tongue. May we, too, call home our wandering thoughts, and wake up our slumbering powers to praise redeeming love. It is a noble word that she uses here: "My soul doth magnify the Lord." I suppose it means, "My soul doth endeavor to make God great by praising him." He is as great as he can be in his being; my goodness cannot extend to him; but yet my soul would make God greater in the thoughts of others, and greater in my own heart. I would give the train of his glory wider sweep; the light which he has given me I would reflect; I would make his enemies his friends; I would turn hard thoughts of God into thoughts of love. "My soul would magnify the Lord." Old Trapp says, "My soul would make greater room for him." It is as if she wanted to get more of God into her, like Rutherford, when he says, "Oh, that my heart were as big as heaven, that I might hold Christ in it"; and then he stops himself—"But heaven and earth cannot contain him. Oh, that I had a heart as big as seven heavens, that I might hold the whole of Christ within it." Truly this is a larger desire than we can ever hope to have gratified; yet still our lips shall sing, "My soul doth magnify the Lord." Oh, if I could crown him; if I could lift him higher! If my burning at the stake would but add a spark more light to his glory, happy should I be to suffer. If my being crushed would lift Jesus an inch higher, happy were the destruction which should add to his glory! Such is the hearty spirit of Mary's song. Again, her praise is very joyful: "My spirit hath rejoiced in God my Savior." The word in the Greek is a remarkable one. I believe it is the same word which is used in the passage, "Rejoice ye in that day and leap for joy." We used to have an old word in English which described a certain exulting dance, a "galliard." That word is supposed to have come from the Greek word here used. It was a sort of leaping dance; the old commentators call it a levalto. Mary in effect declares, "My spirit shall dance like David before the ark, shall leap, shall spring, shall bound, shall rejoice in God my Savior." When we praise God, it ought not to be with dolorous and doleful notes. Some of my brethren praise God always on the minor key or in the deep, deep bass: they cannot feel holy till they have the horrors. Why cannot some men worship God except with a long face? I know them by their very walk as they come to worship: what a dreary pace it is! how solemnly proper and funereal indeed! They do not understand David's psalm:

> Up to her courts with joys unknown,
> The sacred tribes repair.

No, they come up to their Father's house as if they were going to jail, and worship God on Sunday as if it were the most doleful day in the week. It is said of a certain Highlander, when the Highlanders were very pious, that he once went to Edinburgh, and when he came back again he said he had seen a dreadful sight on Sabbath, he had seen people at Edinburgh going to church with happy faces. He thought it wicked to look happy on Sunday; and that same notion exists in the minds of certain good people hereabouts; they fancy that when the saints get together, they should sit down and have a little comfortable misery, and but little delight. In truth, moaning and pining is not the appointed way for worshiping God. We should take Mary as a pattern. All the year round I recommend her as an example to fainthearted and troubled ones. "My spirit hath rejoiced in God my Savior." Cease from rejoicing in sensual things, and with sinful pleasures have no fellowship, for all such rejoicing is evil. But you cannot rejoice too much in the Lord. I believe that the fault with our public worship is that we are too sober, too cold, too formal. I do not exactly admire the ravings of our Primitive Methodist friends when they grow wild; but I should have no objection to hear a hearty "hallelujah!" now and then. An enthusiastic burst of exultation might warm our hearts; the shout of "glory!" might fire our spirits. This I know, I never feel more ready for true worship than when I am preaching in Wales, when the whole sermon throughout, the preacher is aided rather than interrupted by shouts of "glory to God!" and "bless his name!" Why then one's blood begins to glow, and one's soul is stirred up, and this is the true way of serving God with joy. "Rejoice in the Lord alway; and again I say, Rejoice." "My spirit hath rejoiced in God my Savior."

She sings sweetly, in the third place, because she sings confidently. She does not pause while she questions herself, "Have I any right to sing?" but no, "My soul doth magnify the Lord, and my spirit hath rejoiced in God my Savior. For he hath regarded the low estate of his handmaiden." "If" is a sad enemy to all Christian happiness; "but," "peradventure," "doubt," "surmise," "suspicion," these are a race of highwaymen who waylay poor timid pilgrims and steal their spending money. Harps soon get out of tune, and when the wind blows from the doubting quarter, the strings snap by wholesale. If the angels of heaven could have a doubt, it would turn heaven into hell. "If thou be the Son of God" was the dastardly weapon wielded by the old enemy against our Lord in the wilderness. Our great foe knows well what weapon is the most dangerous. Christian, put up the shield of faith whenever you see that poisoned dagger about to be used against you. I fear that some of you foster your doubts and fears. You might as well hatch young vipers, and foster the cockatrice. You think that it is a sign of grace to have doubts, whereas it is a sign of infirmity. It does not prove that you have no grace when you doubt God's promise, but it does prove that you want more; for if you had more grace, you would take God's Word as he gives it, and it would be said of you as of Abraham, that "he staggered not at the promise of God, through unbelief, being fully persuaded that what he had promised he was able also to perform." God help you to shake off your doubts. Oh! these are devilish things. Is that too hard a word? I wish I could find a harder. These are felons; these are rebels, who seek to rob Christ of his glory; these are traitors who cast mire upon the escutcheon of my Lord. Oh! these are vile traitors; hang them on a gallows, high as Haman's; cast them to the earth, and let them rot like carrion, or bury them with the burial of an ass. Abhorred of God are doubts; abhorred of men let them be. They are cruel enemies to your souls; they injure your usefulness; they despoil you in every way. Smite them with "the sword of the Lord and of Gideon"! By faith in the promise, seek to drive out these Canaanites and possess the land. O you men of God, speak with confidence, and sing with sacred joy.

There is something more than confidence in her song. She sings with great familiarity, "My soul doth magnify the Lord, and my spirit hath rejoiced in God my Savior. For he that is mighty hath done to me great things; and holy is his name." It is the song of one who draws very near to her God in loving intimacy. I always have an idea when I listen to the reading of the liturgy, that it is a slave's worship. I do not find fault with its words or sentences; perhaps of all human compositions, the liturgical service of the Church of England is, with some exceptions, the noblest, but it is only fit for slaves or at the best for subjects. The whole service through, one feels that there is a boundary set round about the mountain, just as at Sinai. Its litany is the wail of a sinner, and not the happy triumph of a saint. The service genders unto bondage and has nothing in it of the confident spirit of adoption. It views the Lord far off, as one to be feared rather than loved, and to be dreaded rather than delighted in. I have no doubt it suits those whose experience leads them to put the Ten Commandments near the communion table, for they hereby evidence that their dealings with God are still on the terms of servants and not of sons. For my own part I want a form of worship in which I may draw near to my God, and come even to his feet, spreading my case before him and ordering my cause with arguments; talking with him as a friend talks with his friend or a child with its father; otherwise the worship is little worth to me. Our Episcopalian friends, when they come here, are naturally struck with our service, as being irreverent, because it is so much more familiar and bold than theirs. Let us carefully guard against really deserving such a criticism, and then we need not fear it; for a renewed soul yearns after that very intercourse which the formalist calls irreverent. To talk with God as my Father, to deal with him as with one whose promises are true to me, and to whom I, a sinner washed in blood, and clothed in the perfect righteousness of Christ, may come with boldness, not standing far off; I say this is a thing which the outer-court worshiper cannot understand. There are some of our hymns which speak of Christ with such familiarity that the cold critic says, "I do not like such expressions, I could not sing them." I quite agree with you, Sir Critic, that the language would not befit you, a stranger; but a child may say a thousand things which a servant must not. I remember a minister altering one of our hymns—

Let those refuse to sing
Who never knew our God;
But favorites of the heavenly King
May speak their joys abroad.

He gave it out: "But subjects of the heavenly King." Yes; and when he gave it out, I thought, "That is right; you are singing what you feel; you know nothing of discriminating grace and special manifestations, and therefore you keep to your native level, '*subjects* of the heavenly King.'" But oh, my heart wants a worship in which I can feel, and express the feeling that, I am a favorite of the heavenly King, and therefore can sing his special love, his manifested favor, his sweet relationship, his mysterious union with my soul. You never get right till you ask the question, "Lord, how is it that thou will manifest thyself unto us, and not unto the world?" There is a secret which is revealed to us, and not to the outside world; an understanding which the sheep receive and not the goats. I appeal to any of you who during the week are in an official position; a judge, for instance. You have a seat on the bench, and you wear no small dignity when you are there. When you get home there is a little fellow who has very little fear of your judgeship, but much love for your person, who climbs your knee, who kisses your cheek, and says a thousand things to you which are meet and right enough as they come from him, but which you would not tolerate in court from any man living. The parable needs no interpretation.

When I read some of the prayers of Martin Luther they shock me, but I argue with myself thus: "It is true I cannot talk to God in the same way as Martin, but then perhaps Martin Luther felt and realized his adoption more than I do, and therefore was not less humble because he was more bold. It may be that he used expressions which would be out of place in the mouth of any man who had not known the Lord as he had done." O my friends, sing this day of our Lord Jesus as one near to us. Get close to Christ, read his wounds, thrust your hand into his side, put your finger into the print of the nails, and then your song shall win a sacred softness and melody not to be gained elsewhere.

I must close by observing that while her song was all this, yet *how very humble* it was, and how full of gratitude. The papist calls her "mother of God," but she never whispers such a thing in her song. No, it is "God my Savior"; just such words as the sinner who is speaking to you might use, and such expressions as you sinners who are hearing me can use too. She wants a Savior, she feels it; her soul rejoices because there is a Savior for her. She does not talk as though she could commend herself to him, but she hopes to stand accepted in the Beloved. Let us then take care that our familiarity has always blended with it the lowliest prostration of spirit, when we remember that he is God over all, blessed forever, and we are nothing but dust and ashes; he fills all things, and we are less than nothing and vanity.

III. The last thing was to be—*shall she sing alone?*

Yes, she must, if the only music we can bring is that of carnal delights and worldly pleasures. There will be much music tomorrow which would not chime in with hers. There will be much mirth tomorrow, and much laughter, but I am afraid the most of it would not accord with Mary's song. It will not be, "My soul doth magnify the Lord, and my spirit hath rejoiced in God my Savior." We would not stop the play of the animal spirits in young or old; we would not abate one jot of your relish of the mercies of God, so long as you break not his command by wantonness or drunkenness or excess: but still, when you have had the most of this bodily exercise, it profits little, it is only the joy of the fleeting hour, and not the happiness of the spirit which abides; and therefore Mary must sing alone, as far as you are concerned. The joy of the table is too low for Mary; the joy of the feast and the family grovels when compared with hers.

But shall she sing alone? Certainly not, if this day any of us by simple trust in Jesus can take Christ to be our own. Does the Spirit of God this day lead you to say, "I trust my soul on Jesus?" My dear friend, then you have conceived Christ: after the mystical and best sense of that word, Christ Jesus is conceived in your soul. Do you understand him as the Sin-bearer, taking away transgression? Can you see him bleeding as the substitute for men? Do you accept him as such? Does your faith put all her dependence upon what he did, upon what he is, upon what he does? Then Christ is conceived in you, and you may go your way with all the joy that Mary knew; and I was half ready to say, with something more; for the natural conception of the Savior's holy body was not one tenth so meet a theme for congratulation as the spiritual conception of the holy Jesus within your heart when he shall be in you the hope of glory. My dear friend, if Christ be yours, there is no song on earth too high, too holy for you to sing; no, there is no song which thrills from angelic lips, no note which thrills archangel's tongue in which you may not join. Even this day, the holiest, the happiest, the most glorious of words and thoughts and emotions belong to you. Use them! God help you to enjoy them; and his be the praise, while yours is the comfort evermore. Amen.

Peter's Mother-in-Law: A Lift for the Prostrate

Published on Thursday, March 22, 1906; delivered on Lord's Day evening, September 19, 1875, at the Metropolitan Tabernacle, Newington. No. 2980.

And he [Jesus] came and took her by the hand, and lifted her up; and immediately the fever left her, and she ministered unto them.—MARK 1:31

Peter's wife's mother was sick of a very terrible fever. It was no ordinary one, such as, we are told, is common in the district when she lived; but "Luke, the beloved physician," as Paul calls the Evangelist, tells us that "Simon's wife's mother was taken with a great fever." You know that it is the nature of fever to leave the patient prostrate even when the disease itself departs; but Jesus Christ not only intended to heal Peter's wife's mother, and to heal her at once, but he also meant that she should be so completely cured that she should have no lingering prostration. Christ's cures are always perfect cures, not partial ones. He does not cause the fever to go and permit the prostration to remain, but he takes away both the fever and the prostration.

It is possible that the poor patient had almost given up all hope of recovery; and, probably, those who were round about her would also have despaired if they had not had faith in the great Physician, the Lord Jesus Christ. It was, therefore, for her encouragement, and for theirs also, that our Lord bent over the bed whereon the fevered woman lay, took her by the hand, thus cheering her by showing that he was not afraid to come into contact with her, and then gently lifted her up; and she, yielding to the kindly pressure rose, and sat up—no, not merely sat up, but left the bed, being so perfectly restored that she began at once to minister to them as the housewife whose duty it was to care for their comfort.

I hope that there are many in this congregation whom Jesus Christ means to bless; but they are, at present, in a state of utter prostration; they are so despondent that their spirits sink almost to the point of despair. They cannot believe that there is mercy for them; they have relinquished all hope of that. They did, at one time, have some measure of hope, but it is all gone now.

They are in the prostrate condition of Peter's mother-in-law, and they need Christ to do for them the two things which he did for her. First, *he came into contact with her;* and, second, *he gently lifted her up, and completely restored her.* May he do the like for you!

I. Our first concern, in looking after prostrate souls, is to tell them that *Jesus Christ comes into contact with them.*

You think, my poor distressed friend, that Jesus Christ will have nothing to do with you. You have read and heard about him, but he seems to you to be a long way off, and you cannot reach him; neither does it seem at all probable to you that he will ever come your way and look in pity upon you. Now listen.

In the first place, *Jesus Christ has come into contact with you,* for you are a member of the human race, of which Jesus Christ also became a member by his incarnation. Never forget that, while it is perfectly true that Christ "is over all, God blessed forever," yet it is equally true that he deigned to be born into this world, as the infant of an earthly mother, and that he condescended to live here under the same conditions as the rest of us, suffering the same weakness, and sickness, and sorrow, and death as we do, for our sakes. Never think of Jesus, I pray you, as though he were only a spirit, at whose presence you have cause to be alarmed; but think of him, as a man like yourselves, eating and drinking as others did—not a recluse, shutting himself away from sinners, but living as a man among men, the perfect specimen of manhood, the man Christ Jesus, for thus he has come near to you. You would not be afraid to speak to one of your fellowmen; then, do not be afraid to speak to Jesus. Tell him all the details of your case, for he was never a man of a proud and haughty spirit. He was not one who said, "Stand by, for I am holier than thou"; but he was a man with a great heart of love. He was so full of attractiveness that even children came and clustered around his feet, and when his disciples would have driven them away, he said, "Suffer the little children to come unto me, and forbid them not: for of such is the kingdom of God." He never repelled even the very worst of mankind when they approached him; but he longed to gather them to himself. He wept over the guilty city of Jerusalem, and said, "How often would I have gathered thy children together, even as a hen gathereth her chickens under her wings, and ye would not!" Come, then, distressed spirit, and see, in the very fact that Jesus is Emmanuel, God with us, that he has come near to you, and laid his hand upon you.

"Ah!" you say, "I can comprehend that he has come near to men; but then, I am not merely a man, but a sinful man." Yes, and *Jesus has come near to sinful men,* and his name is called Jesus because he is the Savior from sin. His work in this world was not to seek saints, but "to seek and to save that which was lost." My Master's errand was not to the good, the excellent, the righteous, but to the evil, the unholy, the unrighteous. He said, "They that are whole have no need of the physician, but they that are sick: I came not to call the righteous, but sinners to repentance." If he did not come to save sinners, why did he come as a sacrifice?

Sacrifice is only required where there is sin—an atonement is only needed where there is guilt. Christ comes to you, a guilty sinner, and he lays his hand upon you, even as he laid it upon Peter's wife's mother when she was sick with that great fever.

Do I hear you say, as in a whisper, as if you were afraid that anyone else should hear you, that you are not only a sinner, but a great sinner—that you have sinned beyond the ordinary guilt of the common mass of mankind, that there are some points in which the crimson of your guilt is of a deeper dye than that of any other man? My friend, let me assure you that *Jesus Christ came to save the chief of sinners.* Do you see him, on the cross, enduring those indescribable pangs of death? Can you hear his death cries and that soul-piercing shriek, "My God, my God, why hast thou forsaken me?" and still think that such a death as that was on behalf of little sinners' trifling offenses, mere peccadilloes or mistakes? Ah no! the Son of God came to give his life a ransom for many great sins and many great sinners. The grandeur of the atonement of Christ is a proof that its object was the removal of sin, however great that sin may be. The Son of God is himself the Savior of sinners; there must, therefore, be a colossal greatness about sin to need the Son of God to remove it, and to need that the Son of God should die before the more than Herculean labor of putting sin away could be performed; but, having put away sin by the sacrifice of himself, he is now able to save even the greatest of sinners.

That Jesus has come into contact with great sinners is very clear; or, as you read the record of his life, you see that *his preaching was constantly aimed at just such characters.* If you take a survey of his usual congregations, you will discover that they were largely made up of such characters. The Pharisees said, with contempt, but no doubt with truth, "This man receiveth sinners, and eateth with them." Just at that very time, we have the record, "Then drew near unto him all the publicans and sinners for to hear him." His preaching evidently attracted them, and he never seems to have been surprised that it did, nor to have expressed his disgust that he should have drawn around him such a low and degraded class of hearers. No; but, on the contrary, he said that he was sent to seek lost sheep till he found them, and to welcome the wandering prodigal when he came back to his Father's house. Our Lord Jesus

Christ, from the character of his congregation and the tone of his preaching, evidently came to this world on purpose to come into contact with the very worst of sinners. I want you to realize, dear friend, that my Lord Jesus Christ is a man, and that he is not a man who has come to look for congenial companions who might be worthy to be numbered among his acquaintances; but he has come to look after uncongenial men and women to whom he may bring the blessings of salvation. He has come, not to be ministered unto, but to minister; not to receive, but to bestow boons; his object in being here, in this world, is not to pick out, here and there, a noble and notable character; but to seek after souls that need his grace, and to come to them and bless and save them. So he has, in this respect, come near to you. Remember that commission of his, which he gave to his disciples a little while before he went back to heaven: "Go ye into all the world, and preach the gospel to every creature." On another occasion, after his resurrection, he reminded them "that repentance and remission of sins should be preached in his nation among all nations, beginning at Jerusalem"; that is, beginning at the very place where the people lived who had crucified him. Begin where they live who have stained their hands with my blood. Begin with them, and then go to every other creature in the whole world, and say to sinners in every part of the globe, "Whosoever believeth on the Son of God hath everlasting life." In giving that commission, our Lord Jesus Christ reached his hand across the centuries that he might touch you, and I have come here to obey his commission by preaching the gospel to you, for you are included in the term *every creature*. So Jesus Christ comes into contact with you through the preaching of his word at this very moment.

There is one solemn thought that I should like you to think of; it is this: having entered this house of prayer, and having heard the gospel, as you will have done before this service is over, *the Lord Jesus Christ has so come into contact with you that you will never lose the impress of that contact, whether you are lost or saved.* If you are lost, you will have the additional guilt of having rejected him; neither can you ever clear yourself of that guilt, do what you may. Your ears have heard the Word, so that, if you do not receive it, you will be numbered among those to whom the gospel came, but who judged themselves unworthy of everlasting life, like some of those to whom the apostle Paul preached; and, therefore, it shall condemn you. For, to everybody who hears the gospel, there is a savor in it; to some, it is a savor of death unto death, and to others a savor of life unto life. There is not a man, woman, or child who has understanding enough to know what we mean by preaching the gospel, who will be able to go out of this house of prayer without receiving some token of contact with the Lord Jesus Christ. Either his blood will be upon you to save you, or else there will be realized in you that dreadful curse which the Jews invoked upon themselves, "His blood be on us, and on our children," which abides upon them as a curse unto this day. You shall either be cleansed from guilt by the blood of Jesus, or else you shall be guilty of rejecting him, and so putting yourselves in the same category as the Jews who rejected him, and who nailed him to the accursed tree. One way or other, to be sure of this, "The kingdom of God is come unto you." It is a solemn fact to have to state this, but so it is. Jesus Christ has, in some way or other, put his hand upon you, and he is now in contact with you.

II. Leaving that point, however, I feel joy in passing on to the next one. When Jesus grasped the hand of Peter's wife's mother, *he then began gently to lift her up.*

She, willingly enough, responded to his touch; and, by at once recommencing her household duties, proved that she was perfectly healed.

Now there are some poor, prostrate, desponding souls who need somebody to give them a lift; and I would that the Lord, even while I am preaching, might take some of you by the hand and lift you up. My object will be to mention a few things which may help to give you a lift. You want to be saved; you long to be saved; but you fear that you never will be, and it is that very fear which keeps you from being saved. If you could but hope, your hope would be realized; but you do not feel as if you dared even to hope. Now give me your hand, and let me try to give you a lift.

First, remember that others who were very like what you now are, have been saved. Do you not know some people who used to be very much in the condition in which you are at the present moment? If you do not, then find out the nearest Christian friend among your acquaintance, tell him what you regard as the peculiarity of your condition, and I feel almost certain that he will say to you, "Why, that is not anything peculiar; that is just how I was before I found the Savior." If you do not find it so with the first Christian person whom you meet, you ought not to be surprised, because, of course, all Christians are not alike; but I feel sure that you will not have talked to many Christian people before you will find that what you consider to be very remarkable peculiarities in yourself will turn out to have been very common, for a great many other people have been in just the same state! I challenge you who are very despondent, to see whether you cannot find some who once were as you now are, who have been saved; and when you do find them, the reasoning is very clear. If A be saved, and B is like A, then why should not B also be saved?

"Ah!" say you, "I have very few Christian acquaintances of whom I can make inquiry." Very well, then, I will give you another simple test. Take your Bible, and block out the cases of conversion, and see whether the saved ones were not very much like you now are; and if that should not satisfy you, turn to the various promises that the Lord Jesus has made to coming sinners, and see whether there is not one that is suited to such a sinner as you are. I think that you cannot go far in an honest examination of the promises of the gospel without saying, "Well, now, it really does look as if I could squeeze in there, at any rate; I think that description just exactly meets my case." I should not be surprised if you meet with some text, of which you will say, "Why, that looks as if it had been written entirely for me; it is such an accurate description of my forlorn condition." Well, then, if you find that Christ has invited such sinners as you are, and that, according to the inspired record, he has saved such as you are, why should not you also have hope! Have you been a thief? Remember that—

> The dying thief rejoiced to see
> That fountain in its day;
> And there may you, though vile as he,
> Wash all your sins away.

Have you been a sinner in a more immodest sense? Remember that there was a woman who was "a sinner" in that very sense, who washed Christ's feet with her tears, and wiped them with the hairs of her head. Have you been a swearer? I should think that Simon Peter had been a great swearer before he was converted, or else he would not have used oaths and curses so freely when he denied his Master. Yet in spite of that old habit breaking out again, Simon Peter was not only saved, but he became one of the most useful servants of our Lord Jesus Christ. I might continue to mention all sorts of sinners, and say to you, "Such a one as you now are has been saved, and has gone to heaven; is not that a lift for you? I pray the Lord to make it so. Others like you have been saved, so why should not you also be saved? Wherefore, be of good courage, poor prostrate sinner."

Let me give you another lift. Salvation is all of grace; that is to say, it is altogether of God's free favor. God does not save any man because there is anything in him that deserves salvation. The Lord saves whomsoever he wills to save; this is one of his grand prerogatives, of which he is very tenacious. His own declaration is, "I will have mercy on whom I will have mercy; and I will have compassion on whom I will have compassion"; and Paul's conclusion from that declaration is, "So then it is not of him that willeth, nor of him that runneth, but of God that sheweth mercy." Well, now, if it be God's will to bestow his mercy upon sinners, according to his own sovereign grace in Christ Jesus, irrespective of anything good in them, why should he not show mercy to you? You have been looking for some reason in yourself why he should show mercy unto you, but you cannot find any such reason; and I can tell you that there never was any reason in sinners themselves why God should save them. He has always saved them for reasons known only to himself, which he has never revealed, and which he tells us he will not reveal. He asks, like the householder in the parable, "Is it not lawful for me to do what I will with mine own?" and so he will do. No man has any right to salvation. We have all forfeited all claim of merit; so when the Lord gives his mercy, he gives it wherever he pleases. Why, then, should he not give it to you as well as to anybody else?

I may also remind you that faith in Jesus Christ always does save the soul—simply trusting him, as we were singing just now—

> Only trust him! Only trust him!
> Only trust him now!
> He will save you! He will save you!
> He will save you now!

There have been a great many who have put this to the test, and they have found that faith in Christ has saved them. There are some people, nowadays, who tell us that this is immoral doctrine; they say that we ought to preach up good works. We do preach up good works, in the most forcible manner; for we say that faith in Jesus Christ prevents men from living in sin. We do not preach good works as a ground of salvation. That would be as foolish as children who take flowers, and stick them in the ground, and say, "Oh, what a beautiful garden we have got!" We plant the seeds of the flowers, or the roots of the flowers of grace; for faith in Jesus Christ is the seed and the root of virtue, and he that believes in Jesus Christ is saved, not merely from the punishment of sin, but from the sin itself—from the power of sin, from the habit of sin. If it be still said that this is immoral doctrine, let the thousands of men who have been saved from drunkenness, and lasciviousness, and profanity, by simply believing in Jesus, rise up, and enter their solemn protest against the wicked charge that there is anything immoral in this teaching. Immoral doctrine. Why, it has brought millions to Christ, and millions to heaven. If this doctrine could truly be called immoral, then God himself might be charged with being immoral, for this gospel assuredly came from him, and it is nothing short of blasphemy to call it immoral. Hear this gospel, sinner. You have no good works, and you will never have any until you repent of sin and trust the Lord Jesus Christ. If you try to have any, they will all break down, because the motive at the back of those supposed good works will be this: you will do them in the hope of thereby saving yourself. What is that but sheer selfishness—dead selfishness, which cannot be acceptable with God?

But, sirs, if you will only trust the Lord Jesus Christ, you shall receive the immediate pardon of your sin, and with that pardon will come heartfelt gratitude to him who gives you the pardon; and with that gratitude will come intense hatred of everything that he hates, and fervent love of everything that he loves. And then you will do good works; but from what motive? Why, out of gratitude to him; and not being the result of selfishness, they will really be good works, for they will be done with the view of pleasing God, and not as a means of getting something for yourself.

Every soul, then, that has believed in Jesus has found everlasting life, and deliverance from sin. Very well, then, you also will find the same blessings if you now confide wholly in him. They did "only trust him"; do you the same—"only trust him now." They dropped into the arms of Christ; he caught them and held them fast. Do you the same; drop now into the arms of Christ, who stands beneath you, ready to catch you, and you shall most certainly be saved. This is Christ's own declaration, "He that believeth and is baptized shall be saved." The belief is to come first, and the baptism is to follow as the confession of the belief. Christ commanded his disciples to observe that order: "Go ye therefore, and teach (or make disciples of) all nations, baptizing them (those who are made disciples) into the name of the Father, and of the Son, and of the Holy Ghost." This is what Christ himself said; so if you have believed in him, and have been baptized on profession of that faith, you are saved, just as myriads of others have been saved. I have thus tried to give you a further lift up, and I pray the Lord Jesus to take you by the hand, and lift you up, you fevered and prostrate patients, who cannot rise without his power being poured into you.

Let me try to give you a lift in another way. I think I hear you say, "O sir, I know the gospel; but, somehow, I cannot get hold of it. I know what praying means, but I cannot pray as I would. I know what repenting is, but I cannot repent as I would." Here is a text which will, I hope, give you a lift: "The Spirit also helpeth our infirmities." Can you not look up to heaven, and ask that blessed Spirit to help you now? What though your heart is hard as the nether millstone? The Spirit of God can make it soft in a moment. What though it seems impossible for you to believe in Jesus? The gracious Spirit is ready now to enable you to believe in him. What if now you seem to be the very reverse of what you ought to be? The blessed Spirit can completely change your nature. He can open the blind eye, and unstop the deaf ear, and take away the stony heart out of your flesh, and give you a heart of flesh. I know that you cannot help yourself; but I also know that the Holy Spirit can help you, for nothing is impossible unto him. Come, heavenly wind, and breathe upon these dry bones; quicken them into life and activity, so that, where there was nothing but death, there may be a living army to serve the living Lord! And, blessed be his holy name, he will do it; for wherever there is a true, heartfelt prayer for his presence, he is present already, dictating that prayer; for no one really prays until the Holy Spirit teaches him how to pray. So, you who are like Peter's wife's mother, have we been able to lift you up yet? May the Lord's almighty hand be stretched out to you, for ours alone will be too weak to lift you up.

Here is another lift for you. Notwithstanding all that I have said, you still think that you deserve to be lost, and that you must be lost, for *your being punished will show the justice of God*. That is true, as far as it goes; but let me tell you something else that is equally true. Your being saved will glorify the mercy of God, and "he delighteth in mercy." I recollect the time when I thought that, if Jesus Christ saved me, it would be the biggest thing he ever did. I thought so then, and I do not know but that I think so now; and I feel sure that, when I get to heaven, I shall still have that idea. And if you, dear friend, think the same concerning yourself, I expect you are about right. Jesus Christ, however, loves to do big things; he delights to show great mercy to great sinners; and if there is one man here who seems not to have any good point about him, but whom everybody knows as being a renowned sinner— well, I pray the Lord to save you, my friend, because then the devils in hell will hear of it, and they will be angry, and I like them to be angry for such a reason as that; and the wicked men, with whom you have been accustomed to associate, will hear of it, and they will say, "What! old Jack becomes Christian? Harry turned Baptist? I never would have believed such a thing to be possible." We like to have just such converts as these, and my Lord likes to have them too, for such victories of sovereign grace cause a great stir in the camp of the Philistines, and they begin to tremble and cry, "Who will be the next to turn?" And so the kingdom of heaven grows, and Satan's fame gets dimmed, and the fame of Jesus of Nazareth grows brighter and brighter.

"Ah!" says one, "I never looked at it in that light; for, certainly, if Jesus Christ were to save me, I should be the biggest wonder on earth." Then I think it is very likely that he will save you, for he delights to do great wonders, and to work mighty marvels. How do you think that a doctor gets to have great fame? There are some physicians in London who have so many patients waiting to see them, that the poor sufferers have to wait hour after hour before they can get in. How did those doctors get to be so celebrated? If I were to tell you they got all their fame through curing chapped hands and sore fingers and warts, you would say, "Nonsense! Nobody gets fame through doing such little things as that." How did they get their honor, then? Oh, there was a poor man who was nigh unto death; he had been given up by several other doctors, but this one was enabled by God to heal him. Or there was a man whose leg was about to be amputated, and this doctor said, "I will save that man's limb." Or there was a complicated case of internal disease, and this doctor said, "I understand that case," and he cured it, and everybody talked about the wonderful cure; and now everybody goes to that doctor. He became famous through curing bad cases; one really bad case brought him more credit than fifty minor maladies might have done. So is it with the great Physician and you big sinners with such a complication of disorders that nobody but Christ can cure you. My Lord and Master has a wondrous way of healing those who appear to be incurable; and when he cures such cases as yours, heaven and earth and hell hear of it, and it makes him famous. So I would encourage you to hope that he will save even you, though you are as prostrate as Peter's wife's mother was before Christ took her by the hand, and lifted her up. May my gracious Lord and Master help you to take encouragement from what he has done for others who were in as sad a state as you are now in!

Though your case seems so hopeless to you, or, if you have any hope of recovery, you feel that it will take a long while, I want to remind you that Jesus Christ pardons sinners in an instant. A man is as black as midnight one moment, and as bright as noonday the next. Jesus Christ lifted up upon the cross has such mighty power that, if a man had all the sins of mankind resting upon him, yet, if he did but look to Christ by faith, his sins would be all gone in a moment. Did you ever see that wonderful sculpture which represents the Laocoön and his sons with the monstrous snakes twisted all about their limbs? Well, though you should be another Laocoön, and sinful habits should be twisted all about you, so that it would be impossible for you to free yourself from them, yet, if you look to Jesus by faith, these monsters shall drop dead at your feet. Jesus Christ, the Seed of the woman, sets his foot upon the monster, sin, and breaks its head; and if you believe in Jesus, that pierced foot of his shall crush the life out of your sin, and you shall be delivered from its power. Oh, that you might have grace to trust in Jesus for instantaneous pardon, instantaneous regeneration, instantaneous deliverance from nature's darkness into God's most marvelous light! If you are as prostrate as Peter's wife's mother was, you ought not to lie still any longer when Christ is ready to give you such a lift as that.

But if you do, I bid you remember, poor desponding, despairing sinner, that he who has come to save such as you are is a divine Savior. What a death blow this ought to be to every doubt! You say that there is a difficulty in your case. Yes, there is always a difficulty where there is only finite power; there always will be difficulties where there are creatures with limited capacities; but here is the Creator—the Creator in human flesh—he who made the heavens and the earth has come down to live here as a man, and to die upon the cross, in order that he may save sinners. What difficulty can there be in the presence of Omnipotence? Talk not of difficulty in the presence of the almighty God. He has but to will anything, and it is done; to speak, and it stands fast forever. Jesus Christ, my Lord and Master, is able to save unto the uttermost all them that come unto God by him, and he is able to save them with the greatest possible ease. What an easy thing it was for Christ to bless men and women and children when he was here upon earth! A poor woman came in the crowd, and just touched the hem of his garment—she could not get near enough to touch him—but she just touched the hem of his garment with her finger; there was contact between her and Christ through her finger and the hem of his garment, and she was made whole that very instant. There were other cases in which Christ healed people who were miles away from him at the time. "Go thy way," said he to the nobleman, "thy son liveth." He had not been near him; he could work the miracle just as easily at a distance. O sinner, nothing is impossible with God. If you are sick and near unto death, Jesus Christ is able to save you. If I saw you at the very gates of hell—so long as you had not actually crossed the threshold—if I saw you trembling there, and you said to me, "Can Jesus Christ save me now?" I would reply, "Aye, my brother, look unto him, and he will take you from the gates of hell to the gates of heaven in a single moment." He said when on earth, "All manner of sin and blasphemy shall be forgiven unto men," and it is just as true today. "'Come now, and let us reason together,' saith the LORD: 'though your sins be as scarlet, they shall be as white as snow; though they be red like crimson, they shall be as wool.'"

Only trust him! Only trust him!
Only trust him now!
He will save you! He will save you!
He will save you now!

Oh, that he would bless this word to you! Christ is God as well as man. He suffered in the stead of sinners on the cross, but he lives after the suffering has been accomplished, he lives as the Savior who is mighty to save; and whoever will take him as his or her own Savior shall find it to be so this very hour.

The Samaritan Woman:
Her Mission

Delivered on Lord's Day morning, September 10, 1882, at the Metropolitan Tabernacle, Newington. No. 1678.

And upon this came his disciples, and marveled that he talked with the woman: yet no man said, "What seekest thou?" or, "Why talkest thou with her?" The woman then left her waterpot, and went her way into the city, and saith to the men, "Come, see a man, which told me all things that ever I did: is not this the Christ?" Then they went out of the city, and came unto him.
—JOHN 4:27–30

Behold our Lord and Master with divinely skillful art seeking after a single soul! We must have large congregations or we are disinclined for soul winning. The habit of the age is to do nothing but what is ostentatious; every work must be with beat of drum or sound of tambourine. I pray that the Lord may work in us the steadfast desire to do good on the quiet, by stealth, when no one looks on, when not a single disciple is near. Oh, that we may have such an estimate of the value of a single soul that we count whole days well spent to bring one fallen woman or one drunkard to the Savior's feet. Blessed is he who works on though he is never heard of, and looks for his reward from his Master. In the heat of the day the Lord Jesus found rest and refreshment in speaking to one whom many would scarcely look upon, except with eyes of scorn. Blessed Savior, we do not marvel as the disciples did that you did speak with the woman, but we do wonder with a higher kind of astonishment that ever you did speak to the like of us, who have so sadly fallen, and done you dishonor, and grieved your heart. We are amazed that he who is the glory of heaven, "Light of light, very God of very God," should shroud himself in the likeness of sinful flesh and, being found in fashion as a man, should seek after us unworthy ones. Oh, the compassion of the Redeemer's heart!

Read this chapter through carefully, and see the skill which that compassion taught him. How sweetly ready he was to converse with her and take up her questions. Never imagine that the thirty years of retirement at Nazareth were wasted. I would fain go, if I were young, for thirty years to learn how to talk as he did, if his own Spirit would teach me the lesson. He was a perfect Teacher, because as man he had lent a willing ear to the heavenly instruction of the Holy Ghost, and therefore grew in knowledge and fitness for his work; as says that notable Scripture, "The Lord God hath given me the tongue of the learned, that I should know how to speak a word in season to him that is weary: he wakeneth morning by morning, he wakeneth mine ear to hear as the learned. The Lord God hath opened mine ear, and I was not rebellious, neither turned away back." By communion with God in private, and by watching men in seclusion, he learned both the mind of God and the nature of man, so as to know how to handle the human mind. Men are "kittle cattle," and can only be managed by a wise hand. Many an earnest fool has driven a soul to hell in his endeavor to drag it to heaven by force; for human wills yield not to such rough force, but rebel the more. Souls have to be brought to salvation by a gentleness and wisdom such us the Savior used when he fascinated the Samaritan woman into eternal life and enticed her to the truth: so only can I describe that wondrous power which he exercised over her in the few short but blessed sentences with which he addressed her.

Now turn a moment from that glorious One, that perfect man and yet infinite God, whom we would lovingly adore before we look away from him. Here come his disciples! They have been into the city to buy food—an errand most needful—that they and their Teacher might live. But see! *When they perceive him talking with a woman they marvel,* each in his own way. Some are dumfounded, and cannot explain the phenomenon; others look as if they would interpose if they dared, and would cry to the woman, "Away, you vixen: what right have you here, speaking to such a One as our Leader, whose shoe-latchets even we are not worthy to unloose? Your approach dishonors him: take yourself away." They did say so with their eyes, though awe of their Lord restrained their tongues. For these disciples of Jesus were steeped in the customary antipathies of the age.

First, it was sufficiently offensive that the person with whom Jesus was conversing was a woman. My beloved sisters, you owe much to the gospel, for it is only by its agency that you are raised to your proper place. For what said the rabbis? "Rather burn the sayings of the law than teach them to women"; and, again, "Let no man prolong conversation with a woman; let no one converse with a woman in the streets, not even with his own wife." Women were thought to be unfit for profound religious instruction, and altogether inferior beings. My sisters, we do not think that you are superior to us, though some of you perhaps fancy so; but we are right glad to own your equality, and to know that in Christ Jesus there is neither male nor female. Jesus has lifted you up to your true place, side by side with man. Even the apostles were tainted at first with that horrible superstition which made them marvel that Jesus openly talked with a woman. Moreover, they wondered that he could talk with such a woman! I do not suppose they knew all about her character, but there is a look about the fallen which betrays them; they cannot conceal the boldness which a course of vice usually produces. They may have thought, "If he had talked with an aged matron, a saintly mother in Israel, it might not have been surprising; but how can he converse with such a woman?" They did not as yet understand his mission to rescue the perishing and save the lost.

This poor woman also had the misfortune to be a Samaritan, and above all things Jews hated Samaritans, as aliens and heretics, who dared to call Jacob their father and to believe themselves orthodox. Jews and Samaritans were much alike, and you know the sects that approach nearest to each other usually reserve their bitterest hatred for their next of kin. They will tolerate those who are far removed from them, because they are altogether in the darkness of error, and so are somewhat excusable; but those who have so much light they detest for not seeing eye to eye with themselves. We pity a dumb man, for he cannot speak at all, but we are indignant that one who can say "Sibboleth" will not take a little more trouble and pronounce it "Shibboleth," as we do. Surely he might go that other inch and be quite right. This woman was one of those Samaritan heretics who had dared to set up an opposition temple to the one at Jerusalem, and say that they also were the people of God; so the disciples shrank from her, and marveled that Jesus did not do the same. How could so good a man mix himself up with such people? I have, myself, heard a great deal of foolishness spoken about mixing up with certain people, because we dare to meet with them upon some common ground to accomplish a right purpose. I have sometimes wondered whether people ever read of Abraham when he fought for the cause of the king of Sodom. A horrible man, I have no doubt, that monarch was, yet when his country had been plundered by the invading kings, Abraham marched out on behalf of the king of Sodom; not that he cared for him, but that he desired to deliver his nephew Lot. For that reason he is found in some measure of association with Sodom's king; but when the object upon which they were united was achieved, then see how the princely Abraham washes his hands of the man. He says, "I will not take of thee from a thread even to a shoe-latchet, lest thou shouldest say, 'I have made Abraham rich.'" Thus there may be a temporary union among men, between whom there is the widest difference, and this apparent unity may be lawful and expedient because the end to be gained is altogether good. Our blessed Lord was seeking the good of this unholy woman, and therefore he was fully justified in talking with her. Thereby he rebuked the superstition of his followers more effectually than by words.

There is another side to the question. How could these disciples marvel that he spoke with anybody, after having chosen them and called them? Surely, when they frowned on others they forgot the dunghills where they grew. If they had only remembered where they were when he found them, and how often they had grieved him by their perverseness, they would have reserved their surprise for their own cases. Ah, brethren, ever since the Lord spoke with me, I have never marveled that he spoke with anybody: it has not crossed my mind to make it any subject of wonder that he should stoop to the lowest and meanest now that he has stooped to me; yet I fancy I have seen in certain brethren evident signs that they forget that they were themselves once strangers in Egypt. They forget that grace washed and cleansed them, or else they would have been filthy still, for Paul truly said, "such were some of you." I am sorry when saved ones affect superfine purity and marvelous spirituality, and turn away from such as Jesus would have welcomed. Alas, such disciples have little of the tenderness of their Master! Our divine Lord has more tenderness for sinners than the whole of us put together. There is more love in his soul toward lost ones than there is in all these thousands of believers here present, though I hope that many of your hearts beat high with a loving desire that the guilty may be delivered from the wrath to come.

But look at the disciples! See, yonder is John, that sweet-souled John, and yet he marvels: and there is Peter, good but faulty, and he marvels: and there is Thomas the thoughtful, and he marvels. They are all good men, and yet they are marveling that Jesus is gracious to a poor woman. O Peter and John and James and the rest of you, look into your own hearts, and let a glance of the Holy Spirit lighten up the darkness of your spirits, and you will renounce this self-righteous marveling which grieves the woman, and you will enter into deeper sympathy with your Lord's love. Dear friends, let us never disdain the worst of men or women, but seek with all our might to woo and win them for our Lord. Oh, to have bowels of mercies as Jesus had! This will well become the followers of the compassionate Son of man.

See, as the result of this conduct of the disciples, one of the sweetest conferences that was ever held was broken up, and brought to a close at its very climax. Just when Jesus had said, "I that speak unto thee am he," then it must end, for here they come, these cold, unsympathetic ones. Yet they were disciples, were they not? Oh, yes, and true disciples too; but alas, no breakers of communion are more blamable or more frequent in the offense than Christ's own disciples when they are out of sympathy with their Master. You see, they are thinking about the meat, and about the Savior's need of it: and these thoughts were most proper, but not very elevated or spiritual; and they come wondering that Jesus speaks with a woman, and so the holy conference ends, and the woman must go. Oh, when any of you draw near to Christ, and he is just lifting the silver veil from his dear face, and your eyes are beginning to behold him, mind that you keep your door shut. "Oh, but it is a good man at the door." Yes, but he will be just as likely to mar your fellowship as anybody else. The best of men may sometimes intrude between you and the Well Beloved, and fellowship which seemed as if it must mellow into heaven itself will come to a speedy and sorrowful close. I do not blame Peter that he wanted tabernacles in which to remain upon the top of the mount, for he was pretty well aware of what he might meet upon the plain. Do you not often wish that you could sing—

> Sequestered from the noise and strife,
> The lust, the pomp, and pride of life;
> For heaven I will my heart prepare,
> And have my conversation there.

Although the conference was thus broken up, the consequence thereof was the Lord's glory, even as often out of evil he works good. Since the woman cannot sit and gaze upon the divine face of her Lord, nor hear the strange music which flowed from his blessed lips, she will give herself to holy activity: she goes her way to the city, and she speaks to the men. This is well: there is little to deplore when men's hearts are so right that you cannot take them off from glorifying Christ, do what you may; when if you disturb their private communion they are ready at once for public service. Driven away from sitting, like Mary, at the Master's feet, let us rise to play the Martha, by preparing a table for the Lord. Always reckon, dear friends, whenever you are taken off from your usual course of life, as it were by a jerk, that the Lord has some special work for you to do. Do not fret, or try to buck the engine to get on the old lines again. No, if the switch is turned by the divine Hand, go on; he that has the management of all the railroads of your life knows better which way your soul should go than you yourself can know. I have observed Christian people jerked out of a pious family where they were extremely happy, and placed in the midst of ungodliness, a situation not of their own choosing or seeking, but appointed of the Lord, that they may bring godliness into that house, and shed light in the midst of the darkness. Friend, you, too, may be taken away from this church where your soul has flourished, and you may feel like one banished and bereaved. Well, never mind. If you are sent to some church where everything is dreary and dead, go there like a firebrand to set them on flame. Your Lord would not have permitted the breaking up of your peace unless he had some high service for you. Since you are his servant, find out his will, and do it. God will thus honor himself in you, and by and by he will honor and comfort you also.

Observe that *the woman now becomes a messenger for Christ.* She has to quit conferring with him to go and testify about him. She did not go unbidden though, for she recollected that the Lord had said at an early period of the conversation, "Go, call thy husband, and come hither." So she goes to call her husband. It is well to have a warrant for what we do. Observe, she interprets her orders very liberally. She thought as the Christ had said, "Thou hast had five husbands, and he whom thou now hast is not thy husband," he could not have limited her errand to one who was not her husband except in name, and so she might as well call any of the six men with whom she had dwelled, and therefore she might speak to all the men who were loitering about the public square, and tell them what she had seen. Remember how our Savior gave a large interpretation of his own prophetic mission. He was not sent as a teacher except to the lost sheep of the house of Israel, but he went to the very edge of his diocese, if he did not go over it. He went to the borders of Tyre and Sidon, and when a woman came out of those parts he had healing for her daughter; though he did sow most of his seed upon the acres of the Holy Land, yet he made it fly over the boundary; in fact, he sowed all the ages, and on this once barbarous island there have fallen blessed handfuls which are bringing forth fruit to his glory. Always go to the verge of your commission, never stop short of it. Try to do more good than you can, and it is very possible that you will be successful. Indeed, if you only try to do what you can do, you will do little; but when in faith you attempt what you cannot alone accomplish, God will be at your back, and in your weakness his strength shall be made clear.

Notice that *the woman leaves her waterpot.* The Spirit of God thought well to record this circumstance, and therefore I think there must be a measure of teaching in it. She left her waterpot, first, for speed. Perhaps you have got it into your head that it was an ordinary English waterpot, such as you water the garden with; possibly you so picture it, rose and all. Nothing of the sort: it was a big jar, or large pitcher of earthenware, she had to carry on her head or her shoulder, quite a load for her, and so she left it that she might run the more quickly. She was a wise woman to leave her waterpot when she wanted to move rapidly. Others think she did so because she was so taken up with her errand that she forgot her pitcher. It is blessed forgetfulness which comes of absorption in a holy design. When the King's business requires haste, it is wise to leave behind everything that would hinder. Our Lord Jesus himself forgot his hunger in his zeal to guide a soul to peace, and it is said of him in the psalm, "I forget to eat my bread." He was so absorbed in his heavenly work that he said, "I have meat to eat that ye know not of." A man has hardly felt the power of eternal things unless at times he forgets some earthly matters. If a roan [horse] is called to rush for his life through a room full of crockery there will, probably, be a number of breakages. You cannot think of everything at once; your mind is limited, and it is not advisable that you should divide the strength of your thoughts by having two or more aims. So she left her water-pot. Without thought she hit upon as good an action as thought would have suggested. The waterpot would have hindered her, but it might be useful to the Christ and his disciples. Thus they could give him to drink. He was thirsty, and probably so were they, and with her pitcher they could help themselves. Besides, it was a pledge that she was coming back. She said thereby, "I am running away on an errand, but I shall come back again. I have not listened to the great Teacher for the last time. I shall return and hear him further, till I know him better and trust him more fully." So it was significant that she left her waterpot. Sometimes you will have to leave your shop to win a soul. You will cast up a row of figures wrongly and wonder why; and the reason will be that before your mind there fluttered the soul of a swearer or the figure of a drunkard, or the image of a fallen woman, and your heart was filled with the longing to find the lost sheep. Never mind. I daresay the woman had her waterpot again, and you will get back to business again, and rectify your blunder, and attend to the shop, and set all matters right; and if a soul is saved, you will have made a profit by any loss you have sustained.

We have started the woman on her mission; now I want you to *observe particularly her mode of address,* for there is teaching here. She said to the men, "Come, see a man that told me all things that ever I did: is not this the Christ?" Observe first, when she did go back to the men she had but one aim, and that was to bring them to Jesus. She cries, "Come, see." She did not tell them anything about their sin at the time, nor try to reform their habits; she called them at once to him who could set them right. She knew that if she could bring them to Christ all things would come right inevitably. It is good for you to shoot only at one target. Choose your design and aim at it, and not at two objects. Drive away at the souls of men in the name of God to get them to Christ, and nothing short of him. Labor for this; be willing to live for this, and to die for this, that men may be saved by Emmanuel's love and blood and Spirit. This Samaritan woman aimed at this object and tried to gain it by an exceedingly earnest address. I warrant you she said it very prettily, "Come, come, come, see a man that told me all things that ever I did": perhaps with all her charms, with all the softness of her winsome tongue, with all the entreaty of her bright eyes, she cried, "Come, every one of you; come, see for yourselves, a man which told me all things that ever I did." If you go upon the Lord's errands, take your heart with you; speak every single syllable earnestly; and if you are thoroughly alive you will not need to be taught the way of doing it. The way comes naturally to those whose hearts are set upon the end.

She spoke self-forgetfully: she seemed entirely to have forgotten herself, and yet she remembered herself—a paradox, but not a contradiction. She said, "Come, see a man, which told me all things that ever I did." She quoted herself, and yet if she had thought of herself she would not have said a word on the subject of her own life. She might have feared that the men would have replied, "A pretty story that must be!" They knew her well, and might have turned around and said, "You are a beauty, to come here and talk to us in this style!" No; she let them talk of her as they pleased. "Come, see a man, which told me all things that ever I did." That putting aside of all affectation, that genuine simplicity, was part of her power. Never try to be otherwise than you are. If you have been a great sinner, be ashamed of it, but do not be ashamed of that love which saved you from it, so as to refuse to bear witness to its power. Put away the thought of what people will think of you, and only look to what they will think of Jesus for having forgiven and renewed you.

Note how short she was. Ralph Erskine calls her the female preacher. I am not so sure of the correctness of the title. If women preached just as long as she did, and no longer, no one could find fault with them; her testimony lies all in one verse, and is just an invitation and a question. There needed no more words; no, not another half a word. She said exactly enough; for she was successful in leading the men to Jesus, who could do the preaching far better than she could. I cannot call her words a sermon; at any rate, you would not care for me to preach so briefly. However, brevity is a great virtue. Do not crave to be fluent, only ask to be earnest.

Then, how vivacious she was. "Come, see a man." The words are all alive, and very far from being dull and heavy. "Come, see." It is almost as laconic as Julius Caesar's famous dispatch: "I came, I saw, I conquered." "Come, see a man, which told me all things that ever I did: is not this the Christ?"

Then, it was so sensible. There is a dispute about the exact force of what the woman said, but most of those who give us precise translations differ from our common version. It is what she meant and believed, but not exactly what she said. She probably said, "Come, see a man, which told me all things that ever I did: can this be the Christ?"—or, "This is not the Christ, is he?" She did not say he was, but she suggested it with great modesty for the men to examine. She believed that Jesus was the Christ, but she knew that men do not like to be taught by such as she, and so she humbly threw it out for their examination. "Can this be the anointed One whom we are expecting? Come and judge." She did not express all she believed, lest she should provoke them to opposition; she was adroit and wise. She fished after the manner of her Master, for she could not but feel how dexterously he had fished for her. She was an apt scholar, and humbly copied the Friend who had blessed her: "Come, see a man, which told me all things that ever I did: can this possibly be the Christ?" This led them to come, if it was only to set the woman right. Possibly they thought her a poor, mistaken body; but in their superior wisdom they would look into the matter, and so the thing she desired was granted her. Oh, to have our wits about us for Jesus!

But the argument is exceedingly strong, let her put it how she may. "This man has told me all things that ever I did." She might have said, if she thought it wise to say it, "He must be the Christ"; and that is my last point, namely, the grand argument drawn from herself, and adapted to the men. Observe the force of her reasoning. His power to read her heart and manifest her to herself was conclusive evidence to her that a special anointing was upon him.

But before I get at that, I must have you examine more fully the whole of the woman's little message, of which it was a part. It divides itself into two parts. You have been looking for "first and second" all this while, and now you shall have them. There are two parts in her sermon. The first is the invitation: "Come, see a man, which told me all things that ever I did"; the second is the argument: "Is not this the Christ?"

I. Consider at once *the invitation.*

It is a clever as well as a genuine and hearty invitation. She says, "Come, see." This was putting it most fairly, and men like a fair proposal, and the Holy Spirit works by means which suit the mind. She does not say, "You must and shall believe what I say." No, no; she is too sensible; she says, "Come and see for yourselves," and that is exactly what I want to say to every unconverted person here this morning. My Lord Jesus is the most precious Savior that I ever dreamed of. Come and test him. He is altogether lovely, and he has blessed my soul unspeakably, but I do not want you to believe because of my saying, "Come and see for yourselves." Can anything be fairer? Seek him by prayer; trust him by faith; test his gospel for yourselves. It is an old-fashioned exhortation: "O taste and see that the Lord is good," and, again, "'Prove me now,' saith the LORD of hosts." In fact, this is Christ's own word to the first disciples, "Come and see," and they used it when pleading with others, saying to them, "Come and see."

Moreover, this woman's invitation throws the responsibility upon them. She says, "Come and see." Thus would I say to you—If you do not come and see, I cannot help it, and I cannot help you either. I cannot stand sponsor for you: use your own judgments and clear your own consciences. Come and see on your own accounts. If you do not, then the blame must rest with you. If you do, then your personal investigation will be sure to end in a blessing. O dear hearers, I may preach the gospel to you, but I cannot go to Christ in your stead. It is mine to entreat and persuade, and to use every kind of means by which I may get you to the Savior; but it is a personal matter with each of you. Oh, that the Holy Spirit would lead you to come yourselves to Jesus; for it must be your own act and deed through his blessed working upon your nature. You must come; you must repent; you must believe; you must lay hold on eternal life for yourselves. Nothing but personal religion can possibly save you. The woman's call was a good exhortation in that respect.

Then, is it not pleasantly put, so as to prove the sympathy of the speaker? She does not say, as she might have said, "Go, see a man." No, "Come, see a man," as much as to say, "Come along; I will go with you and lead the way. You shall not say I have seen enough of him and do not care to go again, and now want to send you packing there alone because I am tired of him. No; come! Come along; come with me—we will all go together. The more I have seen of him, the more I want to see. Come, see the wondrous man." Dear friends, when you try to win a soul do not try the "go" system, but use the "come" system. When man cries, "I cannot go to Christ," or, "I will not go to Christ," look at him through your tears and cry out, "Friend, I am a sinner like yourself, and have no hope but in the precious blood of Jesus. Come, let me pray with you, let us go to Jesus together." Then, when you pray, do not say, "Lord, I am one of your saints, and come to you bringing this sinner." That may be true, but it is not a wise way of speaking. Cry, "Lord, here are two sinners that deserve your wrath, and we come to ask you in your pity to give the Savior to us, and renew our hearts by your Spirit." That is the way God helps soul winners to draw others. When we say, "Come," let us lead the way ourselves. What you wish another to do, it will be wise to do yourself, for example has more power than precept. How would you like the sinner to turn around upon you and say, "You may well give away advice when you do not intend to use it yourself." No; but, "Come, see a man, which told me all things that ever I did." A sister's heart spoke out in that word, *come.*

Again, what a blessed vanishing of the speaker there is. I have heard of brethren whose preaching is spoiled because they are so self-conscious. The man wishes you to feel that he is speaking in first-rate style, and is an eminent divine. When he has finished, the common exclamation is "I never heard such a clever man." But he was not so wise as he might have been or should have been, for he who preaches rightly makes you forget himself; in fact, the observation about him, if it comes out at all, is in this fashion: "I did not detect any eloquence; anybody might have talked like that, but somehow I have felt as I never felt before." The fish knows little about the angler, but he knows when he has swallowed the hook. When the truth has gone right home to the hearer's heart, the form of speech is of little consequence. This woman does not say anything to make the Samaritan men admire herself, but she draws to Jesus with the exhortation, "Come, see a man." What she does mention about herself is with the design of extolling the Savior. That is a grand sentence of John the Baptist, "He must increase, but I must decrease." Less, less, less of John, that there may be all the more of Christ. There is but one great universe, and Christ and you are in it. The more space you occupy, there must be so much the less for Jesus. When you get less and less, there is more for Jesus; and when you reach the vanishing point then Jesus is all in all; and that is exactly what you should aim at. This sensible woman's invitation deserves to be copied by every worker.

II. Now for *the argument,* with which I close.

An argument lies concealed here, and if you look at the text a minute or two you will discover it. She conceals it because she is persuaded that they have already agreed to it. It is this: "If Jesus be the Christ, the Anointed, then it is fit that you should come with me and see him." She does not argue that point, because every Samaritan agreed to it. If Jesus be the Christ, then we ought to go and listen to him, look at him, and become his followers. Alas, my dear hearers, I am obliged to urge that argument with many of you, because you are not so practical as these Samaritans. You believe that Jesus is the Christ; I suppose every man and woman of you does that: why, then, do you not believe in him as your Savior? You never had a doubt about his Godhead: why is he not your God? "If I tell you the truth," says Christ, "why do you not believe me?" If this be the anointed One whom God has sent to take away the sins of men, why have you not sought him that he may rid you of your sins? If this be the propitiation which God has set forth, why have you not accepted this propitiation? If this be the fountain wherein sin can be washed away, why are you not washed? There is no reason in your course of action; it is illogical and irrational. If there be a Savior, the man who is taught right reason vows that he will have him; if there be a fountain that can wash away sin, he resolves to be washed in it; if he can get right with God by any process, he hastens to be rectified. I say, this woman did not argue the point, because it did not need arguing. It goes without saying, and there let it stand.

But what she did argue was this: "This man who was just now sitting on the well, is he not the Christ?" How did she prove it? First, she did as good as say, "He must be Christ, *because he has revealed me to myself*: he has told me all things that ever I did." The words are wide. Stop, dear woman; surely he has not revealed all your life, certainly not in words. He has revealed your unchastity, but nothing else. But she was right. Were you ever out in a black and murky night when a single lightning flash has come? It has only smitten one oak in the field, but in so doing it has revealed all the landscape. It struck one object, but all around you was light as day for the moment. So when the Lord Jesus Christ revealed this woman's lustfulness, she saw clearly the whole of her life at a single view, and the Lord had indeed told her all things that ever she did. Do you wonder that she said, "Is not this the Christ?"

Beloved, no one proves himself to be truly anointed unless he begins by showing you your sins. If any teacher leads you to hope that, without repentance, or any sense of sin, you may be saved, he is not of Christ. I charge you fling away any hope which is not consistent with your own entire hopelessness apart from Jesus. If you have not known yourself a sinner, you cannot know Christ as a Savior. Some are preaching up nowadays a dry-eyed faith and men seem to jump into assurance as if there were no new birth, no conviction of sin, and no repentance. But it is not so: "Ye must be born again." That birth is not without pangs. Trust in Christ brings a hatred of sin and a mourning because of it. A man cannot hate what he does not know; but this woman was made to see her sin, and that sight proved that the Messiah was dealing with her. The non-repentance prophets cry, "Peace, peace," where there is no peace: they film [cover] the sore, but Jesus puts the lancet into it, lays it wide open, and makes the patient see the gangrene of the wound, and then he closes it up, and with his heavenly ointment makes a sure cure of it. There is no binding up the heart that was never broken: there is no comforting a man who has always been comfortable: there is no making a man righteous who always was righteous: there is no washing a man who has no filthiness. No, and this is what the Messiah does: he lays bare the disease, and this is a proof that he is sent of God, because he does not adopt the flimsy, flattering mode of deceivers, but goes straight to the truth. Her argument is, he must be the Messiah, for he has revealed me to myself.

Second, *he must be the Messiah, for he has revealed himself to me.* "No sooner did I see my filthiness than I saw at once that he was every way ready to cleanse me." A sinner's eye is never ready to see the Savior till first it has seen the sin. When the man sees despair written across the face of human strength, then he turns and sees hope mildly beaming from the kind eyes of the Son of man: but not till then. Jesus has revealed himself, and now she says, "I see that he knows me, and knows all about me." Wonderful it is how the gospel robe exactly fits a man: when he gets it and puts it on he feels that he who made this garment knew his form. Perhaps you have some special weakness or singular deformity; but you soon perceive that Jesus knew all about it, for his salvation exactly meets the lack. There is a bath: ah, he knew I was filthy. There is a robe: ah, he knew I was naked. There eye salve: he knew that I was blind. Here is a ring for my finger: he knew I wanted a forget-me-not to keep me in memory of mercy received. Here are shoes for my bare feet, and a banquet for my griping hunger. Every want is forestalled, and this proves the omniscience of my Savior. "Therefore," said she, "he knows all about me: he must be infinitely wise; he must be the Christ." This is good arguing, is it not?

Then she seemed to say to them too, "This is more to me a great deal than it can be to you, *for he has dealt personally with me;* therefore I abide in my assurance that he is the Christ: but go and learn the same arguments for yourselves." Brethren, if the Lord Jesus Christ had told this woman all that ever her third husband did, it would have had far less power over her than telling her all she had done herself. When conviction comes personally home, and the discovery is all about your own state and character, it has a special power over your heart and mind to make you say, "This is the Christ." Also, my brethren, at the remembrance of my Lord's surgery when I was wounded and sorely broken, I am ready to cry, "See how he handles me. Never was a hand so strong and yet so tender: never a physician with such a lion's heart and such a lady's hand. I can feel his strength as he upholds me, and I can feel his tenderness as he embraces me. Surely he is the Anointed, and sent of the Lord to bind up the brokenhearted, for he has bound up my broken heart. The case is proved to me: come and experience the like conviction within yourselves."

Moreover, and perhaps there is force in this which has not been noticed, she says, "Come, see," as much as to say, *"You may come, I know,* for when I came to the well, he did not look daggers at me; and when I did not give him water, he did not grow hot with me and say, 'Disrespectful woman, I will not speak to you.' No, but I was at home with him in a moment. Come, see a man who made himself so at home with me that he told me all that ever I did. I am sure he must be the Messiah. The Messiah is to come to open the blind eyes, and he must needs be among the blind to perform the miracle. He is to fetch prisoners out of prison, and they are the lowest class that are in prison, and yet he goes to them. So, come along. I will go first and introduce you to him."

That is the woman's little speech, and how good it is! I am going to add a bit to it which she did not know, but which we know. I wish I knew how to say something that would make you unconverted ones hurry to Christ, but if anything ought to do so it is this. Suppose you never do come to Christ in this life, and die without him. God grant you may not die without having listened to him and received him; but if you do you will be wakened up at the last day from your grave with the blast of a terrible trumpet, and with the cry of "Come to judgment! Come to judgment! Come away!" Whether you will or not, you will have to come, and see a man sitting upon the great white throne, judging the nations; and do you know what he will do with you then? He will tell you all things that ever you did, and as the scenes pass before your mind's eye, and as your own words go ringing again through your ear, you will be sorely distressed. Perhaps this morning's scene will be revived before you, and conscience will tell you, "You were at the tabernacle that morning; the gospel was put plainly to you, by one who in his heart longed for you to be saved; but you did dispute to all those entreaties, and turned away." I tell you it will be your hell for Jesus to tell you all things that ever you did, and you then will see the argument: "Is not this the Christ?" But alas, he will be no Savior to you, for you refused him. He will then tell you, "I called, but you refused; I stretched out my hands, but no man regarded." Still shall proceed that awful tale of all things that ever you did, concluding with this—you refused mercy, you rejected Jesus, you turned away from salvation, you would not have this man to save you, and therefore have you come to have your past made the fuel for your everlasting burning. God grant that no one here may ever come to that. No, if I had the task to select one man out of this congregation that would have to spend an eternity in having his life rehearsed to him, where should I find him? No, I cannot see one that I dare to pitch upon, not one—not one—not even the worst man or woman here. I would not if I could. O God, of thy mercy suffer no one here to know the terror of being driven away forever from thy presence and the glory of thy power, for Jesus' sake. Amen.

The Canaanite Woman: The Little Dogs

◈

Delivered on Lord's Day morning, August 6, 1876, at the Metropolitan Tabernacle, Newington. No. 1309.

But he answered and said, "It is not meet to take the children's bread, and to cast it to dogs." And she said, "Truth, Lord: yet the dogs eat of the crumbs which fall from their masters' table."—MATTHEW 15:26–27

But Jesus said unto her, "Let the children first be filled: for it is not meet to take the children's bread, and to cast it unto the dogs." And she answered and said unto him, "Yes, Lord: yet the dogs under the table eat of the children's crumbs."—MARK 7:27–28

I take the two records of Matthew and Mark that we may have the whole matter before us. May the Holy Spirit bless our meditations thereon.

The brightest jewels are often found in the darkest places. Christ had not found such faith, no, not in Israel, as he discovered in this poor Canaanite woman. The borders and fringes of the land were more fruitful than the center, where the husbandry had been more abundant. In the headlands of the field, where the farmer does not expect to grow much beyond weeds, the Lord Jesus found the richest ear of corn that as yet had filled his sheaf. Let those of us who reap after him be encouraged to expect the same experience. Never let us speak of any district as too depraved to yield us converts, nor of any class of persons as too fallen to become believers. Let us go even to the borders of Tyre and Sidon, though the land be under a curse, for even there we shall discover some elect one, ordained to be a jewel for the Redeemer's crown. Our heavenly Father has children everywhere.

In spiritual things it is found that the best plants often grow in the most barren soil. Solomon spoke of trees, and discoursed concerning the hyssop on the wall and the cedar in Lebanon. So is it in the natural world, the great trees are found on great mountains and the minor plants in places adapted for their tiny roots; but it is not so among the plants of the Lord's right-hand planting, for there we have seen the cedar grow upon the wall—great saints in places where it was apparently impossible for them to exist; and we have seen hyssops growing upon Lebanon—a questionable, insignificant piety, where there have been innumerable advantages. The Lord is able to make strong faith exist with little knowledge, little present enjoyment, and little encouragement; and strong faith in such conditions triumphs and conquers, and doubly glorifies the grace of God. Such was this Canaanite woman, a cedar growing where soil was scant enough. She was a woman of amazing faith, though she could have heard but little of him in whom she believed, and perhaps had never seen his person at all until the day when she fell at his feet and said, "Lord, help me!"

Our Lord had a very quick eye for spying faith. If the jewel was lying in the mire, his eye caught its glitter; if there was a choice ear of wheat among the thorns, he failed not to perceive it. Faith has a strong attraction for the Lord Jesus; at the sight of it, "the king is held in the galleries" and cries, "Thou hast ravished my heart with one of thine eyes, with one chain of thy neck." The Lord Jesus was charmed with the fair jewel of this woman's faith, and watching it and delighting in it, he resolved to turn it around and set it in other lights, that the various facets of this priceless diamond might each one flash its brilliance and delight his soul. Therefore he tried her faith by his silence, and by his discouraging replies, that he might see its strength; but he was all the while delighting in it, and secretly sustaining it, and when he had sufficiently tried it, he brought it forth as gold, and set his own royal mark upon it in these memorable words: "O woman, great is thy faith; be it unto thee even as thou wilt."

I am hopeful this morning that perhaps some poor soul in this place under very discouraging circumstances may nevertheless be led to believe in the Lord Jesus Christ with a strong and persevering faith, and though as yet it enjoys no peace, and has seen no gracious answer to prayer, I trust that its struggling faith may be strengthened this morning by the example of the Canaanite woman.

I gather, from the story of her appeal to the Lord Jesus and her success therein, four facts. The first is, *faith's mouth cannot be closed*; the second is, *faith never disputes with God*; third, I perceive that *faith argues mightily*; and fourth, that *faith wins her suit.*

I. The mouth of faith can never be closed, for if ever the faith of a woman was tried so as to make her cease from prayer, it was that of this daughter of Tyre.

She had difficulty after difficulty to encounter, and yet she could not be put off from pleading for her little daughter, because she believed in Jesus as the great Messiah, able to heal all manner of diseases, and she meant to pray to him until he yielded to her importunity, for she was confident that he could chase the demon from her child.

Observe that *the mouth of faith cannot be closed even on account of the closed ear and the closed mouth of Christ*. He answered her never a word. She spoke very piteously, she came and threw herself at his feet, her child's case was very urgent, her motherly heart was very tender, and her cries were very piercing, and yet he answered her never a word: as if he were deaf and dumb, he passed her by; yet was she not staggered; she believed in him, and even he himself could not make her doubt him, let him try silence even if he would. It is hard to believe when prayer seems to be a failure. I would to God that some poor seeker here might believe that Jesus Christ is able and willing to save, and so fully believe it that his unanswered prayers shall not be able to make him doubt. Even if you should pray in vain by the month together, do not allow a doubt about the Lord Jesus and his power to save to cross your mind. What if you cannot yet grasp the peace which faith must ultimately bring you, what if you have no certainty of forgiveness of your sin, what if no gleams of joy should visit your spirit, yet believe you him who cannot lie. "Though he slay me," said Job, "yet will I trust in him." That was splendid faith. It would be a great deal for some if they could say, "Though he smite me, yet will I trust him," but Job said, "Though he slay me." If he put on the garb of an executioner, and come out against me as though he would destroy me, yet will I believe him to be full of love: he is good and gracious still, I cannot doubt it, and therefore at his feet I will lie down and look up, expecting grace at his hands. Oh, for such faith as this! O soul, if you have it, you are a saved man, as sure as you are alive. If even the Lord's apparent refusal to bless you cannot close your mouth, your faith is of a noble sort, and salvation is yours.

In the next place, *her faith could not be silenced by the conduct of the disciples*. They did not treat her well, but yet perhaps not altogether ill. They were not like their Master, but frequently repulsed those who would come to him. Her noise annoyed them, she kept to them with boundless perseverance, and therefore they said, "Send her away, for she crieth *after us*." Poor soul, she never cried after *them*, it was after their Master. Sometimes disciples become very important in their own eyes, and think that the pushing and crowding to hear the gospel is caused by the people's eagerness to hear them, whereas nobody would care for their poor talk if it were not for the gospel message which they are charged to deliver. Give us any other theme, and the multitude would soon melt away. Though weary of the woman's importunate cries, they acted somewhat kindly toward her, for they were evidently desirous that she should obtain the boon she sought, or else our Lord's reply would not have been appropriate, "I am not sent save to the lost sheep of the house of Israel." It was not her daughter's healing that they cared for, but they consulted their own comfort, for they were anxious to be rid of her. "Send her away," said they, "for she crieth after us." Still, though they did not treat her as men should treat a woman, as disciples should treat a seeker, as Christians should treat everybody, yet for all that, her mouth was not stopped. Peter, I have no doubt, looked in a very scowling manner, and perhaps even John became a little impatient, for he had a quick temper by nature; Andrew and Philip and the rest of them considered her very impertinent and presumptuous; but she thought of her little daughter at home, and of the horrible miseries to which the demon subjected her, and so she pressed up to the Savior's feet and said, "Lord, help me." Cold, hard words and unkind, unsympathetic behavior could not prevent her pleading with him in whom she believed. Ah, poor sinner, perhaps you are saying, "I am longing to be saved, but such and such a good Christian man has dealt very bitterly with me; he has doubted my sincerity and questioned the reality of my repentance, and caused me the deepest sorrow; it seems as if he did not wish me to be saved." Ah, dear friend, this is very trying, but if you have true faith in the Master, you will not mind us disciples, neither the gentlest of us, nor the most crooked of us, but just urge on your suit with your Lord till he deigns to give you an answer of peace.

Her mouth, again, was not closed by exclusive doctrine, which appeared to confine the blessing to a favored few: the Lord Jesus Christ said, "I am not sent save to the lost sheep of the house of Israel," and though properly understood, there is nothing very severe in it, yet the sentence must have fallen on the woman's heart like a talent of lead. "Alas," she might have thought, "then he is not sent to me; vainly do I seek for that which he reserves for the Jews." Now the doctrine of election, which is assuredly taught in Scripture, ought not to hinder any soul from coming to Christ, for if properly understood, it would rather encourage than discourage; and yet often to the uninstructed ear the doctrine of the divine choice of a people from before the foundation of the world acts with very depressing effect.

We have known poor seekers mournfully say, "Perhaps there is no mercy for me; I may be among those for whom no purpose of mercy has been formed." They have been tempted to cease from prayer for fear they should not have been predestinated unto eternal life. Ah, dear soul, if you have the faith of God's elect in you, you will not be kept back by any self-condemning inferences drawn from the secret things of God, but you will believe in that which has been clearly revealed, and you will be assured that this cannot contradict the secret decrees of heaven. What though our Lord was only sent to the house of Israel, yet there is a house of Israel not after the flesh but after the spirit, and therefore the Syrophenician woman was included even where she thought she was shut out, and you may also be comprehended within those lines of gracious destiny which now distress you. At any rate, say to yourself, "In the election of grace others are included who were as sinful as I have been, why should not I? Others have been included who were as full of distress as I have been on account of sin, and why should not I be also?" Reasoning thus you will press forward, in hope believing against hope, suffering no plausible deduction from the doctrine of Scripture to prevent your believing in the appointed Redeemer.

The mouth of faith in this case was not even closed by a sense of admitted unworthiness. Christ spoke of dogs: he meant that the gentiles were to Israel as the dogs: she did not at all dispute it, but yielded the point by saying, "Truth, Lord." She felt she was only worthy to be compared to a dog. I have no doubt her sense of unworthiness was very deep. She did not expect to win the boon she sought for on account of any merit of her own; she depended upon the goodness of Christ's heart, not on the goodness of her cause, and upon the excellence of his power rather than upon the prevalence of her plea; yet conscious as she was that she was only a poor gentile dog, her prayers were not hindered; she cried, notwithstanding all, "Lord, help me." O sinner, if you feel yourself to be the worst sinner out of hell, still pray, believingly pray for mercy. If your sense of unworthiness be enough to drive you to self-destruction, yet I beseech you, out of the depths, out of the dungeon of self-loathing, still cry unto God; for your salvation rests in no measure or degree upon yourself, or upon anything that you are or have been or can be. You need to be saved *from* yourself, not *by* yourself. It is yours to be empty that Jesus may fill you; yours to confess your filthiness that he may wash you; yours to be less than nothing that Jesus may be everything to you. Suffer not the number, blackness, frequency, or heinousness of your transgressions to silence your prayers, but though you be a dog, yes, not worthy to be set with the dogs of the Lord's flock, yet open your mouth in believing prayer.

There was besides this a general tone and spirit in what the Lord Jesus said which tended to depress the woman's hope and restrain her prayer, yet *she was not kept back by the darkest and most depressing influences.* "It is not meet," said the Lord Jesus, "it is not becoming, it is not proper, it is hardly lawful, to take children's bread and throw it to dogs." Perhaps she did not quite see all that he might have meant, but what she did see was enough to pour cold water upon the flame of her hope, yet her faith was not quenched. It was a faith of that immortal kind which nothing can kill; for her mind was made up that whatever Jesus meant, or did not mean, she would not cease to trust him, and urge her suit with him. There are a great many things in and around the gospel which men see as in a haze, and being misunderstood they rather repel than attract seeking souls; but be they what they may, we must resolve to come to Jesus at all risks. "If I perish, I perish." Besides the great stumbling stone of election, there are truths and facts which seekers magnify and misconstrue till they see a thousand difficulties. They are troubled about Christian experience, about being born again, about inbred sin, and all sorts of things; in fact, a thousand lions are in the way when the soul attempts to come to Jesus, but he who gives Christ the faith which he deserves says, "I fear none of these things. Lord, help me, and I will still confide in thee. I will approach thee, I will press through obstacles to thee, and throw myself at thy dear feet, knowing that him that cometh to thee thou wilt in no wise cast out."

II. *Faith never disputes with the Lord.*

Faith worships. You notice how Matthew says, "Then came she and worshiped him." Faith also begs and prays. You observe how Mark says, "She besought him." She cried, "Lord, help me," after having said, "Have mercy on me, O Lord, thou Son of David." Faith pleads, but never disputes, not even against the hardest thing that Jesus says. If faith disputed—I am uttering a solecism—she would not be faith, for that which disputes is unbelief. Faith in God implies agreement with what God says, and consequently it excludes the idea of doubt. Genuine faith believes anything and everything the Lord says, whether discouraging or encouraging. She never has a "but" or an "if," or even a "yet" to put in, but she stands to it, "Thou hast said it, Lord, and therefore it is true: thou hast ordained it, Lord, and therefore it is right." She never goes beyond that.

Observe in our text that *faith assents to all the Lord says*. She said, "Truth, Lord." What had he said? "You are comparable to a dog!" "Truth, Lord; truth, Lord; so I am." "It would not be meet that the children should be robbed of bread in order to feed dogs." "Truth, Lord, it would not be fitting, and I would not have one of thy children deprived of grace for me." "It is not your time yet," said Jesus; "the children must *first* be fed, children at the mealtimes and dogs after dinner; this is Israel's time, and the gentiles may follow after. But not yet." She virtually replies, "I know it, Lord, and agree thereto."

She does not raise a question or dispute the justice of the Lord's dispensing his own grace according to his sovereign good pleasure. She fails not, as some do who cavil at divine sovereignty. It would have proved that she had little or no faith if she had done that. She disputes not as to the Lord's set time and order. Jesus said, "Let the children first be filled," and she does not dispute the time, as many do, who will not have it that now is the accepted time, but are as much for postponing as this woman was for antedating the day of grace. She entered into no argument against its being improper to take the covenant bread from the children and give it to the uncircumcised heathen: she never wished Israel to be robbed for her. Dog as she was she would not have any purpose of God nor any propriety of the divine household shifted and changed for her. She assented to all the Lord's appointments. That is the faith which saves the soul, which agrees with the mind of God, even if it seem adverse to herself, which believes the revealed declarations of God whether they appear to be pleasant or terrible, and assents to God's word whether it be like a balm to its wound or like a sword to cut and slay. If the word of God be true, O man, do not fight against it, but bow before it. It is not the way to a living faith in Jesus Christ, nor to obtain peace with God, to take up arms against anything which God declares. In yielding lies safety. Say "Truth, Lord," and you shall find salvation.

Note that she not only assented to all that the Lord said, but *she worshiped him in it.* "Truth," she said, "but yet thou art my Lord." "Thou callest me 'dog,' but thou art my Lord for all that: thou accountest me unworthy to receive thy bounties, but thou art my Lord, and I still own thee as such." She is of the mind of Job: "Shall we receive good at the hand of the Lord, and shall we not receive evil?" She is willing to take the evil and say, "Whether the Lord gives, or whether he refuses, blessed be his name; he is my Lord still." Oh, this is grand faith, which has thrown aside the disputatious spirit, and not only assents to the Lord's will, but worships him in it. Let it be what it may, O Lord, even if the truth condemns me, yet still thou art Lord, and I confess thy deity, confess thine excellence, own thy crown rights, and submit myself to thee: do with me what thou wilt.

And, you observe, when she said "Truth, Lord," *she did not go on to suggest that any alteration should be made for her.* "Lord," she said, "thou hast classed me among the dogs"; she does not say, "Put me among the children," but she only asks to be treated as a dog is. "The dogs eat the crumbs," says she. She does not want a purpose altered nor an ordinance changed, nor a decree removed: "Let it be as it is: if it be thy will, Lord, it is my will"; only she spies a gleam of hope, where, if she had not possessed faith, she would have seen only the blackness of despair. May we have such a faith as hers, and never enter into controversy with God.

**III. Now I come to an interesting part of our subject, namely, that
faith argues, though it does not dispute.**

"Truth, Lord," said she, "yet the dogs eat the crumbs." This woman's
argument was correct, and strictly logical throughout. It was an argument
based upon the Lord's own premises, and you know if you are reasoning with
a man you cannot do better than take his own statements and argue upon
them. She does not proceed to lay down new premises, or dispute the old ones
by saying, "I am no dog"; but she says, "Yes, I am a dog." She accepts that statement of the Lord, and uses it as a blessed *argumentum ad hominem*, such as was
never excelled in this world. She took the words out of his own mouth, and
vanquished him with them, even as Jacob overcame the angel. There is so
much force in the women's argument, that I quite despair this morning of
being able to set it all forth to you. I would, however, remark that the translators have greatly injured the text by putting in the word *yet,* for there is no
"yet" in the Greek: it is quite another word. Jesus said, "It is not meet to take
the children's bread and cast it to the dogs." "No," said she, "it would not be
meet to do this, because the dogs are provided for, for the dogs eat the crumbs
that fall from their master's table." "It would be very improper to give them
the children's bread, because they have bread of their own." "Truth, Lord, I
admit it would be improper to give the dogs the children's bread, because they
have already their share when they eat the crumbs which fall from the children's table. That is all they want, and all I desire. I do not ask thee to give me
the children's bread, I only ask for the dog's crumbs."

Let us see the force of her reasoning, which will appear in many ways.
The first is this. *She argued with Christ from her hopeful position.* "I am a dog,"
said she, "but, Lord, thou hast come all the way to Sidon; here thou art close
on the borders of my country, and therefore I am not like a dog out in the
street; I am a dog under the table." Mark tells us that she said, "The dogs
under the table eat of the children's crumbs." She as good as says, "Lord, thou
seest my position: I was a dog in the street, far off from thee, but now thou
hast come and preached in our borders, and I have been privileged to listen to
thee. Others have been healed, and thou art in this very house doing deeds of
grace while I look on, and therefore, though I am a dog, I am a dog under the
table; therefore, Lord, let me have the crumbs." Do you see, dear hearer? You
admit that you are a sinner, and a great sinner, but you say, "Lord, I am a sinner that is permitted to hear the gospel, therefore bless it to me. I am a dog,
but I am under the table, deal with me as such. When there is a sermon

preached for the comfort of thy people, I am there to hear it: whenever the saints gather together, and the precious promises are discussed, and they rejoice therein, I am there, looking up, and wishing that I were among them, but still, Lord, since thou hast had the grace to let me be a hearer of the gospel, wilt thou reject me now that I desire to be a receiver of it? To what end and purpose hast thou brought me so near, or rather come so near to me, if after all thou wilt reject me? Dog I am, but still I am a dog under the table. It is a favor to be privileged to be among the children, even if I may only lie at their feet. I pray thee, good Lord, then, since now I am permitted to look up to thee and ask this blessing, do not reject me." To me it seems that this was a strong point with the woman, and that she used it well.

Her next plea was *her encouraging relationship*. "Truth, Lord," she says, "I am a dog, but the dogs eat the crumbs which fall from *their masters'* table." See the stress laid there by Matthew: "from their masters' table." I cannot say that thou art my Father, I cannot look up and claim the privilege of a child, but thou art my Master, and masters feed their dogs; they give at least the crumbs to those dogs which own them as their lord." The plea is very like that suggested to the mind of the poor returning prodigal. He thought to say to his father, "Make me as one of thy hired servants": only his faith was far weaker than hers. "Lord, if I do not stand in relation to thee as a child, yet I am thy creature; thou hast made me, and I look up to thee and beseech thee not to let me perish: if I have no other hold upon thee, I have at least this, that I ought to have served thee, and therefore I am thy servant though I am a runaway. I do belong to thee at least under the covenant of works if I do not under the covenant of grace, and oh, since I am thy servant, do not utterly reject me. Thou hast some property in me by creation, at any rate; Oh, look upon me and bless me. The dogs eat what falls from their masters' table; let me do the same." She spies out a dog's relation to its master, and makes the most of it with blessed ingenuity, which we shall do well to imitate.

Notice next, she pleads *her association with the children*. Here I must tell you that it is a pity that it was not, I suppose, possible for our translators to bring clearly out what is after all the pith of the passage. She was pleading for her *little* daughter; and our Lord said to her, "It is not meet to take the children's bread and cast it to the *little* dogs." The word is a diminutive, and the woman pitched upon it. The word *dogs* could not have served her turn one half as well as that of *little dogs,* but she said, "Truth, Lord, yet the little dogs eat of the crumbs." In the East, as a rule, a dog is not allowed indoors; in fact, dogs are there looked upon as foul creatures, and roam about uncared for and half wild. Christianity has raised the dog, and made him man's companion, as it will raise all the brute creation, till the outrages of vivisection, and the cruelties of the vulgar, will be things unheard of except as horrors of a past barbarous age. In the East a dog is far down in the scale of life, a street wanderer, prowling for scanty food, and in temper little better than a reformed wolf. So the adult Easterners do not associate with dogs, having a prejudice against them, but children are not so foolish, and consequently the Eastern children associate with the little dogs. The father will not have the dog near him, but his child knows no such folly, and seeks out a little dog to join him in his sports; thus the little dog comes to be under the table, tolerated in the house for the child's sake.

The woman appears to me to argue thus—"Thou hast called me and my daughter whelps, little dogs, but then the little dogs are under the children's table; they associate with the children, even as I have been with thy disciples today. If I am not one of them, I have been associating with them and would be glad to be among them." How heartily do I wish that some poor soul would catch at this and say, "Lord, I cannot claim to be one of thy children, but I love to sit among them, for I am never happier than when I am with them. Sometimes they trouble and distress me, as little children pinch and hurt their little dogs, but oftentimes they caress me, and speak kindly and comfortably to me, and pray for me, and desire my salvation; so Lord, if I am not a child, yet thou callest me a little dog, so I am, but give me a little dog's treatment; give me the crumb of mercy which I seek."

Her argument goes further, *for the little dog eats the crumbs of the children's bread with the child's full consent.* When a child has its little dog to play with while he is eating, what does the child do? Why, of course, it gives a little bit to the dog every now and again, and the doggie himself takes great liberties and helps himself as much as he dares. When a little dog is with the children at mealtime, it is sure to get a crumb from one or other of its playmates; and none will object to its eating what it can get. So the woman seems to say, "Lord, there are the children, thy disciples; they do not treat me very well; little children do not treat little dogs always so kindly as they might; but still, Lord, they are quite willing that I should have the blessing I am seeking. They have a full portion in thee; they have thy presence; they have thy word; they sit at thy feet; they have obtained all sorts of spiritual blessings. I am sure they cannot grudge me so much less a boon; they are willing that I should have the devil cast out of my daughter, for that blessing compared with what they have is but a crumb, and they are content that I should have it. So Lord, I answer thine argument. Thou sayest it is not meet until the children are filled to give bread to dogs, but, Lord, the children are filled and are quite willing to let me have my portion, they consent to allow me the crumbs; wilt thou not give them to me?"

I think there was another point of force in her plea: it was this, *the abundance of the provision*. She had a great faith in Christ, and believed big things of him, and therefore she said, "Lord, there is no great strength in thine argument if thou dost intend to prove that I ought not to have the bread for fear there should not be enough for the children, for thou hast so much that even while the children are being fed, the dogs may get the crumbs, and there will be enough for the children still." Where it is a poor man's table, and he cannot afford to lose a crumb, dogs should not be allowed; but when it is a king's table where bread is of small account, and the children are sitting and feeding to the full, the little dogs may be permitted to feed under the table for the mere droppings—not the bread the master casts down, but the crumbs which *fall* by accident are so many that there is enough for the dogs without the children being deprived of a mouthful. "No, Lord," said she, "I would not have thee take away the bread from thine own children; God forbid that such a deed should be done for me; but there is enough for thy children in thine overflowing love and mercy, and still enough for me, for all I ask is but a crumb compared with what thou art daily bestowing upon others."

Now here is the last point in which her argument had force. *She looked at things from Christ's point of view.* "If, great Lord," said she, "thou lookest at me as a dog, then behold I humbly take thee at thy word, and plead that if I be a dog to thee then the cure I ask for my daughter is but a crumb for thy great power and goodness to bestow on me." She used a diminutive word too, and said, "a little crumb."

The little dogs eat of the little crumbs which fall from the children's table. What bold faith this was! She valued the mercy she sought beyond all price; she thought it worth ten thousand worlds to her, but yet to the Son of God she knew it to be a mere crumb, so rich is he in power to heal and so full of goodness and blessing. If a man give a crumb to a dog, he has a little the less, but if Jesus gives mercy to the greatest of sinners he has none the less, he is just as rich in condescension and mercy and power to forgive as he was before. The woman's argument was most potent. She was as wise as she was earnest, and best of all, she believed most marvelously.

I shall close this outline of the argument by saying that, at bottom, the woman was, in reality, arguing according to the eternal purpose of God—for what was the Lord's grand design in giving the bread to the children, or, in other words, sending a divine revelation to Israel? Why, it always was his purpose that through the children the dogs should get the bread; that through

Israel the gospel should be handed to the gentiles. It had always been his plan to bless his own heritage that his way might be known upon earth, his saving health among all nations; and this woman somehow or other, by a divine instinct, fell into the divine method. Though she had not spied out the secret, or at least it is not told us that she did so in so many words, yet there was the innate force of her argument. In other words, it ran thus—"It is through the children that the dogs have to be fed: Lord, I do not ask thee to cease giving the children their bread; nor do I even ask thee to hurry on the children's meal, let them be fed first, but even while they are eating let me have the crumbs which drop from their well-filled hands, and I will be content." There is a brave argument for you, poor coming sinner. I leave it in your hands, and pray the Spirit of God to help you to use it, and if you can turn it to good account you shall prevail with the Lord this day.

IV. Our last and closing head is this: *faith wins her suit.*

This woman's faith first *won a commendation for herself.* Jesus said, "O woman, great is thy faith." She had not heard of the prophecies concerning Jesus; she was not bred and born and educated in a way in which she was likely to become a believer and yet did become a believer of the first class. It was marvelous that it should be so, but grace delights in doing wonders. She had not seen the Lord before in her life, she was not like those who had associated with him for many months: and yet, with but one view of him, she gained this great faith. It was astonishing, but the grace of God is always astonishing. Perhaps she had never seen a miracle: all that her faith had to rest upon was that she had heard in her own country that the Messiah of the Jews was come, and she believed that the Man of Nazareth was he, and on this she relied. O brethren, with all our advantages, with the opportunities that we have of knowing the whole life of Christ, and understanding the doctrines of the gospel as they are revealed to us in the New Testament, with many years of observation and experience, our faith ought to be much stronger than it is. Does not this poor woman shame us when we see her with her slender opportunities nevertheless so strong in faith, so that Jesus himself commending her says, "O woman, great is thy faith."

But her faith prevailed further, that it *won a commendation for the mode of its action,* for, according to Mark, Jesus said, "Go thy way; *for this saying* the devil is gone out of thy daughter"; as if he rewarded the saying as well as the faith which suggested it. He was so delighted with the wise and prudent and humble yet courageous manner in which she turned his words against himself, that he said, "For this saying the devil is gone out of thy daughter." The

Lord who commends faith afterward commends the fruits and acts of faith. The tree consecrates the fruit. No man's actions can be acceptable with God till he himself is accepted, but the woman having been accepted on her faith, the results of her faith were agreeable to the heart of Jesus.

The woman also *gained her desire*: "The devil is gone out of thy daughter," and he was gone at once. She had only to go home and find her daughter on the bed taking a quiet rest, which she had not done since the demon had possessed her. Our Lord, when he gave her the desire of her heart, gave it in a grand manner; he gave her a sort of *carte blanche,* and said, "Be it unto thee even as thou wilt." I do not know that any other person ever had such a word said to him as this woman, "Be it unto thee even as thou wilt." It was as if the Lord of glory surrendered at discretion to the conquering arms of a woman's faith. The Lord grant to you and me in all times of our struggling to be able thus by faith still to conquer, and we cannot imagine how great will be the spoil which we shall divide when the Lord shall say, "Be it unto thee even as thou wilt."

The close of all is this: this woman is a lesson to all outsiders, to you who think yourselves beyond the pale of hope, to you who were not brought up to attend the house of God, who perhaps have been negligent of all religion for almost all your lifetime. This poor woman is a Sidonian; she comes of a race that had been condemned to die many centuries before, one of the accursed seed of Canaan, and yet for all that, she became great in the kingdom of heaven because she believed, and there is no reason why those who are reckoned to be quite outside the church of God should not be in the very center of it, and be the most burning and shining lights of the whole. O you poor outcasts and far-off ones, take heart and comfort, and come to Jesus Christ and trust yourselves in his hands.

This woman is next of all an example to those who think they have been repulsed in their endeavors after salvation. Have you been praying, and have you not succeeded? Have you sought the Lord, and do you seem to be more unhappy than ever? Have you made attempts at reformation and amendment, and believed that you made them in the divine strength, and have they failed? Yet trust in him whose blood has not lost its efficacy, whose promise has not lost its truth, and whose arm has not lost its power to save. Cling to the cross, sinner. If the earth sink beneath you, cling on; if storms should rage, and all the floods be out, and even God himself seem to be against you, cling to the cross. There is your hope. You cannot perish there.

This is a lesson, next, to every intercessor. This woman was not pleading for herself, she was asking for another. Oh, when you plead for a fellow sinner, do not do it in a coldhearted manner; plead as for your own soul and your own life. That man will prevail with God as an intercessor who solemnly bears the matter upon his own heart and makes it his own, and with tears entreats an answer of peace.

Last, recollect that this mighty woman, this glorious woman, is a lesson to every mother, for she was pleading for her little daughter. Maternal instinct makes the weakest strong, and the most timid brave. Even among poor beasts and birds, how powerful is a mother's love. Why, the poor little robin, which would be frightened at the approach of a footstep, will sit upon its nest when the intruder comes near when her little ones are in danger. A mother's love makes her heroic for her child; and so when you are pleading with God, plead as a mother's love suggests to you, till the Lord shall say to you also, "O woman, great is thy faith; the devil is gone out of thy daughter; be it unto thee even as thou wilt." I leave that last thought with parents as an encouragement to pray. The Lord stir you up to it, for Jesus' sake. Amen.

The Infirmed Woman: The Lifting Up of the Bowed Down

Delivered on Lord's Day morning, July 14, 1878, at the Metropolitan Tabernacle, Newington. No. 1426.

*And he was teaching in one of the synagogues on the sabbath. And, behold, there was a woman which had a spirit of infirmity eighteen years, and was bowed together, and could in no wise lift up herself. And when Jesus saw her, he called her to him, and said unto her, "Woman, thou art loosed from thine infirmity." And he laid his hands on her: and immediately she was made straight, and glorified God.—*LUKE 13:10–13

I believe that the infirmity of this woman was not only physical but spiritual: her outward appearance was the index of her deep and long-continued depression of mind. She was bent double as to her body, and she was bowed down by sadness as to her mind.

There is always a sympathy between body and soul, but it is not always so plainly seen as in her case; many sad sights would meet us on all hands if it were so. Imagine for a moment what would be the result upon the present congregation if our outward forms were to set forth our inward states. If someone having an eye like that of the Savior could gaze upon us now, and could see the inward in the outward, what would be the appearance of this crowd? Very deplorable sights would be seen, for in many a pew dead persons would be sitting, looking forth from the glassy eyes of death, bearing the semblance of life and a name to live, but all the while being dead as to spiritual things. My friend, you would shudder as you found yourself placed next to a corpse. Alas, the corpse would not shudder, but would remain as insensible as ungodly persons usually are, though the precious truth of the gospel rings in their ears—ears which hear but hear in vain. A large number of souls will be found in all congregations, "dead in trespasses and sins," and yet sitting as God's people sit, and not to be discerned from the living in Zion. Even in those cases in which there is spiritual life, the aspect would not be altogether lovely. Here we should see a man blind, and there another maimed; and a third twisted from perfect uprightness.

Spiritual deformity assumes many forms, and each form is painful to look upon. A paralyzed man with a trembling faith, set forth by a trembling body, would be an uncomfortable neighbor, and a person subject to fits of passion or despair would be equally undesirable if his body suffered from fits also. How sad it would be to have around us persons with a fever upon them, or shivering with ague, hot and cold by turns, burning almost to fanaticism at one moment and then chilled as with a northern wind with utter indifference. I will not try to sketch in further detail the halt [crippled], lame, blind, and impotent folk who are assembled in this Bethesda. Surely if the flesh were shaped according to the spirit, this tabernacle would be turned into a hospital, and each man would flee from his fellow, and wish to run from himself. If to any one of us our inward ailments were to be set forth upon our brow, I warrant you we should not linger long at the glass, nor scarcely dare to think upon the wretched objects which there our eyes would behold. Let us quit the imaginary scene with this consoling thought, that Jesus is among us notwithstanding that we be sick folk, and although he sees nothing to delight his eye if he judges us according to the law, yet, since his mercy delights to relieve human misery, there is abundant scope for him here in the midst of these thousands of ailing souls.

In that synagogue on the Sabbath, this poor woman described in the text must have been one of the least observed. Her particular disease would render her very short in stature; she was dwarfed to almost half her original height, and in consequence, like other very short persons, she would be almost lost in a standing crowd. A person so bent down as she was might have come in and gone out and not have been noticed by anyone standing upon the floor of the meeting place; but I can imagine that our Lord occupied a somewhat elevated position, as he was teaching in the synagogue, for he had probably gone to one of the higher places for the greater convenience of being seen and heard, and for this reason he could more readily see her than others could. Jesus always occupies a place from which he can spy out those who are bowed down. His quick eye did not miss its mark. She, poor soul, was naturally the least observed of all the people in the company, yet was she the most observed, for our Lord's gracious eye glanced over all the rest, but it lighted upon her with fixed regard. There his tender look remained till he had worked the deed of love.

Peradventure, there is someone in the crowd this morning the least observed of anybody, who is yet noticed by the Savior; for he sees not as man sees, but observes most those whom man passes over as beneath his regard. Nobody knows you, nobody cares for you; your peculiar trouble is quite unknown, and you would not reveal it for the world. You feel quite alone; there is no solitude like that which is to be found in a dense throng; and you are in that solitude now. Be not, however, quite despairing, for you have a friend left. The preacher's heart is going after you, but that will little help you: there is far more joy in the fact that, as our Master observed most the least-observed one on that Sabbath in the synagogue, so we trust he will do this day, and his eye shall light on you, even you. He will not pass you by, but will deal out a special Sabbath blessing to your weary heart. Though by yourself accounted to be among the last, you shall now be put upon the first by the Lord's working a notable miracle of love upon you. In the hope that this may be so, we will proceed, by the help of the Holy Spirit, to look into the gracious deed which was done to this poor woman.

I. Our first subject for consideration is, *the bowing down of the afflicted.*

We read of this woman that "she had a spirit of infirmity and was bowed together, and could in no wise lift up herself." Upon which we remark first, that she had lost all her natural brightness. I can imagine that when she was a girl, she was light of foot as a young roe, that her face was dimpled with many a smile, and that her eyes flashed with childish glee. She had her share of the brightness and beauty of youth, and walked erect like others of her race, look-ing up to the sun by day, and to the sparkling stars at night, rejoicing in all around her, and feeling life to be a joy. But there gradually crept over her an infirmity which dragged her down, probably a weakness of the spine: either the muscles and ligatures began to tighten so that she was bound together, and drawn more and more toward herself and toward the earth; or else the mus-cles commenced to relax, so that she could not retain the perpendicular posi-tion, and her body dropped forward more and more. I suppose either of these causes might cause her to be bowed together, so that she could in no wise lift herself up.

At any rate, for eighteen years she had not gazed upon the sun; for eigh-teen years no star of night had gladdened her eye; her face was drawn down-ward toward the dust, and all the light of her life was dim: she walked about as if she were searching for a grave, and I do not doubt she often felt that it would have been gladness to have found one. She was as truly fettered as if bound in iron, and as much in prison as if surrounded by stone walls. Alas, we know certain of the children of God who are at this moment in much the same condition. They are perpetually bowed down, and though they recollect happier days, the memory only serves to deepen their present gloom. They sometimes sing in the minor key:

Where is the blessedness I knew
When first I saw the Lord?
Where is the sweet refreshing view
Of Jesus and his word?

What blissful hours I then enjoyed!
How sweet their memory still!
But they have left an aching void
The world can never fill.

They seldom enter into communion with God now; seldom or never behold the face of the Well Beloved. They try to hold on by believing, and they succeed; but they have little peace, little comfort, little joy: they have lost the crown and flower of spiritual life, though that life still remains. I feel certain that I am addressing more than two or three who are in such a plight at this moment, and I pray the Comforter to bless my discourse to them.

This poor woman was *bowed toward herself and toward that which was depressing.* She seemed to grow downward; her life was stooping; she bent lower and lower and lower, as the weight of years pressed upon her. Her looks were all earthward; nothing heavenly, nothing bright could come before her eyes; her views were narrowed to the dust, and to the grave. So are there some of God's people whose thoughts sink evermore like lead, and their feelings run in a deep groove, cutting evermore a lower channel. You cannot give them delight, but you can readily cause them alarm: by a strange art they squeeze the juice of sorrow from the clusters of Eshcol; where others would leap for joy, they stoop for very grief, for they draw the unhappy inference that joyous things are not meant for the likes of them. Cordials expressly prepared for mourners they dare not accept, and the more comforting they are, the more are they afraid to appropriate them. If there is a dark passage in the Word of God, they are sure to read it, and say, "That applies to me"; if there is a thundering portion in a sermon, they recollect every syllable of it, and although they wonder how the preacher knows them so well, yet they are sure that he aimed every word at them. If anything occurs in providence, either adverse or propitious, instead of reading it as a token for good, whether they might rationally do so or not, they manage to translate it into a sign of evil. "All these things are against me," say they, for they can see nothing but the earth, and can imagine nothing but fear and distress.

We have known certain prudent, but somewhat unfeeling, persons blame these people, and chide them for being low spirited; and that brings us to notice next, that *she could not lift up herself.* There was no use in blaming her.

There may have been a time, perhaps, when her older sisters said, "Sister, you should keep yourself more upright; you should not be so round shouldered; you are getting quite out of figure; you must be careful or you will become deformed." Dear me, what good advice some people can give! Advice is usually given gratis, and this is very proper, since in most cases that is its full value. Advice given to persons who become depressed in spirit is usually unwise, and causes pain and aggravation of spirit. I sometimes wish that those who are so ready with their advice had themselves suffered a little, for then, perhaps, they would have the wisdom to hold their tongues. Of what use is it to advise a blind person to see, or to tell one who cannot lift up herself that she ought to be upright, and should not look so much upon the earth? This is a needless increase of misery. Some persons who pretend to be comforters might more fitly be classed with tormentors. A spiritual infirmity is as real as a physical one. When Satan binds a soul it is as truly bound as when a man binds an ox or an ass. It cannot get free, it is of necessity in bondage; and that was the condition of this poor woman. I may be speaking to some who have bravely attempted to rally their spirits: they have tried change of scene, they have gone into godly company, they have asked Christian people to comfort them, they have frequented the house of God, and read consoling books; but still they are bound, and there is no disputing it. As one that pours vinegar upon niter, so is he that sings songs to a sad heart: there is an incongruity about the choicest joys when forced upon broken spirits. Some distressed souls are so sick that they abhor all manner of meat, and draw near unto the gates of death. Yet if any one of my hearers be in this plight, he may not despair, for Jesus can lift up those who are most bowed down.

The worst point, perhaps, about the poor woman's case was that *she had borne her trouble for eighteen years,* and therefore her disease was chronic and her illness confirmed. Eighteen years! It is a long, long time. Eighteen years of happiness!—the years fly like Mercuries, with wings to their heels: they come, and they are gone. Eighteen years of happy life—how short a span! But eighteen years of pain, eighteen years of being bowed down to the earth, eighteen years in which the body approximated rather to the fashion of a brute than to that of a man, what a period this must be! Eighteen long years—each with twelve dreary months dragging like a chain behind it! She had been eighteen years under the bond of the devil; what a woe was this! Can a child of God be eighteen years in despondency? I am bound to answer, yes. There is one instance, that of Mr. Timothy Rogers, who has written a book upon *Religious Melancholy,* a very wonderful book too, who was, I think, twenty-eight years in despondency: he tells the story himself, and there can be no question as to his accuracy. Similar instances are well known to those familiar with religious biographies. Individuals have been locked up for many years in the gloomy den of despair, and yet after all have been singularly brought out into joy and comfort. Eighteen years' despondency must be a frightful affliction, and yet there is an escape out of it, for though the devil may take eighteen years to forge a chain, it does not take our blessed Lord eighteen minutes to break it. He can soon set the captive free. Build, build your dungeons, O fiend of hell, and lay the foundations deep, and place the courses of granite so fast together that none can stir a stone of your fabric; but when *he* comes, your Master who will destroy all your works, *he* does but speak, and like the unsubstantial fabric of a vision your Bastille vanishes into thin air. Eighteen years of melancholy do not prove that Jesus cannot set the captive free; they only offer him an opportunity for displaying his gracious power.

Note further about this poor woman, that bowed down as she was both in mind and body, *she yet frequented the house of prayer.* Our Lord was in the synagogue, and there was she. She might very well have said, "It is very painful for me to go into a public place; I ought to be excused." But no, there she was. Dear child of God, the devil has sometimes suggested to you that it is vain for you to go any more to hear the word. Go all the same. He knows you are likely to escape from his hands so long as you hear the word, and therefore if he can keep you away, he will do so. It was while in the house of prayer that this woman found her liberty, and there you may find it; therefore still continue to go up to the house of the Lord, come what may.

All this while, too, she was a daughter of Abraham. The devil had tied her up like an ox or an ass, but he could not take away her privileged character. She was still a daughter of Abraham, still a believing soul trusting in God by humble faith. When the Savior healed her, he did not say, "Thy sins be forgiven thee." There was no particular sin in the case. He did not address her as he did those whose infirmity had been caused by sin; for, notwithstanding her being thus bowed down, all she needed was comfort, not rebuke. Her heart was right with God. I know it was, for the moment she was healed, she began to glorify God, which showed that she was ready for it, and that the praise was waiting in her spirit for the glad opportunity. In going up to the house of God, she felt some measure of comfort, though for eighteen years she was bowed down. Where else should she have gone? What good could she have gained by staying at home? A sick child is best in its father's house, and she was best where prayer was wont to be made.

Here, then, is a picture of what may still be seen among the sons of men, and may possibly be your case, dear hearer. May the Holy Spirit bless this description to your hearts' encouragement.

II. I invite you, second, to notice *the hand of Satan in this bondage.*

We should not have known it if our Lord had not told us, that it was Satan who had bound this poor woman for eighteen years. *He must have bound her very cunningly to make the knot hold all that time,* for he does not appear to have possessed her. You notice in reading the Evangelists that our Lord never laid his hand on a person possessed with a devil. Satan had not possessed her, but he had fallen upon her once upon a time eighteen years before, and bound her up as men tie a beast in its stable, and she had not been able to get free all that while. The devil can tie in a moment a knot which you and I cannot unloose in eighteen years. He had in this case so securely fastened his victim that no power of herself or others could avail: in the same way, when permitted he can tie up any one of God's own people in a very short time, and by almost any means. Perhaps one word from a preacher, which was never meant to cause sadness, may make a heart wretched; one single sentence out of a good book or one misunderstood passage of Scripture, may be quite enough in Satan's cunning hand to fasten up a child of God in a long bondage.

Satan had bound the woman to herself and to the earth. There is a cruel way of tying a beast which is somewhat after the same fashion: I have seen a poor animal's head fastened to its knee or foot, and somewhat after that fashion Satan had bound the woman downward to herself. So there are some children of God whose thoughts are all about themselves: they have turned their eyes so that they look inside and see only the transactions of the little world within themselves. They are always lamenting their own infirmities, always mourning their own corruptions, always watching their own emotions. The one and only subject of their thoughts is their own condition. If they ever change the scene and turn to another subject, it is only to gaze upon the earth beneath them, to groan over this poor world with its sorrows, its miseries, its sins, and its disappointments. Thus they are tied to themselves and to the earth and cannot look up to Christ as they should, nor let the sunlight of his love shine full upon them. They go mourning without the sun, pressed down with cares and burdens. Our Lord uses the figure of an ox or an ass tied up, and he says that even on the Sabbath its owner would loose it for watering.

This poor woman was restrained from what her soul needed. She was like an ass or an ox which cannot get to the trough to drink. She knew the promises; she heard them read every Sabbath day; she went to the synagogue and heard of him who comes to loose the captives; but she could not rejoice in the promise or enter into liberty. So are there multitudes of God's dear people who are fastened to themselves and cannot get to watering, cannot drink from the river of life, nor find consolation in the Scriptures. They know how precious the gospel is, and how consolatory are the blessings of the covenant, but they cannot enjoy the consolations or the blessings. Oh, that they could. They sigh and cry, but they feel themselves to be bound.

There is a saving clause here. Satan had done a good deal to the poor woman, but *he had done all he could do.* You may rest assured that whenever Satan smites a child of God, he never spares his strength. He knows nothing of mercy, neither does any other consideration restrain him. When the Lord delivered Job into Satan's hand for a time, what destruction and havoc he made with Job's property. He did not save him chick or child or sheep or goat or camel or ox; but he smote him right and left, and caused ruin to his whole estate. When, under a second permit, he came to touch him in his bone and in his flesh, nothing would satisfy the devil but covering him from the sole of his foot to the crown of his head with sore boils and blains. He might have pained him quite sufficiently by torturing one part of his body, but this would not suffice, he must glut himself with vengeance. The devil would do all he could, and therefore he covered him with running sores. Yet, as in Job's case, there was a limit, so was there here; Satan had bound this woman, but he had not killed her. He might bend her toward the grave, but he could not bend her into it; he might make her droop over till she was bent double, but he could not take away her poor feeble life: with all his infernal craft, he could not make her die before her time. Moreover, she was still a woman, and he could not make a beast of her, notwithstanding that she was thus bowed down into the form of the brute. Even so the devil cannot destroy you, O child of God. He can smite you, but he cannot slay you. He worries those whom he cannot destroy and feels a malicious joy in so doing. He knows there is no hope of your destruction, for you are beyond shot of his gun; but if he cannot wound you with the shot, he will frighten you with the powder if he can. If he cannot slay, he will bind, as if for the slaughter; yes, and he knows how to make a poor soul feel a thousand deaths in fearing one. But all this while Satan was quite unable to touch this poor woman as to her true standing: she was a daughter of Abraham eighteen years before when first the devil attacked her, and she was a daughter of Abraham eighteen years afterward, when the fiend had done his worst. And you, dear heart, if you should never have a comfortable sense of the Lord's love for eighteen years, are still his beloved; and if never once he should give you any token of his love which you could sensibly enjoy, and if by reason of bewilderment and distraction you should keep on writing bitter things against yourself all this while, yet still your name is on the hands of Christ, where none can erase it. You belong to Jesus, and none shall pluck you out of his hands. The devil may bind you fast, but Christ has bound you faster still with cords of everlasting love, which must and shall hold you to the end.

That poor woman was being prepared, even by the agency of the devil, to glorify God. Nobody in the synagogue could glorify God as she could when she was at last set free. Every year out of the eighteen gave emphasis to the utterance of her thanksgiving. The deeper her sorrow, the sweeter her song. I should like to have been there that morning, to have heard her tell the story of the emancipating power of the Christ of God. The devil must have felt that he had lost all his trouble, and he must have regretted that he had not let her alone all the eighteen years, since he had only been qualifying her thereby to tell out the more sweetly the story of Jesus' wondrous power.

III. I want you to notice in the third place *the Liberator at his work*.

We have seen the woman bound by the devil, but here comes the Liberator, and the first thing we read of him is that he saw her. His eyes looked round, reading every heart as he glanced from one to another. At last he saw the woman. Yes, that was the very one he was seeking. We are not to think that he saw her in the same common way as I see one of you, but he read every line of her character and history, every thought of her heart, every desire of her soul. Nobody had told him that she had been eighteen years bound, but he knew all about it—how she came to be bound, what she had suffered during the time, how she had prayed for healing, and how the infirmity still pressed upon her. In one minute he had read her history and understood her case. He saw her; and oh, what meaning there was in his searching glance. Our Lord had wonderful eyes; all the painters in the world will never be able to produce a satisfactory picture of Christ, because they cannot copy those expressive eyes. Heaven lay calmly reposing in his eyes; they were not only bright and penetrating, but they were full of a melting power, a tenderness irresistible, a strength which secured confidence. As he looked at the poor woman, I doubt not the tears started from our Lord's eyes, but they were not tears of unmingled sorrow, for he knew that he could heal her, and he anticipated the joy of doing so.

When he had gazed upon her, he called her to him. Did he know her name? Oh, yes, he knows all our names, and his calling is therefore personal and unmistakable. "I have called thee by thy name," says he, "thou art mine."

See, there is the poor creature, coming up the aisle; that pitiful mass of sorrow, though bowed to the earth, is moving. Is it a woman at all? You can hardly see that she has a face, but she is coming toward him who called her. She could not stand upright, but she could come as she was, bent and infirm as she was. I rejoice in my Master's way of healing people, for he comes to them where they are. He does not propose to them that if they will do somewhat, he will do the rest, but he begins and ends. He bids them approach him as they are, and does not ask them to mend or prepare. May my blessed Master this morning look on some of you till you feel, "The preacher means me, the preacher's Master means me," and then may there sound a voice in your ears saying, "Come to Jesus just as you are." Then may you have grace to reply—

> Just as I am—poor, wretched, blind,
> Sight, riches, healing of the mind,
> Yea, all I need, in thee to find,
> O Lamb of God, I come.

When the woman came, *the great Liberator said to her, "Woman, thou art loosed from thine infirmity."* How could that be true? She was still as bent as she was before. He meant that the spell of Satan was taken off from her, that the power which had made her thus to bow herself was broken. This she believed in her inmost soul, even as Jesus said it, though as yet she was not at all different in appearance from her former state.

Oh, that some of you who are God's dear people would have power to believe this morning that the end of your gloom has come, power to believe that your eighteen years are over, and that your time of doubt and despondency is ended. I pray that God may give you grace to know that when this morning's sun first gilded the east, light was ordained for you. Behold, I come today to publish the glad message from the Lord. Come forth, you prisoners; leap, you captives, for Jesus comes to set you free today.

The woman was liberated, but she could not actually enjoy the liberty, and I will tell you why directly. Our Lord proceeded to give her full enlargement in his own way: *he laid his hands on her.* She suffered from want of strength, and by putting his hands upon her, I conceive that the Lord poured his life into her. The warm stream of his own infinite power and vitality came into contact with the lethargic stream of her painful existence, and so quickened it that she lifted up herself. The deed of love was done: Jesus himself had done it. Beloved mourners, if we could get you away this morning from thinking about yourselves to thinking about our Lord Jesus, and from looking down upon your cares to thinking of him, what a change would come over you. If his hands could be laid upon you, those dear pierced hands which bought you, those mighty hands which rule heaven and earth on your behalf, those blessed hands which are outstretched to plead for sinners, those dear hands which will press you to his bosom forever: if you could feel these by thinking of him, then would you soon recover your early joy, and renew the elasticity of your spirit, and the bowing down of your soul would pass away like a night dream, to be forgotten forever. O Spirit of the Lord, make it to be so.

IV. I will not linger there, but invite you now to notice *the loosing of the bound*.

She was made straight we are told, and that at once. Now, what I want you to notice is this, that she must have lifted herself up—that was her own act and deed. No pressure or force was put upon her, she lifted up herself; and yet she was "made straight." She was passive insomuch as a miracle was worked upon her, but she was active too, and, being enabled, she lifted up herself. What a wonderful meeting there is here of the active and the passive in the salvation of men.

The Arminian says to the sinner, "Now, sinner, you are a responsible being; you must do this and that." The Calvinist says, "Truly, sinner, you are responsible enough, but you are also unable to do anything of yourself. God must work in you both to will and to do." What shall we do with these two teachers? They fell to fighting, a hundred years ago, most frightfully. We will not let them fight now, but what shall we do with them? We will let both speak, and believe what is true in both their testimonies.

Is it true what the Arminian says, that there must be an effort on the sinner's part or he will never be saved? Unquestionably it is. As soon as ever the Lord gives spiritual life, there is spiritual activity. Nobody is ever lugged into heaven by his ears or carried there asleep on a feather bed. God deals with us as with responsible, intelligent beings. That is true, and what is the use of denying it?

Now what has the Calvinist to say? He says that the sinner is bound by the infirmity of sin and cannot lift up himself, and when he does so, it is God that does it all, and the Lord must have all the glory of it. Is not that true too? "Oh," says the Arminian, "I never denied that the Lord is to have the glory. I will sing a hymn with you to the divine honor; and I will pray the same prayer with you for the divine power." All Christians are thorough Calvinists when they come to singing and praying, but it is a pity to doubt as a doctrine what we profess on our knees and in our songs. It is most true that Jesus alone saves the sinner, and equally true that the sinner believes unto salvation. The Holy Ghost never believed on behalf of anybody: a man must believe for himself and repent for himself, or be lost; but yet there never was a grain of true faith or true repentance in this world except it was produced by the Holy Ghost. I am not going to explain these difficulties, because they are not difficulties, except in theory. They are plain facts of practical everyday life. The poor woman knew at any rate where to put the crown; she did not say, "I straightened myself," no, but she glorified God, and attributed all the work to his gracious power.

The most remarkable fact is that *she was made straight immediately;* for there was something beyond her infirmity to be overcome. Suppose that any person had been diseased of the spine, or of the nerves and muscles, for eighteen years, even if the disease which occasioned his being deformed could be entirely removed, what would be the effect? Why, that the result of the disease would still remain, for the body would have become set through long continuance in one posture. You have doubtless heard of the fakirs and others in India: a man will hold his hand up for years in pursuance of a vow, but when the years of his penance are over, he cannot bring his hand down: it has become fixed and immovable. In this case the bond which held the poor bowed body was taken away, and at the same time the consequent rigidity was removed, and she in a moment stood up straight; this was a double display of miraculous power. O my poor, tried friend, if the Lord will visit you this morning, he will not only take away the first and greatest cause of your sadness, but the very tendency to melancholy shall depart; the long grooves which you have worn shall be smoothed, the ruts in the road of sorrow which you have worn by long continuance in sadness shall be filled up, and you shall be strong in the Lord and in the power of his might.

The cure being thus perfect, *up rose the woman to glorify God.* I wish I had been there; I have been wishing so all the morning. I should have liked to have seen that hypocritical ruler of the synagogue when he made his angry speech: I should have liked to have seen him when the Master silenced him so thoroughly; but especially I should have rejoiced to have seen this poor woman standing upright, and to have heard her praise the Lord. What did she say? It is not recorded, but we can well imagine. It was something like this: "I have been eighteen years in and out among you; you have seen me, and know what a poor, miserable, wretched object I was; but God has lifted me up all in a moment. Blessed be his name, I have been made straight." What she spoke with her mouth was not half of what she expressed. No reporter could have taken it down; she spoke with her eyes, she spoke with her hands, she spoke with every limb of her body. I suppose she moved about to see if she was really straight, and to make sure that it was not all a delusion. She must have been all over a living mass of pleasure, and by every movement she praised God from the sole of the foot to the crown of the head. Never was there a more eloquent woman in the universe. She was like one newborn, delivered from a long death, joyous with all the novelty of a fresh life. Well might she glorify God.

She made no mistake as to how the cure was worked; she traced it to a divine power, and that divine power she extolled. Brother, sister, cannot you glorify Christ this morning that he has set you free? Though bound so long, you need not be bound any longer. Christ is able to deliver you. Trust him, believe him, be made straight, and then go and tell your kinsfolk and acquaintances, "You knew how depressed I was, for you cheered me in my sorrow as best you could, but now I have to tell you what the Lord has done for my soul."

V. Fifth, let us reflect upon *our reason for expecting the Lord Jesus to do the same thing today* as he did eighteen hundred years and more ago.

What was his reason for setting this woman free? According to his own statement, it was, first of all, *human kindness*. He says, "When you have your ox or your ass tied up, and you see that it is thirsty, you untie the knot, and lead the poor creature away down to the river, or the tank, to water. None of you would leave an ox tied up to famish." This is good reasoning, and leads us to believe that Jesus will help sorrowing ones. Tried soul, would you not loose an ox or an ass if you saw it suffering? "Yes," you say. And do you think the Lord will not loose you? Have you more bowels of mercy than the Christ of God? Come, come, think not so meanly of my Master. If your heart would lead you to pity an ass, do you think his heart will not lead him to pity you? He has not forgotten you: he remembers you still. His tender humanity moves him to set you free.

More than that, there was *special relationship*. He tells this master of the synagogue that a man would loose his ox or his ass. Perhaps he might not think it his business to go and loose that which belonged to another man, but it is his own ass, his own ox, and he will loose him. And do you think, dear heart, that the Lord Jesus will not loose you? He bought you with his blood, his Father gave you to him, he has loved you with an everlasting love: will he not loose you? You are his property. Do you not know that he sweeps his house to find his lost goat, that he runs over hill and dale to find his lost sheep? And will he not come and loose his poor tied-up ox or ass? Will he not liberate his captive daughter? Assuredly he will. Are you a daughter of Abraham, a child of faith, and will he not set you free? Depend upon it, he will.

Next, there was *a point of antagonism* which moved the Savior to act promptly. He says, "This woman being a daughter of Abraham, whom Satan hath bound." Now, if I knew the devil had tied anything up I am sure I would try to unloose it, would not you? We may be sure some mischief is brewing when the devil is working, and, therefore, it must be a good deed to undo his work. But Jesus Christ came into the world on purpose to destroy the works of the devil; and so when he saw the woman like a tied-up ox he said, "I will unloose her if for nothing else that I may undo what the devil has done." Now, dear tried friend, inasmuch as your sorrow may be traced to satanic influence, Jesus Christ will prove in your case more than a match for the devil, and he will set you free.

Then think of *her sorrowful condition.* An ox or an ass tied up to the manger without water would soon be in a very sad plight. Pity it, poor thing. Hear the lowing of the ox, as hour after hour its thirst tells upon it. Would you not pity it? And do you think the Lord does not pity his poor, tried, tempted, afflicted children? Those tears, shall they fall for nothing? Those sleepless nights, shall they be disregarded? That broken heart which fain would but cannot believe the promise, shall that forever be denied a hearing? Hath the Lord forgotten to be gracious? Hath he in anger shut up the bowels of his mercy? Ah no, he will remember your sorrowful estate and hear your groanings, for he puts your tears into his bottle.

Last of all, there was this reason to move the heart of Christ, that *she had been eighteen years in that state.* "Then," said he, "she shall be loosed at once." The master of the synagogue would have said, "She has been eighteen years bound, and she may well wait till tomorrow, for it is only one day." "No," says Christ, "if she has been bound eighteen years, she shall not wait a minute; she has had too much of it already; she shall be set free at once." Do not, therefore, argue from the length of your despondency that it shall not come to an end, but rather argue from it that release is near. The night has been so long, it must be so much nearer the dawning. You have been scourged so long that it must be so much nearer the last stroke, for the Lord does not afflict willingly, nor grieve the children of men. Therefore take heart and be of a good courage. Oh, that my divine Master would now come and do what I fain would do but cannot, namely, make every child of God here leap for joy.

I know what this being bound by Satan means. The devil has not tied me up for eighteen years at a stretch, and I do not think he ever will, but he has brought me into sad bondage many a time. Still, my Master comes and sets me free, and leads me out to watering: and what a drink I get at such times! I seem as if I could drink up Jordan at a draft when I get to his promises, and quaff my fill of his sweet love. I know by this that he will lead other poor souls out to the watering; and when he does so to any of you, I pray you drink like an ox. You may be tied up again; therefore drink as much as you can of his grace, and rejoice while you may. Eat that which is good, and let your soul delight in fatness. Be glad in the Lord, you righteous, and shout for joy all you that are upright in heart, for the Lord looses the prisoners. May he loose many now. Amen.

Mary of Bethany: To Lovers of Jesus—An Example

◆◦◆

Intended for reading on Lord's Day, April 12, 1885; delivered on November 2, 1884, at the Metropolitan Tabernacle, Newington. No. 1834.

She hath wrought a good work on me.—MARK 14:6

This holy woman had *displeased the disciples*. She must have been very sorry to do that. She would not have willfully grieved the least servant of her Lord. But she did so without the slightest blame on her part: it was the unexpected consequence of a most blessed action, and the fault lay with those who complained of her holy deed, and not with her. I do not know whether all the disciples felt grieved, but we are told by Matthew that "they had indignation," and he seems to speak of them as a body; from which I gather that those who love Jesus much must not measure their conduct by that of Christ's ordinary disciples, indeed it might fare ill with them even if apostles became their judges. They must not tone down the fervor of their zeal to the lukewarmness of the general order of Christian men: they must not measure the consecration of their lives by the little which many professors present upon the altar to God. No, my brother or sister, you must not be too much distressed if the best of the household misjudge you, for it has happened to many favored sons before you. You, O man, greatly beloved, cannot abide to be lukewarm, and be not surprised if the lukewarm cannot agree with you! Count it no strange thing if, in your ardor, you should come to be accused of fanaticism, want of prudence, rashness, forwardness. Do not break your heart over it if they should even call you mad, or suspect that you have more zeal than knowledge; for Mary, whom we would be glad to imitate, came under this kind of censure; and David, and your Lord, the Son of David, were each thought to be madmen.

This honored woman performed a notable act, which is to be rehearsed wherever the gospel is preached, and yet thereby she stirred the wrath of the brotherhood of the disciples: of how small account is the judgment of men!

Chiefly, she called down upon her head the censure of Judas. As far as Judas was known to his brethren, he was reckoned among the best of them. They never suspected him of playing the traitor, or they would have caviled at his being their treasurer: they once had indignation at James and John, but the canny Judas had their respect. I should think he was the most businesslike man of the whole company—which is not saying much for business, is it? He was a leading spirit among that little band. He was one who would be selected because of his prudence—and that is not saying much for prudence, is it? Doubtless Judas abounded in that cool, calculating shrewdness which makes a man fit to deal with monies and purchases. He had far more business ability than impetuous Peter, or affectionate John, or thoughtful Thomas. He was the right man in the right place, if he had but happened to have been an honest man. Wonderful it was that he could conceal the deep meanness of his spirit from all his fellows during the years in which they lived together; but he had done so, and therefore his opinion carried weight with it. Among the apostles, the censure of Judas meant the calm condemnation of a judicious person. His judgment was not what you and I would esteem it to be, for we should think nothing of his censure now, because we know that he betrayed his Lord; but the disciples could not foresee this, and in their judgment that which Judas would condemn must be very censurable; at least it must be unbusinesslike; it must lack common sense; it must be imprudent and wasteful. Was not Judas the perfect model of economy? Was he not the sort of man who in these days many a father would point out to his boy as an example? Hear him say, "Boy, if you want to get on in the world, imitate Judas Iscariot; he is the model man, he is a Christian, and yet he has a keen eye for his own advantage, and is a sharp man of business."

It was a hard thing for a timid woman to bear such a censure from one so highly respected in the college of apostles; but she had this solace, which I will warrant you, put quite out of her mind all care about the censure of disciples, even of the biggest of them: she pleased her Master. She could see by the very look of him that he accepted what his followers condemned. She knew in her conscience that she had the approbation of the Lord, even though she had the disapprobation of the servants. O brothers and sisters, let us always carry our case into the highest court, and live before the Lord, and not as the slaves of men! If we are conscious that we have sincerely done what we have done as unto the Lord, and if we feel sure that *he* has approved our service, it is of the smallest consequence possible what men shall say of us. Let us never provoke our brethren to be ill-tempered to us, neither let us do anything that can be rightly censured out if we have gone somewhat beyond common custom in the fervor of our spirit; let us reply with young David to his envious brethren,

"Is there not a cause?" The opinions of other men are no rule to us: we have
our own obligations to discharge, and as our debt of love is larger than usual,
let us take liberty to be as full of love and zeal as we can be, only regretting
that we cannot go still further in the way of sacred service.

"Well," says one, "but do those who love Christ encounter the frowns of
men at this time?" Oh yes, and of their own Christian brethren too! If you con-
sort with the common ruck of brethren, and travel on the road to heaven so
slowly that it is a question whether you are going there at all, then you will
escape criticism: if you keep with those who practice the snail's march they
will call you a good easy man, a right respectable person. But if you run for it,
if you put out all the energy of your nature, and are determined to live at a
high pitch for Christ, you will get the cold shoulder, even from many of his
disciples, for you will be practically condemning their halfheartedness; and
who are you to be such a troubler in Israel? The more prudent among your
brethren will say that your pride and the naughtiness of your heart make you
so forward and presumptuous, and they will try to put you down or put you
out. You cannot commit a greater crime against some people than to be more
useful than they are. When a person reckons himself to be the standard of
holiness, he looks upon one who excels him as guilty of a kind of blasphemy.
If you outrun others, do not reckon upon smiles, but count upon black looks.
You will be called impudent and thought impertinent. Bear it all and fret not.
Go to your Lord, and tell him that you have done and are doing all you can as
unto him, and entreat him to smile upon you. Crave his acceptance of your
poor doings, and then go about your business, occupying till he shall come.
Sow the seed of duty, and care not whether in human judgment it shines or
rains. "He that regardeth the clouds shall not reap"; if you regard not the
clouds at all, you will do your sowing and your reaping with the comfort of
true faith, and God will bless you.

I am going to talk about this blessed woman at this time with this hopeful
desire—that you and I may imitate her ever-memorable example. I shall have
nothing to say but to open up the meaning of our Lord, as far as I know it,
when he said, "She hath wrought a good work on me" or "in me." The passage
might be rendered—only the translators do not like to use the term—"She
hath wrought a beautiful work on me"—a comely work. "A thing of beauty is
a joy forever" [John Keats]. This was a thing of beauty, which is a joy forever to
the church of God, in that constant memorial of her which is blended with the
preaching of the gospel of Christ; for as long as the gospel is proclaimed, this
Mary of Bethany shall have a memorial, because of what she did.

What was there beautiful about her work—the breaking of the alabaster vase, and the pouring out of the liquid nard? What was there beautiful about that? I will try to show you.

I. There were seven beauties in it, and the first and chief beauty, perhaps, was that *it was altogether glorifying of Jesus.*

She meant when she poured that ointment on his head to honor *him* personally; every drop of it was for himself, out of reverence for his actual personality.

She was not so much thinking of his deeds of love, or of his words of truth, as of his own unrivaled and most precious self. She had seen his deeds of love when Lazarus was raised; she had heard his words of truth when she sat at his feet: but now she felt an adoring reverence for his thrice-blessed Person, and she brought that box of precious spikenard, and offered it to him as her Teacher, her Friend, her Lord, her all. Suggestion was made that she should have sold it and given it to the poor; but she longed to present one offering *to him* directly, and not by any roundabout method. Doubtless she was not behindhand in her gifts to the poor, but she felt that when she had done *that* she had not satisfied the cravings of her grateful heart toward *him* who had become poorest of the poor for her sake. She wanted to give something *to him*—something suitable for such a One as she conceived him to be—something suitable for the time and circumstances then present with regard to him.

I think this holy woman knew more about our Lord than all his apostles put together. Her eyes had peered within the veil. You remember that only a day or two after this, he rode in triumph through Jerusalem a proclaimed king. Should he not first be anointed? And who would anoint him to the kingdom visibly with oil but this consecrated woman? She was come to give him a royal anointing preparatory to his proclamation in the streets of his capital city. At any rate her spikenard must be poured out alone *for him*. She forgot the poor just then as she quite forgot the disciples. Martha was busy at the table waiting upon them all, disciples and Master; but Mary had concentrated all her thoughts on Jesus. She "saw no man save Jesus only." Blessed exclusiveness of vision! What she did must not be for Peter and James and John with Jesus, but it must be for him alone, who indeed is alone, above and beyond all others, worthy of a homage all his own. Because she had a love for him beyond all others that she had ever heard of, her heart must find expression in a deed of love which must be entirely, wholly, only toward himself.

Now this is, as we have read the text, a beautiful thing. It will be beautiful on your part and mine if, having taken care of the poor according to our ability, having discharged the claims of our relationships to our fellowmen, we then feel that we must do something for Jesus—distinctly for our Lord. Do you ask me what you shall do for him? No, but, sister, I must not tell you; your own heart must originate the thought, as your own hand must carry it out. "Oh," cries a brother, "tell me what I could do for Jesus!" No, but, brother, I must not tell you. The better part of the whole matter will lie in the hallowed ingenuity of your spirit in inventing something for him out of your own fervent soul. The holy woman's deed had been somewhat spoiled if there had been a command for her to bring the alabaster box, and pour the ointment on his head: her love commanded her, and that was better than a formal precept. Her deed had not possessed half its worth if Simon had suggested to her, "I have not sufficient spikenard to anoint our guests; fetch you a box from home." The very glory of it lay in the spontaneous suggestion of her own heart that she must do something which should be all for Jesus.

She must do it herself personally, and not by proxy; and she must do it unto him distinctly, directly, openly. Others might smell the spikenard. That she did not wish to prevent; but still the perfume was never meant for them, but for him exclusively. She poured it on *his* head; she poured it on *his* feet; she would anoint *him* from head to foot with this token of her intense and reverent gratitude, and her boundless love: she felt wrapped up in *him*, her Lord and her God, and so her willing offering was for him, and for him alone. What a joy to be permitted to do anything for him whose great love holds us fast! I feel as if I would fain at once retire from you all to indulge my heart in this rare luxury.

Alas, good Lord, how little have you of this devotion in these calculating days! Instead of "all for Jesus," how seldom we do anything for Jesus! Brethren, when you sing your hymns, do you "sing a hymn to Jesus"? When you are in prayer, do you pray *to* Jesus, and *for* Jesus? Is it not written, "Prayer also shall be made for him continually, and daily shall he be praised"? When you come to this communion table, I pray that you may forget all that come with you in this assembly, and cry, "I will remember *thee*." In the chief place, at any rate, let Jesus fill your thoughts. Set him alone upon the throne, and think only of eating his flesh and drinking his blood, and receiving him into your very self, that there may be a vital union between the Christ of God and your own souls. To my mind this is the beauty of our fellowship in the holy Supper, that we feed on Jesus only. Let us make him our soul's sole meat and drink; and then let us live for him. My heart craves now to know what I shall do that I may imitate her who gave to "Jesus only" that box of spikenard, very costly. O you lovers of my Lord who have been washed in his precious blood, who owe your all to him, think of his matchless beauties now, and as you look up into that face where shines your heaven, think to yourselves, "What can we do for him—for him absolutely, directly, and personally?" There is the first beauty of this woman's act of homage: it was for Jesus, for Jesus only, for Jesus wholly.

II. A second beauty lay in this: that *it was an act of pure love, altogether of love to Jesus.*

The other woman—blessed was she also among women—I refer to that woman who was a sinner: she also came and brought an alabaster box, and did much the same thing as this Mary of Bethany. But she did what Mary did not do: she mingled weeping with her ointment: she washed his feet with tears, and wiped them with the hairs of her head. That was a beautiful act in its own way, but Mary's deed is a beautiful thing in another way. In this lies the distinction: there does not seem to have been in Mary's act any remembrance of personal sin, though, doubtless, that feeling was in her heart, and had brought her to the higher stage of adoration of her pardoning Lord. Her sin was put away long ago. Mary had sat at Jesus' feet, and had chosen the good part, and the matter of pardon for sin had been transacted a long while before; and now, although in her heart there is deep gratitude for it, and for the raising of her dear brother Lazarus, yet it seems to be quite absorbed in the deeper thought of her soul, for she had attained to an all-consuming love of himself. She never would have known that kind of love if she had not learned to sit at his feet, but to sit long there has a wonderful operation on the human mind; it causes even things that are good in themselves to be overshadowed by matters that are less and less in relation to self. It is a blessed thing to love Christ because we escape from hell by him; it is a blessed thing to love Christ because he has opened the kingdom of heaven to all believers; but it is a still higher thing to forget yourself, and to contemplate with delight the ineffable perfections of him whom heaven and earth acknowledge to be chief among ten thousand, and altogether lovely. "We love him because he first loved us"; here we begin, and this beginning always remains; but on it we pile tier after tier of precious stones of love, which are crowned with pinnacles of inexpressible affection for the great Lord himself. He in himself has won our hearts, and carried our spirits by storm, and now we must do something which will express our love to him. That love is not alone a gratitude for benefits received from him, but an intense affection for his glorious, adorable person.

Come, dear friends, do you feel that kind of emotion in your hearts at this time? Do you even now feel that so perfectly has Christ won the verdict of your understanding, so completely has he bound in silken fetters every movement of your affections, that you want to be doing something which shall have but this one aim, to express your love to him who has made you what you are? Indulge the emotion, crown it with action, continue it through life. In this point be not slow to be imitators of the sister of Martha and Lazarus. O sweet love of Jesus, come and fill our souls to the brim, and run over in delicate personal service!

III. The third beauty of the action was that *it was done with considerable sacrifice.*

There was an expense about it, and that of no trifling character to a woman who was neither queen nor princess. I shall always feel obliged to Judas for figuring up the price of that box of costly nard. He did it to blame her, but we will let his figures stand, and think the more of her the more he put down to the account of waste. I should never have known what it cost, nor would you either, if Judas had not marked down in his pocket book that it "might have been sold for much." How he grudged that "much." He calculated the value at three hundred pence. He did well to put it in pence, for his sordid soul reveled in small monies which make up the pounds. Pence, indeed, when the expense is for him to whom the silver and the gold belong! Yet I like his calculation in pence, for it is suggestive, since a Roman penny was a day's wages; and take a day's wages now—say four shillings—and you get some £60. It was a large sum of money for a woman in her state of life in Bethany. It was £10 of their money, but money then was of a different value from what it is now, and it was a great sum for her to expend in one single deed of love.

Her gift was costly, and the Lord Jesus deserved to be served at the best rate, and at the highest cost. There was a woman who served the Lord at a higher rate than this: she only spent two mites in the doing of it, but then you know it was all that she had. I do not know how much Mary had, but I feel persuaded that it was pretty well all she had, and that all she could get together seemed to her to be far too little for the Lord Jesus Christ. If his head was to be anointed, plenty of ordinary oil might have been procured at Bethany. The Mount of Olives was hard by. But she would have scorned the thought of pouring common olive oil on him: she must find an imperial unguent such as Caesar might have accepted. If he is to be anointed, there is nard to be bought in the bazaars at Jerusalem at a very reasonable rate. Why must you, Mary, seek after this liquid ointment of the East, this oil distilled from myriads of roses, of which it needs leagues of gardens to make a drop? Why must you buy the "very precious" nard, and spend such a deal of money upon that which will only last half an hour, and then the wind will have carried it away, and its perfume will have vanished? Yes, but the glory of service to Christ is to serve him with the best of the best!

He deserves, if we serve him with sermons, that we preach the best discourses mind can frame or tongue deliver; or if we serve him with teaching in the class, he deserves that we teach in the tenderest fashion, and feed his lambs with the best of the grass; or if we serve him with the pen, that we write not a line that may need to be erased; or if we serve him with money, that we give with liberality of the best we have, and much of it. We must see to it that in everything we do not serve Christ with the lean sheep of the flock, or with such as are wounded, and broken, and torn by beasts; but that he has the fat of our offerings. We should not be content if we are rich to give him out of our estate the cheese parings and candle ends, such as we dare not keep back for very shame. Usual donations have little beauty in them—those monies dragged out of people by importunity—that guinea dribbled out by custom because it is a respectable amount. There is nothing to satisfy love in the slender oblations which come forth like an unwilling taxation, which a miser could scarcely withhold. But oh, to give to the Lord Jesus freely, richly, whatever it is with which he has entrusted us, whether it be gold or genius, time or words—whether it be the minted coinage of the purse, or the living courage of a loving heart, or the labor of an earnest hand! Let us give our Well Beloved the best we have, and he will call it beautiful. Mary's gift was all for him, and all for love, and it was done at great expense, and therefore it was beautiful.

IV. Next, remember, that part of the beauty of Mary's action lay in this, that *it was done with preparation.*

We are told by John what we should not else have known, "Against the day of my burying hath she kept this." "Kept this." It was not that seeing Jesus there at the feast, and being seized with a sudden thought, she rushed back to her stores, and fetched out the little vase of spikenard, and broke it in a passion of affection, which in cooler moments she might regret. Far from it: she was now consummating the long thought of weeks and months. We have known warm-spirited brethren and sisters both say and do and give grandly, under a certain spur and impulse, what they never thought of doing when they entered into the assembly. I shall not blame them; rather do I commend them for obeying gracious impulses; but it is not the best way of doing service to our ever-blessed Master. Passion seldom gives so acceptably as principle. Mary did not perform a thoughtless action under a tempestuous force of unusual zeal. No, she had kept this. She had kept this choice unguent on purpose till a fitting time should come for putting it to its most appropriate use. My own belief is that, when she sat at Jesus' feet, she learned much more than any of the disciples had ever gathered from his public preaching. She had heard him say that the Son of man would be delivered to the scribes and Pharisees, and that he would be spat upon and scourged, and they would put him to death, and the third day he would rise again; and she believed it. She thought it over, and she studied it, and made out more of the meaning of it than any one of the apostles had done. She said to herself—he is going to die as a sacrifice at the hands of wicked men, and I will, therefore, render him special honor. I should not wonder if she began to read the Old Testament with that light, "This is he whom God hath sent, upon whom he hath laid the iniquities of us all, and he shall be given up to judgment, and he shall bear the sin of man." Then she thought within herself, "If that is so, I will get the spikenard ready to anoint him for his burial." Perhaps she intended as much as that, for so the Lord himself interpreted the deed. At any rate, she thought, "Alas, for my Lord! If he dies he will need to be embalmed, and I will be ready to aid in his burial." Therefore she kept this.

"Against the day of my burying hath she kept this." Brethren, there is great beauty in an action which is the outcome of a long time of loving careful consideration. It is ill to delay a good deed which might be done at once; but if a deed must be delayed, it is well to be doing it at once by preparing for it. When a person feels, "The time is not yet, but I will be prepared when it does come," it shows that the heart is occupied with a love of a very engrossing character. We sing—

> Oh, what shall I do
> My Savior to praise?

And it were well if the question were constantly in our minds. Let each man resolve in his heart—I will not offer my Lord the hasty fruit of impulse, or that which shall cost me nothing, but I will consider what I can do for him. Of what will there be a need? In what direction can I do him homage where else he might lack that honor? I will turn it over and meditate and consider, and then I will perform. This last the preacher would repeat with emphasis, for o my brothers, it is a custom with many of us to get a grand thought and then, as we turn it over, to let it evaporate without its leaving even a drop of practical result behind! This holy woman was no mere planner and purposer, but a doer of holy deeds. She could keep her alabaster box as long as was prudent, and yet she did not arrive at the tempting conclusion to keep it altogether. She allowed her heart to weigh the project; and the more she weighed it, she became the more resolved to do it—to do it when the due time came. When she believed that the hour had come, she did not delay for an instant. She was as prompt as she had been thoughtful. The Passover was drawing very near; it was within six days, and so she brought out what she had held in reserve. Blessed are the punctualities of service which are the result of earnest endeavor to honor the Lord in the best possible way.

There is something beautiful in seeing, as we have seen, some poor woman saving her little bits, and putting them by for years till she could accomplish a secret purpose by which Jesus would be glorified. It is striking to see, as you and I did see, a woman of moderate wealth discarding all the comforts of life that she might save sufficient that there might be an orphanage in which children might be cared for; not, as she said, for the children's sake, but for Christ's sake, that he might be glorified. The Stockwell Orphanage is the alabaster box which a devout woman presented to her Lord. Her memory is blessed. Its perfume is recognized in all parts of the earth at this moment, to the glory of the Lord she loved. Such a thoughtful deed is what Jesus would call a beautiful thing. Let us abound in such beautiful things. For a man to say, "There will come a crisis when I shall have to stand out for God and his truth, and it will be a serious loss to me," and then so to ponder it as to be almost eager for the occasion, is a beautiful thing. To feel like the Lord Jesus, "I have a baptism to be baptized with, and how am I straitened till it be accomplished!" is a beautiful thing. A courageous, self-sacrificing decision for the truth is a beautiful thing, when its action is well considered, and carried out with enthusiasm. God give us to mix thought and impulse, reason and affection, and thus serve him both with the mind and the heart!

V. There is a fifth point of beauty. *Mary did her great deed without a word.*

Dear sisters, you will pardon me for commending this holy woman for her wise and fitting silence all through her gracious act. She did not talk about it beforehand, she said not a word while she did it, and she said nothing afterward. Martha was the worker, and rather the talker too; but I think that all you will find Mary saying is, "Lord, if thou hadst been here, my brother had not died"; and she was so scant of words that she had to borrow those from Martha. Martha said a great deal more than that; but Mary was quite satisfied to be as brief as possible. She was a great thinker, a great sitter at Jesus' feet, and a great learner, but not a great talker. When the time came, she was a great worker, for it is very curious, though Martha bears the palm for work in our ordinary talk, yet Mary, the thinker, did more than Martha, the worker. "She," said Christ, "hath wrought a good work on me," which he never said of Martha, good as Martha was. He a little censured the elder sister for being cumbered with much serving; but Mary's work he commended, and decreed that it should be remembered as long as the world stands. Though she does not bear the name of a worker in the vulgar judgment, yet is she the queen in the kingdom of good works.

Yet, I remind you, she did not say a word. There is such a thing as spoiling what you do by making so great a fuss before you do it, that when the mouse is born people are only astonished that such a small creature should be the only fruit of the dreadful throes of the mountain. Moreover, there is such a thing as talking so much afterward of what we have done that it spoils it all. It seems as if we must let all the world know something about ourselves; whereas the joy and bliss of it all is not to let yourself be seen, but to let the oil go streaming upon the Master till he is anointed with perfume, and we ourselves sink back into our natural insignificance. Silent acts of love have musical voices in the ear of Jesus. Sound no trumpet before you, or Jesus will take warning and be gone.

If we could all *do* more and *talk* less, it might be a blessing to ourselves at least, perhaps to others. Let us labor in our service for the Lord to be more and more hidden; as much as the proud desire to catch the eye of man, let us endeavor to avoid it.

"I should like to know," says one, "how to do holy work." Go and do it, and consult not with flesh and blood. "I have done my work, and now I should dearly like to hear what you think of it." You should rise above such idle dependence upon man's opinion; what matters it to you what your fellow servant thinks? To your own Master you stand or fall. If you have done a good thing, do it again. You know the story of the man who comes riding up to the captain, and says, "Sir, we have taken a gun from the enemy." "Go and take another," said the matter-of-fact officer. That is the best advice which I can render to a friend who is elated with his own success. So much remains to be accomplished that we have no time to consider what has been done. If we have done holy service, let us do it a second time, and do it a third time, and continue to do it, ever praying the Lord to accept our persevering service. In any case let our consecrated life be for our Lord's eye alone, a spring shut up, a fountain sealed. Anything like sounding a trumpet before us is hateful to the lowly Lord; secrecy has a charm for Jesus, and the more carefully we preserve it, the better.

VI. Next, and sixth, there was this beauty about the action of Mary—that *she did it in reference to our Lord's death.*

The disciples shrank from thinking of that sad subject. Peter said, "That be far from thee, Lord." But Mary, bearing her Master's heart very near her own, and sympathizing with him in his glorious enterprise, instead of drawing back from the thought of that death, performed her work in connection with it. I am not certain to what degree she was conscious that it was so, but there is the fact—the anointing had reference to the burial of the Lord. It seems to me that the best and tenderest duty that Christians do for their Lord Jesus is that which is touched with the blood mark—which bears the stamp of the cross. The best preaching is "We preach Christ crucified." The best living is "We are crucified with Christ." The best man is a crucified man. The best style is a crucified style: may we drop into it! The more we live beholding our Lord's unutterable griefs, and understanding how he has fully put away our sin, the more holiness shall we produce. The more we dwell where the cries of Calvary can be heard, where we can view heaven and earth and hell, all moved by his wondrous passion—the more noble will our lives become. Nothing puts life into men like a dying Savior. Get you close to Christ, and carry the remembrance of him about you from day to day, and you will do right royal deeds. Come, let us slay sin, for Christ was slain. Come, let us bury all our pride, for Christ was buried. Come, let us rise to newness of life, for Christ has risen. Let us be united with our crucified Lord in his one great object—let us live and die with him, and then every action of our lives will be very beautiful.

VII. The seventh beauty, to my mind, is this: you may think it a little far-fetched, but I cannot help mentioning it, for it touches my heart. I believe that *Mary had in this anointing of the Savior some little glimpse of his resurrection from the dead*, and of his after existence.

For I would ask of you—Why do nations at all embalm their dead? Why not consume them in the fire? A mysterious something makes the ordinary Christian man shudder at the thought of cremation. That must surely be an acquired taste: unsophisticated nature does not court the furnace or covet the flame; we prefer to lie beneath the green hillock with our fathers. Many nations of antiquity, and especially the Egyptians and other Orientals, took great care to anoint the bodies of the departed with precious perfumes, and to lay them asleep in gems and fine linen. What for? Because there darkly shone upon their minds some thought of the hereafter. There remained with man, long after the fall, a glimmering, undefined belief in immortality. That truth was so universally received that the Old Testament takes it for granted. The existence of God and the immortality of the soul lie at the basis of Old Testament teaching. The afterlife of the body was accepted also in a manner more or less clear. Immortality was not brought to light, but there it was, and they who reject that doctrine go back into a darkness denser than that in which the heathens themselves dwelled. Why did the Egyptian king embalm his father and lay him in spices, but that he thought that somehow or other there was another life, and he would, therefore, take care of the body? They would not have wasted precious linen and gems and spices, if they had thought that the body was mere rottenness for worms to consume forever. Mary had deeper and clearer thoughts than that, for she expected that something would happen to that blessed body after Christ had died; and she must, therefore, anoint it, and bring the most precious spices that she could procure for his burial. At any rate, let your service of the Lord Jesus be the service of a risen Christ. Come not hither to worship one who died years ago—a hero of the past; but come to adore the ever-living Jesus.

> *He lives, your great Redeemer lives.*

He will certainly come in his own person to reward his saints; and ere he comes he sees what you are doing. "We live," said one, "in the great Taskmaster's eye." I care not for that title. I have no Taskmaster. It is far more an impulse to my life that I live within the sight of him whom, having not seen, I love, because he loved me and gave himself for me. If this does not quicken you, what will? If this does not nerve you to tireless diligence in holy service, what can? Our Lord Jesus Christ lives. Let us find some way of anointing his dear and reverend head—some way of crowning him who wore the crown of thorns for our sake. Ours it is to know that he lives, and that we live in him. On him would we expend the full force of our being, counting it all joy to spend and to be spent for his sake.

I am not going to stir you up, my fellow Christians, to do anything for Christ, for I fear to spoil the freeness of your love's life. I do not want to be pleading with you to enter into his service more fully; for the work of pressed men is never so much prized as that of happy volunteers. Yet as I love you, I would have you love your Lord more and more. It is so sweet to belong to Christ, that the more fully we can belong to him the more free we are. I like that of Paul, where he calls himself the *doulos* of Christ, the slave of Jesus. He says exultingly, "Let no man trouble me. I bear in my body the marks of the Lord Jesus," as if he gloried to think of himself as the branded slave of his

Lord. He had been beaten and scourged, and he retained upon his back the marks of his lashings, and therefore he was wont to say to himself, and smile all the while, "These are my Master's marks. I am branded with his name." Oh, sweet service, in which if it could be slavery it would be joy! I would not have a hair of my head that was not my Lord's if I could help it, nor a drop of my blood that did not flow for him if I could help it. My liberty—and I speak for you all—my liberty, if I might choose it, would be liberty never to sin again; freedom to do Christ's bidding, and that alone. I would fain lose my free will in his sweet will, and find it again as I never found it before in having yielded it up completely to his command.

I will not, therefore, so much intrude upon the sanctity of your heart's love as to suggest what you can do for Jesus. As the best juice flows from the cluster with the least pressure, so shall the best service be that which is most spontaneous. Do not let me push you on, or draw you on, or drag you on; but be eager on your own account. Say to the Lord himself, "Draw me: I will run after thee." Have you not a certain private reason why you should love your Lord better than any other of his redeemed? I repeat it; I will not pry into your sacred secrets, but leave you to commune with your own heart, and with your Lord. Only let us so love him that when we look at him he shall say, "Thou hast ravished my heart, my sister, my spouse; thou hast ravished my heart with one of thine eyes, with one chain of thy neck." Then shall we know what to do for our Well Beloved, and, what is better, we shall do it without further exhortation.

There I leave it. May the Holy Ghost bless the word!

As for you that do not love the Lord Jesus, God be merciful to you! I will not pronounce upon you an "Anathema Maranatha," but I tremble lest it fall upon you. I am sorely grieved for your sakes. I am, moreover, sorely vexed for Christ's sake, that he should be deprived of your love and service. What has he done that you should slight him? O blind eyes, that cannot see his beauties, and deaf ears, that cannot hear the charms of his voice! God be merciful to you, and help you to trust your Savior, and then you will love him for his salvation! It is no wonder that the saved ones love their Lord: it is a marvel that they do not love him ten thousand times more. The Lord be with you for Christ's sake! Amen.

A Repentant Woman:
A Gracious Dismissal

Intended for reading on Lord's Day, January 11, 1891; delivered at the Metropolitan Tabernacle, Newington. No. 2183.

And he said to the woman, "Thy faith hath saved thee; go in peace."
—LUKE 7:50

The main part of my subject will be that gracious dismissal, "Go in peace." To her who had been so lately blessed, the word *go* sounded mournfully; for she would fain have remained through life with her pardoning Lord; but the added words *in peace* turned the wormwood into honey—there was now peace for her who had been so long hunted and harried by her sins. Rising from the feet she had washed with tears, she went forth to keep her future footsteps such as those of a believing, and therefore saved, woman ought to be.

We like a motto to begin the year with, and it has been useful to some spirits to choose a motto with which to enter on a new course of life. We climb the hill of enterprise, or dare the wave of trial, with an inspiring word upon our lip. To certain young men a word has come in life's early morning, wet with the dew of heaven, and that word of their day dawn has kept with them. The echoes of that life-evoking word have followed them long after it was spoken; amid strange scenes it has come to them like a voice from the unseen. It has whispered to them within the curtains of their dying bed: it has murmured consolation amid Jordan's swelling waves. That first word of joy and peace from Jesus with which they began the new life came to them over again just as they were melting away into the invisible land: so they began the service of the Redeemer, and so he declared that their work was finished. Perhaps that love note will be their welcome at the very gates of heaven.

Our Lord, in the instance before us, sent a penitent away from the chill atmosphere of self-righteous caviling, and thus relieved her of a controversy for which she was not fitted; but I see more than that in this benediction. It looks to me as if our divine Master, when he found this poor sinner so full of love to him that she washed his feet with tears, and wiped them with the hairs of her head, having by a parable explained to the Pharisee the reason for the greatness of her love, then said to her, "Go in peace"—meaning that word not only to be cheering for the necessary purpose of the moment, but to go with her, and to attend her all the rest of her life, until, when she came into the dark valley, she should fear no evil, for she would still hear that sweet voice saying, "Go in peace." What music to have heard! What music still to hear!

Now, I would to God that the word which I shall speak at this time might be honored of the Lord to serve that sacred purpose to some here present. May it be a life-word to certain of you! May it be to others of us who have long known the Savior a revival of our rest, and may we get such a draft of peace from Jesus that we may never thirst again! The lips of our divine Lord are a wellspring of delight; each word is a chalice brimmed with sweetness. Imbibing this, we shall go our way henceforth even to our journey's end, after the manner of the hymn which we sang just now—

> Calm in the hour of buoyant health,
> Calm in my hour of pain;
> Calm in my poverty or wealth,
> Calm in my loss or gain;
>
> Calm me, my God, and keep me calm,
> Soft resting on thy breast;
> Soothe me with holy hymn and psalm,
> And bid my spirit rest.

Oh, that our life may be as a sea of glass! May the sacred circle of our fellowship be within the golden line of the peace of God! You who did bid us come to you and rest, now bid us "go in peace."

I am going to say a little in my opening upon a *delightful assurance* which constituted the reason why the woman went in peace: "Thy faith hath saved thee"; or, as in verse 48, "Thy sins are forgiven thee." Upon the strength of the assurance that she was saved, she might safely go in peace. When we have talked a little upon that subject, we will then come to a *considerate precept*: the Savior directed her, in the moment of trial, to "go in peace." There was an assurance for her comfort, and a precept for her guidance.

I. First, then, consider *a delightful assurance.*

The ground upon which the penitent woman might go in peace was that she had been saved. The Savior assured her: "Thy faith hath saved thee."

She was not saved otherwise than we are saved; but she received the common salvation by like precious faith. The way of salvation to her was faith in Christ. There is the same way for us, but she had what some of you, no doubt, would greatly like to have: she had *an assurance that she was saved, from the Lord's own mouth.* I think I hear some saying, "I should go in peace, I am sure, if the Lord Jesus would but appear to me, and speak, and say with his own lips, 'Thy faith hath saved thee.'" It is natural that you should think so; it must have been rapture to receive a benediction from the mouth of our King, our Savior. Yet, dear friends, we must not hang our confidence upon a mere circumstance. For a mere circumstance it is, whether Christ shall literally stand before you in the flesh, and say, "Thy faith hath saved thee," or whether he shall say it to you by the infallible record of his own Word. It does not make much difference as to my faith in what my father says to me, whether I meet the venerable man in the morning in my garden, and there hear his voice, or whether I get a letter by post in his handwriting, and he says to me upon that paper just what he would have said if I had met him face to face. I do not require him always to come up the hill to my house to tell me everything that he has to say: I should think myself an idiot if I did. If I were to say, "My dear father, you have assured me of your love by letter; but somehow, I cannot credit it unless you come and look me in the face, and take my hand, and assure me of your goodwill," surely he would say to me, "My dear son, what ails you? You must be out of your mind. I never knew you to be so childish before: my handwriting has always been enough. I can hardly think you mean it when you say that you cannot credit me unless I stand manifest before your eyes, and with your ears you hear me speak."

Now what I would not do to my earthly father, I certainly would not do to my heavenly Savior. I am perfectly satisfied myself to believe what he writes to me; and if it be so written in his Book, it seems to me to be quite as true and sure as if he had actually come from heaven, and had talked with me, or had appeared to me in the visions of the night. Is not this the reasoning of common sense? Do you not at once agree with me?

"Well," say you, "we go with you there, dear sir; but, then, he spoke that word to her personally. We should never have any more doubts, but should go in peace, if he said that word of assurance to us. You see, it is not merely that Jesus himself spoke, and said, 'Thy faith hath made thee whole,' but he looked that way; he turned toward her, and she knew that he referred to her. There was no mistaking to whom the assurance was given. There were other people in the room, but he did not say it to Simon; he did not say it to Peter; he did not say it to James and John. She knew by the look of him that he meant it for her, and for her alone, for she was the only person to go, and consequently the only one to 'go in peace.' Our Lord put it in the singular number, and said, 'Thy faith hath saved thee.' I want it to come home just so to me."

Yes, but I think that this is a little unreasonable too; is it not? Because if my father (to carry on my figure) were to speak to me, and to my brothers and to my sisters, and were to say, "Dear children, I have loving thoughts concerning you, and I have laid up in store for your needs," I do not think that I should say to him by and by, "Now, Father, do you know that I did not believe you, or derive any pleasure from what you said, because you spoke to others besides myself? I did not think your statement of love could be true, because you included my brothers and my sisters. You did not use the singular, but you put it in the plural; and you spoke to all my brothers and sisters, as well as to myself; and therefore I felt that I could not take any comfort out of your tender assurances." I should be a most unreasonable kind of body if I were to talk in that way; and my father would begin to think that his son was qualifying for a lunatic asylum. If he did not attribute it to unkindness of heart, he certainly would ascribe it to imbecility of head. Why, surely, surely, if my father says the same to each one of his children as he says to me, his words are all the more likely to be true, instead of being less worthy of belief; and therefore I derive comfort from his promises of love being put in the plural rather than in the singular. Surely, it should not be less easy to believe that God would deal graciously with me in company with thousands of others than that he should pursue a solitary plan with me as the lone object of his love. Is it not so?

"Ah yes!" says one, "but you have not hit on it yet. I want to know that I am one that is in that plural, and I want to know that I really am one of those to whom Jesus speaks in his Word." My anxious friend, you may know it; and you may know it most certainly. It is written, "He that believeth on him hath everlasting life." It need never be a question whether you believe in him or not; if you trust him, that is the gist of the matter. You can readily ascertain whether you do really trust him, or do not trust him. If you do trust him, you are his, and every promise of his covenant is made to you. You have faith, and when the Lord lays it down as a general statement that faith saves—the statement is applicable to all the world, in every place, and in all time, until the present age shall end, and men shall have passed into the fixed state of retribution, where no gospel of faith is preached. "Thy faith hath saved thee": if you have faith at all—if you believe that Jesus is the Christ—you are born of God. If you can say to the Lord Jesus,

All my trust on thee is stayed,
All my help from thee I bring,

that is faith, and Jesus testifies, "Thy faith hath saved thee." Now, because the infallible Witness says this of all who have faith, I do not think you ought to doubt it. It is true you do not hear his voice, because he says it rather by the written Word than by word of mouth; but surely this does not affect your faith. We believe a true man whether he writes or speaks: indeed, if there be any choice, we prefer that which he has deliberately put upon paper; for this remains when the sound of the voice is clean gone. It is most profitable for us that we should read our Lord's declaration over and over again, and put it in all sorts of shapes, and see how it remains evermore faithful and true. It is more assuring to you to find it in the volume of the Book than it would be if the Savior met you tonight, and said to you, "Thy sins are forgiven thee. Thy faith hath saved thee." The record excels the voice.

"No," say you, "I cannot see that." Well now, Peter was with Christ on the Mount of Transfiguration, and nothing could shake Peter's conviction that he had been there in the midst of that heavenly glory; and yet, for all that, Peter says, concerning the inspired Word, "We have a more sure word of testimony [prophecy]." He felt that even the memory of that vision, which he had assuredly seen, did not always yield to him so much assurance as did the abidingly inspired Word of God. You ought to feel the same. If I were conscious tonight that, at some period of my life, I had seen the Lord, and that he had spoken to me, the very spot of ground on which it occurred would be exceedingly dear and sacred to my spirit; but I am certain that when I grew depressed, when darkness rushed over my soul, as it does sometimes, I should be sure to say to myself, "You never saw anything of the kind. It was a delusion, a figment of imagination, a delirium, and nothing more." But, beloved, when I get to this Book, and see before me the sacred lines, I know that I am not deluded. There it stands, "God so loved the world, that he gave his only begotten Son, that whosoever believeth in him should not perish, but have everlasting life." I am sure about that, and I am sure that I believe, and therefore I am sure that I am saved. I like to put my finger right down on the passage, and then say, "Lord, I know you cannot lie. I have never had a question about this being your Book. Whatever other doubts have plagued me, this has not. You have so spoken it home to my soul, that I am as assured that this is your Book as I am assured of my own existence; and, hence, you have done better for the removal of my doubts, and for the assurance of my soul's eternal salvation, by putting your promise in your Book, than if you had yourself personally appeared to me, and spoken with your own voice."

O my hearer, the written Word is most sure! If you believe, you are saved, as surely as you are alive. If you believe, heaven and earth may pass away, but the Word of the Lord shall stand fast for you. "He that believeth in him hath everlasting life." He has eternal life in present possession. Our Lord has put it thus: "He that believeth and is baptized shall be saved." "He that with his heart believeth, and with his mouth maketh confession of him, shall be saved." There are no "ifs" or "buts" about these words of promise. Salvation is put as a present thing, and as an abiding thing, but in every case as a certain thing; and why should we be worried and worn about the matter? It is so, and let us take the comfort of the fact. We must either throw away this Book by beginning to talk about "degrees of inspiration" and all that foul rubbish, or else we are logically bound to be sure of our hope, and to rejoice in it. I warrant you, O my hearer, that as long as you stand fast by the belief that this is a sure word of testimony, you will know that you are saved! If this Book be true, every believer in Jesus is as safe as Jesus himself. To say "I believe, but I am afraid I am not saved" is to say, only in a roundabout way, that you do not believe at all; for, if you believe, then you believe that God speaks the truth; and this is the testimony, that "God hath given us eternal life, and that life is in his Son." This is the testimony of the great Father, and the testimony of the eternal Spirit; and we must not dare to doubt it. You may doubt whether you believe or not; but given that you do really and unfeignedly put your trust in the Lord Jesus, then, as effect follows cause, it is certain that the cause of faith will be followed by its sure effect—salvation. "Thy faith hath saved thee: go in peace."

Do not worry any longer: go in peace. Have done with questioning; end debate; go in peace. Go about your business, for the work of salvation is done. You are a saved soul: go and rejoice in finished salvation, and ask no more questions. "Wherefore criest thou unto me?" said God to Moses. "Speak unto the children of Israel, that they go forward." Wherefore do you question and doubt any longer? Go forward to enjoy what God has prepared for you; and as you are saved and justified in Christ, now seek sanctification, and all the other blessings of the covenant of grace which lie before you in Christ Jesus your Lord. The promise is sure; be sure that it is so, and in perfect rest of soul enjoy the good which God provides you.

I think I have thus brought out as clearly as I can that delightful assurance which is the ground of the command, "Go in peace."

II. We come, second, to hearken to *a considerate precept*.

Our Lord, with wise tenderness, dismissed the beloved object of his pardoning love, and bade her "go in peace." May the Holy Spirit bless this to us!

This precept divides itself into two parts. There is, first, "go," and then there is "go in peace."

There is "*go.*" Now in "*go,*" there are two things: to go *from* and to go *to.* *Where was she to go from?* First, she was *to go from these quibblers.* Simon and the Pharisees are as full of objections as a swarm of bees is full of stings. They say in their hearts one to another, "Who is this that forgiveth sins also?" They have even dared to question the character of the perfect One, and have hinted a suspicion of his purity for allowing such a woman to come so near him, and to wash his feet with her tears. Therefore the Savior says to her "*go.*" This was not a happy place for a childlike love to linger in. Her soul would have been among lions. Jesus seems to say, "Do not stay to be tormented by these cavilers. Thy faith hath saved thee; go. You have gained a great blessing; go home with it. Let these people argue with each other; you have a rich prize, take it out of the reach of these pirates."

Oftentimes I believe that the child of God would find it to be his greatest wisdom, whenever he is in company that begins to assail his Lord, or to denounce his faith, just to go about his business, and let the scoffers have their scoffing to themselves. Some of us have thought it our miserable duty to read certain books that have been brought out against the truth, that we might be able to answer them; but it is a perilous calling. The Lord have mercy upon us when we have to go down into these sewers; for the process is not healthy!

"Oh," says a man, "but you must prove all things!" Yes, so I will; but if one should set a joint of meat on his table, and it smelled rather high, I would cut a slice, and if I put one bit of it in my mouth, and found it far gone, I should not feel it necessary to eat the whole round of beef to test its sweetness. Some people seem to think that they must read a bad book through; and they must go and hear a bad preacher often before they can be sure of his quality. Why, you can judge many teachings in five minutes! You say to yourself, "No, sir, no, no, no! This is good meat—for dogs. Let them have it, but it is not good meat for me, and I do not intend to poison myself with it." The Savior does not tell the woman, "Stop, now, and hear what Simon has got to say. Dear good woman, you have been washing my feet with tears, and here is a highly intelligent gentleman, a Pharisee, who has a very learned prelection to deliver; give him a fair hearing. You have to prove all things; therefore, stop and hear him. And here are more gentlemen who object to my pardoning your sins; and their objections are fetched from deep veins of thought. Listen to them, and then I will meet their questions, and have peace: do not stop till you lose it. You have your comfort and joy: refuse to be robbed of them." Why, if you were in a room, and you saw a certain number of gentlemen of a suspicious character, and you had your watch with you, you would not feel it necessary to stop and see whether they were able to extract your watch from you, but you would say to yourself, "No; I am best out of this company." We are safest out of the society of those whose great object it is to rob us of our faith. "Thy faith hath saved thee. Go home. Leave them. Go in peace."

I think that he meant, besides going away from the men, *"Go away from the publicity into which you have unwillingly stepped."* If our Savior had been like some excellent people of the present day, he would have said, "Stand before all these men, and tell your experience. I shall require you to be at half a dozen meetings this week, and you must speak at every one of them." A splendid woman, was she not, who washed the Savior's feet with tears, and wiped them with the hairs of her head? She might have exhibited her eyes and her hair, and told their gracious story. Who can tell but several would have been impressed by the narrative? The Savior said to the woman—so excitable, for she was all that, as well as grateful, "Thy faith hath saved thee: go in peace." As much as to say, "There are certain of your own sex that you can speak to. You will find some poor fallen woman to whom you can quietly tell of my pardoning grace. But yours is a case in which the very beauty of your character will lie in the quietude of your future life. 'Thy faith hath saved thee.' That is enough for you. You have come upon the stage of action by that splendid act of your love; but do not acquire the habit of winning publicity. Do not aspire to display yourself in a bold and heroic attitude, but go in peace." He almost seems to say, "Subside now into your family. Take your place with the rest of your sisters. Adorn by your future purity my doctrine, and let all men see what a change has been worked in you; for, maybe, that very weakness of yours, which made you what you were as a sinner, may put you in danger even as a saint. Therefore I do not ask you to tarry here, and join my disciples, and follow me publicly through the streets, but your faith has saved you: go in peace."

I think that the Master taught a great deal of wisdom here, which some of those who are leaders in the church of God would do well to copy. Yes, I think that I shall go a little further, and say, that *I think the Savior there and then dismissed her from that high ministry which, for once in her life, she had carried out.* She washed his feet with tears, and wiped them with the hairs of her head. It was the action of a love which had risen to a passion. It was an action such as shall be told for a memorial of her everywhere; and we may well imitate her penitence, and her heroic courage, as well as her love to Christ. But, at the same time, we cannot always be doing heroic actions: life is mainly made up of common deeds. It would not be possible to be always washing feet with tears, nor to be always unbraiding tresses to use them as a towel. The difficulty with some people is that they are always wanting to practice the sublime. Alas! they often fail by just one step, and become ridiculous. They are always straining after effect; and hearing of what has been done once, by one choice person, they must do it themselves, and they must keep on doing it.

O my sister! there may come a time when you will have to speak for Christ, and speak openly before many; but tomorrow you had better go home, and see to the children, and make home happy for your husband. You will glorify Christ by darning stockings, and mending the socks of the little ones, quite as surely as by washing his feet with tears. You make a great mistake if you have not a piety which will take you into domestic life—which will help you to make the common drudgery of life a divine service.

We want men that can serve God with the axe and plane or behind a counter or by driving a quill. These are the men we want; but there are many that crave to vault at once into a conspicuous place and perform an astounding deed. Having done it once, they become unsettled all the rest of their lives; and do not seem as if they ever could take to plainly keeping the Ten Commandments, and walking in the steps of Jesus. I wish that those who must flash and blaze would hear the Lord Jesus say to them, "Go in peace." I mean any of you who really did distinguish yourselves on one occasion, and deserved much praise from your Christian friends. I fear lest you should pine for unusual and even undesirable forms of service and become useless in the ordinary course of life. Now do not be spoiled for life by having been allowed in one unusual deed, but hear the Master say, "Thy faith hath saved thee: go in peace. Serve me in the daily avocations of life, and bring glory to my name at home. Go from the strain of publicity to the gentler pressures of family duty."

Do you not think that he even meant that she was now to cease *from that singular fellowship with him that she had enjoyed*? She had been very close to him; but she was, perhaps, never to be quite so near to him again. In spirit she should be; but certainly not physically. It happens that those who take to the contemplative life—and there is no life higher than that—are apt to think that they must forget the practical life. But it must not be so. We must do that which the Master bids us do, as well as sit at his feet.

I am tempted to tell a story which most of you must know concerning the famous man of God, who, in his cell, thought he saw the Lord Jesus, and under that persuasion he worshiped with rapt delight. But just then the bell at the convent gate rang, and it was his turn to stand at the door and deal out bread to the hungry. There was a little battle in his mind as to which he should do—tarry with his Lord or go to hand out bread to the poor mendicants. At last, he felt that he must do his duty even at the cost of the highest spiritual bliss. He went and distributed the bread, and when he came back, to his great delight, the vision was still there, and a voice said to him, "If you had stayed, I would have gone; but as you have gone, I have therefore stayed still to commune with you." The path of duty must be followed, and no spiritual enjoyment can excuse us from it. Never offer one duty to God stained with the blood of another. Balance your duties and let not one press out another. "Thy faith hath saved thee: go in peace." Do not think that you need to be all day long at your Bible, or all the evening at your prayer. There is time for everything. Let every holy work have its place, that your life may be a fair mosaic of brilliant colors, all set according to the divine pattern, to make up a perfect character. "Thy faith hath saved thee. Go in peace, and do the next thing, and the next, without weariness."

That leads me to speak of *what she was to go to*. It seems to me that the Savior said, "Now go home. You have been a fallen woman: home is the place for you. Go home to your mother and father, or other relatives. Seek a home. Be domesticated. *Attend to your own work.* Whatever your place is, go to it. Leaving daily duty was the source of your temptation; return to walks of usefulness, and habits of order, and this will be your safety. You will be less likely to be led away if you have work to occupy head and heart and hands."

Did he not mean, *"Go now to your ordinary life-trial"*? Do you think yourself a very peculiar person—a sort of saint, that has to float in the air, or live upon roses? Do not fancy such a thing. I have heard of the Chinese, that they sell shoes with which you can walk on the clouds; and I believe that some people must have bought a pair of these remarkable articles; for their lives are spent in cloudland, walking as in a dream, upon high stilts of fond imaginations. Do not think great things of yourself. You are but a commonplace man or woman. Do such duty as your fellow Christians do, and do not think yourself a superior person. The worst people in the world to work with are superior people. Those are of no importance who think they are of great importance. Poor creature! it is not the grace of God which turns your brain, but your own silly conceit.

Go forth to your further service: "Go in peace. There are some to whom you can tell of my love. Oh, how you will tell it! You that have washed my feet with your tears, go and shower those tears over fallen ones like yourself. Go, use those eyes, that you may look my love right into their hearts as you are speaking to them. Go all your life in peace, and do for me all that I shall put in your way to do for me." That is what I think our Lord meant. Brethren, do not think of sitting here to enjoy yourselves; but go off, and glorify your Redeemer's name. Go!

But then here is the point of it: he said, *"Go in peace."* O my brethren, I desire that all of us who love the Lord may go henceforth all the rest of our life journey in peace. May pardoning love put us at peace concerning all our sins! O pardoned one, you love much, for you have had much forgiven; let your thoughts all run to love, and none to fear. Fret not about the past—the dark, dishonorable past. The hand that was pierced has blotted it all out. The great Lord has frankly forgiven you all your debt. Let not that disturb you any longer. Go in peace. What a rest it is to be rid of the burden of sin, and to know of a certainty, from the teaching of God's own Word, that your sins are forgiven you! This is peace which passeth all understanding.

Our Lord meant, next, *"go in peace" in reference to all the criticisms of all these people who have looked at you.* Do not mind them. Do not trouble about them. What have they to do with you? It is enough for a servant if his master accepts him: he need not mind what others have to say about his service. Your faith has saved you. Forget all the unkind things they have said, and do not trouble your heart about the cruel speeches they may yet make. Go in peace, and be under no alarm as to upbraiding tongues.

And then I think he meant, *"Go in peace about what thou hast done."* I know the mood of a word like that. I have preached the gospel: I have thrown my whole soul into it; and after it is all over, I have felt bound to chide myself that I did not do much better as to style or spirit or length, or some other matter. Oh, but if the Master accepts it, one may go in peace about it! This woman had done a very extraordinary thing in washing Christ's feet with tears, and wiping them with the hairs of her head; and when she got away, she might have said to herself, "I wonder that I was so bold. Was I not immodestly conspicuous? How could I have done it? How must I have looked when I was bathing his feet? For me, too—such a sinner as I am—for me to have done it to the blessed and holy One! I fear he must have felt vexed at my rudeness!" Have you not sometimes done a brave thing for Christ, and then afterward felt just like that. "I was a bold minx," say you, "after all, to push myself so forward." The good young man, who has just preached for the first time, says, "Well, I got through it this time, but I will never attempt it again, for I am sure that I am not fit for such holy work." So the Master says to this woman, "Go in peace. I have accepted thee and thy loving service. Do not trouble about what thou hast done. It is all sweet to me, and has a rich perfume of thy great love. Never fret about what you have done. You have done the right thing. Thy faith hath saved thee. Go in peace." I want us to have just that kind of peace—peace about what we have done for our Lord, even as we have peace about sin forgiven, and peace about human criticisms. "Go in peace." Oh, to possess, from this time forth, a holy quiet! We are so apt to grow fretful. I know some good brethren who have a swollen vein of suspicion about them, that bleeds every now and then, and pains them greatly, and alarms other people. I know some sisters: they are very good, but unreasonably fearful. They say that they are "nervous." Perhaps that is the fact; and so I will say no more. But oh, that we could get them cured of this disease of the nerves! I would they could be quieted! I admire the members of the Society of Friends for this virtue beyond almost any other which they exhibit: they seem to be so steady, self-contained, and equable. They are a little slow, perhaps; but then they are very sure and firm and steadfast and calm. We are some of us too much in a hurry to go fast. If we were a little slower, we should be quicker. If we left our affairs more entirely with God, our peace might be like a river.

Yes, I would to God, dear friends, that we might feel henceforth a constant joy. Why not? Nothing ought to trouble us, for we know that all things work together for good. If we live by faith, nothing can trouble us; for between here and heaven we shall keep company with you, you blessed One! And if the way you take be rough, the fact of your being with us shall make it smooth to us. We will travel merrily with this as our march music: "Thy faith hath saved thee; go in peace."

Still, to come back to where I began, I daresay that the good woman thought that she would like to speak a word for the Lord. When they said that he could not forgive sin, would not she have liked to say, "But he did forgive my sin, and he changed my nature. How dare you speak thus"?

But the Savior said, go. She was not called to contend. Thank God every child of God is not called to fight with the adversary: those of us who are men of war from our youth up take no pleasure in strife. We wish that, like this holy woman, we could be exempt from this warfare. She might well rejoice in her escape from the sacred conscription. Many a cuff and blow she thus avoided; and as her Captain sent her off the field, she might go home right happily.

She might have lost the blessed frame of mind in which she then was, and this would have been a real injury to her. She was sweetly wrapped up in love, and there her Lord would have her abide.

He seems to say, "You are too precious to be battered and bruised in battle. Go—go in peace. Dear soul, you are so full of love to me that I do not want you to be worried with fighting and contending and controverting. Go in peace." She would have done no good, I dare say, if she had ventured into a fray for which she was so unfitted. If she had spoken, she would have said something which the cruel Pharisees would have turned into a jest. So he said to her, "Go in peace." Why should her feebleness give them an occasion for unholy triumph? All true hearts are not fit for fight. Besides, she had her Lord to be her Advocate, and there was no need for her to speak. Therefore he said, "I can manage them without your presence. Go in peace." When we may believingly leave a difficulty with our Lord, it is faith's duty to go home quietly. No doubt, by going in peace, she would be doing greater service than she would by using her tongue upon these ungodly men. A quiet, happy life is often the noblest witness that we can bear for Christ. Therefore I say to everyone who loves the Lord, there are times when he will say to us, "Do not enter into any of this conflict and turmoil and muddle. Thy faith hath saved thee. Go in peace."

The last word I have to say is this. There are many poor souls who talk about coming to Christ who are not yet saved; and they are always hearing about faith, and thinking of it, and yet they never do, in very truth, believe. Now do not hear or debate any more about faith, but *believe*. Trust Jesus Christ, and think no more about your own trusting. You shall think of it as a thing done, I mean, but not as a thing to be done. God help you now to believe in Jesus, and so pass over the bridge of belief to the golden shore of Jesus himself!

Well, but I notice some say that they believe, but it is not believing, because if it were believing, they would "go in peace." A person comes to the bank with a check. He believes it to be honestly his, and the signature to be correct. He puts it down on the counter, and the clerk puts out the money. But see! The man does not take it. He stands and loafs about; and the clerk looks at him, and wonders what he is at. At last, when the person has been there long enough to wear the good man's patience out, the clerk says, "Did you bring that check to have the money?" "Yes, I handed it in." "Well, then, why do you not take the money and go about your business?" If he is a sensible man, he delays no longer; no, he would not have delayed so long. He takes the money, and departs in peace. Now, dear soul, if you have a promise from God—"He that believeth is not condemned," or, "He that believeth hath everlasting life"—do you believe? Then take the blessing, and go about your business. Do not keep on saying, "Perhaps it is so," and, "Perhaps it is not so." Do you believe that God speaks the truth? If so, then take the promised blessing and enjoy it; for you are a saved man. "But I have been going to a place of worship for years, and I have been believing in a sort of a way; but I have never dared to say that I was saved." Then you are acting the part of an unbeliever.

If you do not know that you are saved, how dare you go to sleep tonight? How should a man dare to eat his meals, and go about his business, and yet say, "I do not know whether I am saved or not"? You may know it, and you ought to know it. If you believe, you are saved: if you doubt that fact, you are rather an unbeliever than a believer. Take up your money and go home. "O thou of little faith, wherefore didst thou doubt?" Trust Jesus! Your faith has saved you. Go in peace.

The Lord help you truly to believe, for Jesus' sake! Amen.

Mary and Martha: The Master Calls

⁂

Delivered at the Metropolitan Tabernacle, Newington. No. 1198.

She . . . called Mary her sister secretly, saying, "The Master is come, and calleth for thee."—JOHN 11:28

I suppose by Martha's whispering the words "the Master" in Mary's ear, that it was the common name by which the sisters spoke of our Lord to one another in his absence. Perhaps it was his usual name among all the disciples, for Jesus said, "Ye call me Master and Lord: and ye say well; for so I am." It often happens that for persons whom we love, we have some special title by which we speak of them familiarly when we are in the circle of those who join in our esteem of them. Instead of always using their official titles or their actual names, there is some one name which we have attached to them, which calls up happy associations, or reminds us of endearing traits in their character, and therefore it is very sweet in our mouths. So I suppose that most of the disciples called Jesus "the Master," many of them coupling with it the word Lord.

Mary, I should suppose, was peculiarly given to the use of the term—it was *her* name for the Lord. I fancy that she called him *"my* Master," only, of course, Martha could not say to her, "your Master is come," for that would have been to cast suspicion on her own loyalty to Jesus, and perhaps she did not feel exactly in a frame of mind to say, "our Master," remembering that he was Master of so many more besides, and half hoping that he might be Master over death himself. She therefore said, *"the* Master." It was an emphatic title, *"The* Master is come."

Very remarkable is it that minds of a kindred spirit to Mary have always loved this title of "the Master," and more especially that wondrous, sweet, mystic poet and dear lover of his Lord, George Herbert, who, whenever he heard the name of Jesus mentioned, would always say "my Master." He has given us that quaint poem, called "The Odor," which begins,

How sweetly doth my Master sound, my Master.

There must needs be something exceedingly precious about the title for a Mary and a Herbert thus to be enamored of it above all others. Jesus has many names, all full of music; this must be choice indeed to be selected before them all as the title which his best beloved prefer to apply to him. There are many among us who are ourselves accustomed to speak of the Lord as the Master, and, though there are many other titles, such as the Well Beloved, the Good Shepherd, the Friend, the Bridegroom, the Redeemer, and the Savior, yet we still cherish a very special affection for this one name, which gives forth to us "an oriental fragrancy," with which "all day [we] do perfume our mind" [George Herbert].

You are aware that the word might just as well be translated the "Teacher," the authoritative Teacher, for that is the gist of its meaning. I am glad to pronounce it Master, because usage and sweet association have enshrined the word, and also because we have still among us the custom of calling the chief teacher in a school or college *the master*, but still, had our version given us "the Teacher is come," it would have been nearer the mark.

I. I shall speak a few words, first, upon *the deep propriety of this title as applied to our Lord.*

He is, indeed, the Master—the Teacher. What if I put the two together, and say the Master-Teacher? He has a peculiar fitness for this office. To be a master-teacher a man must have *a masterly mind.* Certainly all minds are not cast in the same mold and are not possessed with the same vigor, depth, force, and quickness of action. Some mental organizations are princely by their very formation; though they may belong to plowboys, the imperial stamp is on them. These minds cannot be smothered by a peasant's smock frock, nor kept down by the load of poverty; master minds are recognized by an innate superiority, and force their way to the front. I say nothing of the moral qualities of Napoleon, but a mind so vast as his could not have been forever hidden away among the soldiers in the ranks; he must become a captain and a conqueror. So, too, a Cromwell or a Washington must rise to be masters among men, because the caliber of their minds was masterly. Such men see a thing quickly; they hold it with a comprehensive grasp; and they have a way of infusing faith into others about it which, before long, pushes them into a master's position, with the common consent of all around them. You cannot have for a master-teacher a man with a little soul. He may insinuate himself into the chair of the teacher, but everyone will see that he is out of place and no one will delight to think of him as his master. Many painters there are, but there have been few Raphaels or Michelangelos, few who could found schools to perpetuate their names. Many songsters have there been, but few poets have founded schools of tuneful thought in which they have been the beloved choirmasters. Many philosophers have there been, but a Socrates or an Aristotle will not be found every day; for great teachers must have great minds, and these are rare among men. The teacher of all teachers, the master of all the teachers must needs be a grand, colossal spirit, head and shoulders above other men.

Such a soul Mary saw in her Lord Jesus Christ, and such we see there also, and we therefore challenge for our Lord the name of the Master. There we have divinity itself, with its omniscience and infallibility, and at the same time a complete, full-orbed manhood, harmonious in all its qualities, a perfect equilibrium of excellence, in which there is no excess and no deficiency. You find in him a perfect mind, and that mind so human, as to be intensely manly, and sweetly womanly also. In Jesus there was all the tenderness and sympathy of woman, joined with the strength and courage of man. His love was feminine, but not effeminate; his heart was masculine, but not hard and stern. He was *the* complete man, unfallen manhood in its perfectness.

Our Lord was a man who impressed all who came near him; they either hated him intensely or loved him fervently. Wherever he was, he was seen to be a prince among the sons of men. The devil recognized him and tempted him beyond all others. He saw in him a foeman worthy of his steel, and took him into the wilderness to have a duel with him, hoping to defeat the race by vanquishing its manifest chief. Even scribes and Pharisees, who despised everyone who made not broad the borders of his garment, could not despise this man; they could hate him, but their hate was the unconscious reverence which evil is forced to render to superlative goodness and greatness. Jesus could not be ignored and overlooked. He was a force in every place, a power wherever he might be. He is a master, yes, "the Master." There is a grandeur about his whole human nature, so that he stands out above all other men, like some mighty Alpine peak, which overtops the minor hills, and casts its shadow all down the vales.

But to make a master teacher, a man must not only have a master mind, but he must have *a master knowledge* of that which he has to teach; and it is best if that be acquired by experience rather than by instruction. Such was the case with our Lord Jesus. He came to teach us the science of life, and in him was life; he experienced life in all its phases, and was tempted in all points like as we are, though without sin. The highest were not above him, the lowest he did not regard as beneath him, but he condescended to their infirmities and sorrows. There are no dreary glens of melancholy which his feet have not trodden, nor lofty peaks of joy which he has not scaled; wondrous was the joy as well as the sorrow of our Lord Jesus Christ. He leads his people through the wilderness, and, like Hobab of old, he knows where they should encamp in the wilderness, and understands all the way which they must traverse to reach the Promised Land. He was made "perfect through suffering." He teaches us no truth as mere theory, but as matter of actual experiment on his own person. The remedy he gives to us he has tested. If there be bitterness for us, he has quaffed full bowls of it, and if there be sweetness in his cup he gives us of his joy; all things that have to do with this life and godliness, the whole science of salvation from the gates of hell up to the throne of God, he understands right well, by personal acquaintance therewith. There is not a single chapter of the book of revelation which he does not comprehend, nor a solitary page of the book of experience which he does not understand; and therefore he is fit to teach, having both a master mind and a master knowledge of that which he comes to inculcate.

Moreover, our great Master while here below had *a masterly way of teaching*, and this also is essential, for it is not every man of vast knowledge and great mind that can teach others. Aptness to teach is required. We know some whose utterances never seem to be in the tongue of ordinary men. If they have anything to say, they say it in a jargon of their own, which they probably comprehend, and a few of their disciples, but it is Greek to commonplace people. Blessed is that teacher who teaches what he understands himself in a way which enables others to understand him. I like the style of old Cobbett when he said, "I not only speak so that men can understand me, but so that they *cannot misunderstand* me"; and such a teacher was Christ to his own disciples. When they sat at his feet, he made truth so clear that wayfaring men, though fools, need not err therein. By homely parables and phrases which caught the ear and won the heart, he brought down celestial truths to ordinary comprehensions, when the Spirit of God had once cleansed those comprehensions, and made them able to receive the truth. He taught, moreover, not only plainly, but lovingly. So gently did he open up things to his own disciples that it must have been a pleasure to be ignorant, in order to require to be taught, and a greater pleasure still to learn—to learn in such a way. The way in which he taught was as sweet as the truth he taught. Everybody that came into Christ's school felt at home, felt pleased with their Master, and confident that if they could learn anywhere, they must learn at his feet.

The Master gave, in connection with his teaching, a measure of the Holy Spirit—not the full measure, for that was reserved until he had ascended up on high, and the Spirit should baptize the church, but he gave to each of his people a measure of the Spirit of God, by which truths were not taught to their ears only but to their hearts also. Ah, my brethren, we are not such teachers as Christ; for, when we have done our best, we can only reach the ear. We cannot give the Holy Spirit, but he can; and when the Spirit this day comes from Christ, and takes of his things and reveals them unto us, then we see yet more of our Lord's masterly modes of teaching and learn what a Master Jesus is, who writes his lessons, not on the blackboard, but on the fleshy tablets of the heart; who gives us school books, no, is himself the Book; who sets us lessons, yes, is himself the Lesson; who performs before us that which he would have us do, so that when we know him we know what he has to teach, and when we imitate him we have followed the precepts which he gives. Our Lord's way of embodying his instruction in himself is a right royal one, and none can rival him in it. Do not children learn infinitely more by example than ever they do by precept? And this is how our Master teaches us. "Never man spake like this man" is a grand Christian proverb; but it might be eclipsed by another: "Never man *acted* like this man"; for this man's deeds and words tally with each other, the deeds embody and enforce the words, give them life, and help us to understand them. He is a prophet like unto Moses, because he is mighty both in word and in deed, and so he is of prophets and teachers *the Master*. Here a master mind, a master experience, and a master mode of teaching: well is he called the Master.

Withal, dear friends, there was, over and above this—if I have not comprehended it in what I have already said—*a master influence* which Jesus, as a teacher, had over those who came within his range. They did not merely see, but feel; they did not only know, but love; they did not merely prize the lesson, but they worshiped the Teacher. What a master was this Christ, whose very self became the power by which sin was checked, and ultimately cast out, and by which virtue was implanted, and the new life commenced, nourished, and brought to perfection. To have one to teach you who is very dear to you is to make lessons easy. No child learns better than from a mother qualified to teach, who knows how to make her lessons sweet, by crystallizing them in the sugar of her own affection. Then it is pleasure, as well as duty, to learn.

But no mother ever won her child's heart (and there have been tender and affectionate mothers too) so thoroughly as Jesus won the heart of Mary; or, I may say, as Jesus has won your heart and mine, if you feel as my heart feels to my Lord. From him we want no reasonings to prove what he says; he is himself instead of reason and of argument. His love is the logic which proves everything to us. With him we hold no debate; what he has done for us has answered every question we could raise. If he tells us what we do not understand, we believe it. We ask if we may understand it, and if he tells us no, we stay where we are and believe the mystery. We love him so that we are as glad *not* to know as *to* know, if such should be his will; we believe his silence to be as eloquent as his speech, and that which he conceals to be as kindly intended as that which he reveals. Because we love him he exercises such an influence over us that, straightaway, we prize his teaching and receive it; and the more we know him, and the more his inexpressibly delightful influence dominates our nature, the more completely we yield up imagination, thought, reason, everything, to him.

Men may call us fools for it, but we have learned at Jesus' feet that "the world by wisdom knew not God," and that except we be converted, and become as little children, we shall in no wise enter the kingdom of heaven, and therefore we are not confounded when the world thinks us childish and credulous. The world is growing more manly and more foolish, and we are growing more childlike and more wise. We reckon that to grow downward into our Lord Jesus is the surest and truest growth; and when we shall have grown clean down to nothing, and lower still, till we are less than nothing, then we shall be full grown in the school of Jesus, and shall take a high degree in true learning, knowing the love of Christ which passes knowledge.

We may well call him Master who has a masterly mind, a masterly experience, and a masterly way of teaching; and, moreover, wields a masterly influence over his pupils, so that they are forever bound heart and soul to him, and count him to be himself his own highest lesson, as well as the chief of all instructors.

Having proved that our beloved Lord is fairly entitled to the name, let me add that he is by office the sole and alone Master of the church. There is in the Christian church no authority for a doctrine but Christ's Word. The inspired Book which he has left us, charging us never to diminish a letter or add a syllable, that is our code imperial, our authorized creed, our settled standard of belief. I hear a great deal said of sundry "bodies of divinity," but my own impression is that there never was but one Body of divinity, and there never will be but one, and that is Jesus Christ, in whom "dwelleth all the fullness of the Godhead bodily." To the true church, her body of divinity is Christ. Some churches refer to other standards, but we know no standard of theology but our Master. "I, if I be lifted up," says he, "will draw all men unto me"; we feel no drawings toward any other master. He is the standard—"Unto him shall the gathering of the people be."

We are not of those who will go no further than Martin Luther. Blessed be God for Martin Luther! God forbid that we should say a word in depreciation of him. But were we baptized unto Martin Luther? I believe not. Some can never budge an inch beyond John Calvin, whom I reverence first of all merely mortal men; but still John Calvin is not our master, but only a more advanced pupil in the school of Christ. He teaches, and, as far as he teaches as Christ taught, he is authoritative, but where Calvin goes apart from Jesus, he is no more to be followed than Voltaire himself. There be brethren whose one reference for everything is to the utterances of John Wesley. "What would Mr. Wesley have said?" is a weighty question with them. We think it a small matter what he would have said, or what he did say for the guidance of Christians, now so many years after his departure; far better is it to inquire what Jesus says in his Word. One of the grandest of men that ever lived was Wesley, but he is no master of ours. We were not baptized in the name of John Wesley or John Calvin or Martin Luther. "One is our Master, even Christ." And now the parliament of our country is about to set apart a learned judge to decide what is right in a so-called church of Christ, and he is to say, "This garment you may wear, and that you shall not; hitherto your ritual shall go but no further." In his person the House of Commons is to be recognized as the creator and lord and master of the Church of England, to whom he will say, "do this," and she will do it, or, "refrain," and she will stay her hand. She must crouch and bend, and take her meat like any dog from the hand that patronizes her, and her collar, made of what brass or leather Caesar chooses to ordain, shall bear this motto, "His servants ye are whom ye obey." Why, the poorest minister in the most despised of our churches, whose poverty is thought to make him contemptible, but whose poverty is his glory if he bears it for Christ's sake, would scorn to have any spiritual act of his church submitted to the judgment of the state, and would sooner die than be dictated to in the matter of divine worship. What has the church to do with the state? Our Master and Lord has set up a kingdom which owns no other King but himself; and we cannot bow, and will not bow, before decrees of Parliament and lords and kings in spiritual things. Christ's church has but one head, and that is Christ, and the doctrines which the church has to teach cannot be tested by a Court of Arches, or a bench of bishops, or a synod of ministers, or a presbytery, or a conference.

The Lord Jesus Christ has taught us this and that: if his teaching be contradicted, the contradiction is treason against his crown. Though the whole church were assembled, and that church the true one, if it should contradict the teaching of Christ, its decrees ought to be no more to a Christian than the whistling of the wind upon the mountain wilds, for Christ is Master, and none but Christ. Though an apostle or an angel from heaven preach any other doctrine than that of our Lord, "let him be accursed." I would God that all Christians stood up for this. Then would

> *Sects and names and parties fall,*
> *And Jesus Christ be all in all.*

He is the sole Teacher and the sole Legislator. A church has a right to execute Christ's laws, but she has no right to make a law. The ministers of Christ are bound to carry out the rules of Christ, and when they so do, what is bound on earth is bound in heaven; but if they have acted upon any rules but those of this Book, their laws are only worthy of contempt; be they what they may, they bind no Christian heart. The yoke Christ puts on us, it shall be our joy to wear, but the yoke which prelates would thrust upon us it shall be our glory to trample on. "If the Son make you free, you shall be free indeed." "Stand fast therefore in the liberty wherewith Christ hath made you free, and be not entangled again with the yoke of bondage."

"*The Master.*" That is the name Christ should receive throughout the whole church, and he should be regarded always, and on all occasions, and in reference to all spiritual subjects, as the last court of appeal, whose inspired word is

> *The judge that ends the strife*
> *Where wit and reason fail.*

Thus much upon the propriety of the title.

II. But now, second, let us consider *the peculiar recognition which Mary gave to Christ as the Master.*

How did she give that recognition? *She became his pupil*: she sat right reverently at his feet. Beloved, if he be our Master, let us do the same. Let us take every word of Jesus, weigh it, read it, mark it, learn it, feed on it, and inwardly digest it. I am afraid we do not read our Bibles as we should, or attach such importance as we ought to every shade of expression which our Master uses. I should like to see a picture of Mary sitting at the Master's feet. Great artists have painted the virgin Mary so often that they might take a change, and sketch this Mary looking up with a deep, fixed gaze, drinking all in, and treasuring all up; sometimes startled by a new thought and a fresh doctrine, and then inquiringly waiting till her face beams with unspeakable delight as new light floods her heart. Her attentive discipleship proved how truly Jesus was her Master.

Then, mark, she was not only his disciple, but *she was a disciple of nobody else.* I do not know whether Gamaliel was in fashion then, but she did not sit at his feet. I daresay there was some Rabbi Ben Simon, or other famous doctor of the period, but Mary never spent an hour with him, for every moment she could set apart was joyously spent at the feet of a far dearer Rabbi. I wonder whether she was a little deaf, and so sat close to the teacher for fear of losing a word! Perhaps she feared she might be slow of heart, and so she got as near the preacher as others do who have a little deafness in their ears; anyhow, her favorite place was close at his feet. That shows us, since we are always dull of hearing in our souls, that it is good to get very close to Jesus when we are hearing him, and commune while we listen. She did not change from him to someone else for variety's sake. No, the Master, her Master, her only Master, was the Nazarene, whom others despised, but whom she called her Lord.

She was a willing scholar, for "Mary hath chosen the good part," said Jesus. Nobody sent her to sit at Jesus' feet. Jesus drew her, and she could not help coming, but she loved to be there. She was a willing and delighted listener. Never was she so happy as when she had her choice, that choice being always to learn of him. Children at school always learn well if they want to learn. If they are driven to school, they learn but little comparatively, but when they want to go, and when they love the teacher, it is quick learning with them; and happy is the teacher who has a class that has chosen him to teach them. Mary could well call him "the Master," for she rendered him her sole attention, her loving and delighted attention. And, mark you, in choosing Christ for Master, *she perseveringly stuck to him.* Her choice was not taken away from her, and she did not give it up. Martha looked very cross one day. How was she to see to the roast meat and the boiled at once? How could she be expected to prepare the table, and to look to the fire in the kitchen too? Why could not Mary come? And she scowled, I do not doubt. But it did not signify. Mary sat there still. Perhaps she did not even notice Martha's face; I think she did not, for the saints do not notice other countenances when Christ's beauty is to be seen: there is something so absorbing about him. He takes you all into himself, and bears you right away, drawing not only all men, but all *of* men to himself, when he does draw; and so she sat there still, and listened on. Those children will learn who stick to their books, who come not sometimes to study, but are always learning. So Mary recognized the Lord Jesus Christ's master-teachership by giving to him that persevering attention which such a Master-Teacher had a right to claim.

She went humbly to him; for while she sat at his feet for nearness, she sat there too out of deep humiliation of spirit. She felt it her highest honor to be sitting in the lowest place, for lowly was her mind. They shall learn most of Christ who think least of themselves. When a place at his feet seems to be too good for us, or at any rate we are more than content with it, then will his speech distill as the rain and drop as the dew, and we shall be as the tender herbs that drink in sweet refreshment, and our souls shall grow.

Blessed were you, O Mary! And blessed is each one of you, if you can call Christ your Master and prove it as she did. You shall have the good part which shall not be taken away from you.

III. Now I come to my third point, which is this—*the special sweetness of the name to us.*

I have shown why it was peculiarly recognized by Mary, and now I would show that it has a peculiar sweetness for us also. *"The Master"* or *"My Master"* or *"My Teacher."*

I love that name in my own soul, because it is *as a teacher* that *Jesus Christ is my Savior.* The best illustration I can give you is that of one of those poor little boys in the street, an urchin without father and mother, or with parents worse than none; the poor child is covered with filth and rags, he is well known to the policemen, and has seen the inside of many a jail; but a teacher of a ragged school has laid hold of him, and instructs him, and he is now washed and clothed and happy. Now that poor boy does not know the sweetness of "my father" or "my mother"; he does not recognize anything in those titles. Perhaps he never knew them or only knew such a form of them as to disgust him. But with what a zest does he say, *"My teacher!"* These little children say, "My teacher," with quite as much affection as others speak of their mother. Where there has been a great moral change worked by the influence of a teacher, the name "my teacher" has great sweetness in it. Now hear the parable of the ragged boy and his teacher! I was that ragged child. Truly, I did not think myself ragged, for I was foolish enough to think my rags were fine garments, and that my filth was my beauty. I knew not what I was. My Teacher saw me, he knew how foul I was and how ragged I was, and he taught me to see myself, and also to believe that he could wash me whiter than the snow. Yes, he went further and actually washed me till I was clean before the Lord. My Teacher showed me a wardrobe of snow-white linen garments, and clothed me in them. My Teacher has taught me a thousand things and worked innumerable good works upon me; I owe my salvation wholly to my Teacher, my Master, my Lord. Cannot you say the same?

I know you can if you are indeed disciples of Jesus. "My Teacher" means to you "my Savior," for he saved you by teaching you your disease and your remedy, teaching you how wrong you were, and making you right by his teaching. The word master or teacher has to us a delightful meaning, for it is by his teaching that we are saved.

Let me tell you how as a preacher I love that name, "my Master." I like to feel that what I said to those people on Sunday was not mine. I preached my Master, and I preached what my Master told me. Some find fault with the doctrine; I do not mind that, because it was none of mine, it was my Master's. If I were a servant and went to the front door with a message, and the gentleman to whom I took it did not like the message, I should say, "Do not be vexed with me, sir. I have told you my master's message to the best of my ability, and I am not responsible for it. It is my master's word, not mine." When there are no souls converted, it is dreary work, and one's heart is heavy, but it is sweet to go and tell your Master; and when souls are converted, and your heart is glad, it is a happy and a healthy thing to give all the glory to your Master. It must be an awkward thing to be an ambassador from the English court in some far-off land where there is no telegraph, and where the ambassador has to act on his own responsibility. He must feel it a serious burden. But, blessed be God, between every true minister and his Master there is a telegraphic communication; he need never do anything on his own account. He may imitate the disciples of John, who, when they had taken up the Baptist's mangled body, went and told Jesus. That is the thing to do. There are difficulties in all churches, troubles in all families, and cares in all businesses, but it is good to have a Master to whom you can go as a servant, feeling, "He has the responsibility of the whole concern—not I; I have only to do what he bids me." If we once step beyond our Lord's commands, the responsibility rests on us, and our trouble begins, but if we follow our Lord we cannot go astray.

And is not this a sweet name to quote when you are troubled, dear friends? Perhaps some of you are in trouble now. How it removes fear when you find out that he who sent the trouble is the Teacher who teaches you by the trouble—the Master who has a right to use what form of teaching he likes. In our schools much is learned from the blackboard, and in Christ's school much is learned from affliction. You have heard the story often, but I venture to repeat it again, of the gardener who had preserved with great care a very choice rose; and one morning when he went into the garden it was gone, and he scolded his fellow servants and felt very grieved, till someone said, "I saw the master coming through the garden this morning, and I believe he took the rose." "Oh, then," said he, "if the master took it, I am content." Have you lost a dear child or a wife or a friend? It was he that took your flower. It belonged to him. Would you wish to keep what Jesus wants? We are asked to pray sometimes for the lives of good people, and I think we may, but I have not always exercised faith while pleading, because it seemed to me that Christ pulled one way and I pulled the other. I said, "Father, let them be here," and Jesus said,

"Father, I will that they be with me where I am"; and one could not pull very hard then. Only feel that Christ is drawing the other way, and you give up directly. You say, "Let the Master have it. The servant cannot oppose the Master." It is the Lord; let him do what seemeth him good. I was dumb with silence; I opened not my mouth because thou didst it.

Our Master learned that lesson himself which he teaches to us. That is a very striking expression, "Father, I thank thee that thou hast hid these things from the wise and prudent, and hast revealed them unto babes; even so, Father, for so it seemed good in thy sight." It pleased God to pass by the wise and prudent, and therefore it pleased Christ that it should be so. It is well to have our hearts like that poor shepherd to whom a gentleman said, "I wish you a good day." Said he, "I never knew a bad day." "How is that, my friend?" "The days are such as God chooses to make them, and therefore they are all good." "Well," said the other, "but some days please you more than others?" "No," said he, "what pleases God pleases me." "Well, but have you not a choice?" said the other. "Yes, I have a choice, and that is, I choose that God should choose for me." "But have you not a choice whether you would live or die?" "No," said he, "for if I am here Christ will be with me, and if I am in heaven I shall be with him." "But suppose you had to choose." "I would ask God to choose for me," said he. Oh, sweet simplicity which leaves everything with God; this is calling Jesus Master to perfection:

Pleased with all the Lord provides,
Weaned from all the world besides.

Once again, dear friends, is it not sweet to us to call Jesus Master, because in so doing we take a position easy to reach, and yet most delightful. To call him Bridegroom—what an honor is it to be so near akin to the Son of God! Friend is a familiar and honorable title; to call him Master, however, is often easier, and it is quite as sweet, for his service, if we take no higher place, is pure delight to us. If our hearts are right, to do the Lord's bidding is as much as we can ask for. Though we are sons now and not slaves, and therefore our service is of a different character from what it ever was before, yet service is delight. What will heaven be but perpetual service? Here we labor to enter into rest; there they enter into rest while they labor. Their rest is the perfect obedience of their fully sanctified spirits. Are you not panting for it? Will it not be one of your greatest joys in heaven to feel that you are his servants? The glorified ones are called his servants in heaven. "His servants shall serve him, and they shall see his face, and his name shall be on their foreheads." Rid us of sin, and we should be in heaven now; earth would be heaven to us.

I want you, dear brethren in Christ, to go away rolling this sweet word under your tongue: "my Master, my Master." You will never hear better music than that: "my Master, my Master." Go and live as servants should live. Mind you make him truly your Master, for he says, "If I be a Master where is my honor?" Speak well of him, for servants should speak well of a good master, and no servant ever had so dear a Master as he is.

But there are some of you who cannot say this. I wish you could. Jesus is not your Master. Who is, then? You have a master somewhere, for "his servants you are whom ye obey." Now, if you obey the lusts of the flesh, your master is your flesh, and the wages will be corruption; for that is what flesh comes to—corruption, and nothing better. Or your master is the devil, and his wages must be death. Run away from such a master. Mostly when servants leave their masters, they are bound to give notice, but here is a case in which no notice should ever be given. When the prodigal son ran away from feeding the swine, he never stopped to give notice that he was going to leave the pigs, but started off directly, and I recommend every sinner to run by the grace of God straightaway from his sins. Stopping to give notice is the ruin of many. They mean to be sober, but they must treat their good resolution to another glass or two; they intend to think about divine things, but they must go to the theater once more; they would fain serve Christ, but tomorrow, not tonight. If I had such a master as you have—you who live in sin—I would up and away at once, by the grace of God, and say, "I will have Christ for my Lord." Look at your black master. Look at his cunning eyes! Can you not see that he is a flatterer? He means your ruin. He will destroy you as he has destroyed myriads already. That horrid leer of sin, that painted face, consider them and abhor them. Serve not a master who, though he gives you fair promises, labors for your destruction! Up and away, you slaves of sin! Eternal Spirit, come and break their chains! Sweet star of liberty, guide them to the free country, and let them find in Jesus Christ their liberty! My Master rejoices to receive runaways. His door is open to vagrants and vagabonds, to the scum of the earth and the offscouring of all things, to men that are dissatisfied with themselves, to wretches who have no joy of their lives, and are ready to lie down and die. "This man receiveth sinners." He is like David, who went into Adullam, and every man that was in debt and discontented came to him, and he became a captain over them. As Romulus and Remus gathered the first population of new Rome by harboring escaped slaves and robbers, whom they trained into citizens and made to be brave soldiers, so my Master has laid the foundation of the new Jerusalem, and he looks for his citizens—yes, the noblest of them, over yonder there, where sin and Satan hold them captive; and he bids us sound out the silver trumpet, and tell the slaves of sin that if they flee to him he will never give them up to their old master, but he will emancipate them, make them citizens of his great city, sharers of his bounties, partakers in his triumphs; and they shall be his in the day when he makes up his jewels.

I recollect preaching in this strain once, and an old sea captain told me after the sermon that he had served under the black flag for fifty years, and by the grace of God he would tear the old rag down, and run up the bloodred cross at the masthead. I recommended him not merely to change his flag, but to see that the vessel was repaired, but he wisely replied that repairing would be of no use to such an old waterlogged hulk, and he had better scuttle the old ship and have a new one. I reckon that is the best thing to do, to be dead indeed unto sin and made alive in Christ Jesus; for you may do what you will with the old wreck of fallen nature, you will never keep it afloat. The old man must be crucified with Christ. It must be dead and buried and sunk fifty thousand fathoms deep, never to be heard of again. In the new vessel which Jesus launches in the day of our regeneration, with the blessed flag of atoning blood above us, we will sail to heaven convoyed by irresistible grace, giving God the glory forever and ever. Amen.

Two Marys: "Over Against the Sepulcher"

Delivered on Lord's Day morning, March 24, 1878, at the Metropolitan Tabernacle, Newington. No. 1404.

Sitting over against the sepulcher.—MATTHEW 27:61

Mary Magdalene and the other Mary were last at the Savior's grave. They had associated themselves with Joseph and Nicodemus in the sad but loving task of placing the body of their Lord in the silent tomb, and after the holy men had gone home they lingered still near the grave. Sitting down, perhaps upon some seat in the garden, or on some projection of the rock, they waited in mournful solitude. They had seen where and how the body was laid, and so had done their utmost, but yet they sat watching still: love has never done enough, it is hungry to render service. They could scarcely take their eyes away from the spot which held their most precious treasure, nor leave, till they were compelled to do so, the sacred relics of their Best Beloved.

The virgin Mary had been taken by John to his own home. She had sustained too great a shock to remain at the tomb, for in her were fulfilled the words, "Yea, a sword shall pierce through thine own heart also." She was wise to leave to others those sorrowful offices which were beyond her own power; exceedingly wise, also, from that hour to her life's end, to remain in the shade, modestly bearing the honor which made her blessed among women. The mother of Zebedee's children, who also lingered late at the tomb, was gone home too, for as she was the mother of John it is exceedingly probable that John resided with her, and had taken the Virgin to her home: hence she was needed at home to act as hostess and assist her son, and thus she would be obeying the last wish of her dying Lord when he said, "Son, behold thy mother," and explained his meaning by a look. All having thus departed, the two Marys were the sole watchers at the tomb of Christ at the time of the going down of the sun. They had work yet to do for his burial, and this called them away, but they stayed as long as they could—last to go and first to return.

This morning we shall with the women take up the somewhat unusual post of "sitting over against the sepulcher." I call it unusual, for as none remained save these two women, so few have preached upon our Redeemer's burial. Thousands of sermons have been delivered upon his death and resurrection, and in this I greatly rejoice, only wishing that there were thousands more; but still the burial of our Lord deserves a larger share of consideration than it generally obtains. "He was crucified, dead, and buried," says the creed, and therefore those who wrote that summary must have thought his burial an important truth; and so indeed it is. It was the natural sequence and seal of his death, and so was related to that which went before; it was the fit and suitable preparation for his rising again, and so stood in connection with that which followed after. Come, then, let us take our seat with the holy women "over against the sepulcher," and sing—

> *Rest, glorious Son of God: thy work is done,*
> *And all thy burdens borne;*
> *Rest on that stone till the third sun has brought*
> *Thine everlasting morn.*

> *How calmly in that tomb thou liest now,*
> *Thy rest how still and deep!*
> *O'er thee in love the Father rests: he gives*
> *To his beloved sleep.*

> *On Bethel pillow now thy head is laid,*
> *In Joseph's rock-hewn cell;*
> *Thy watchers are the angels of thy God,*
> *They guard thy slumbers well.*

I. Supposing ourselves to be sitting in the garden with our eyes fixed upon the great stone which formed the door of the tomb, we first of all *admire that he had a grave* at all.

We wonder how that stone could hide him who is the brightness of his Father's glory; how the Life of all could lie among the dead; how he who holds creation in his strong right hand could even for an hour be entombed. Admiring this, we would calmly reflect, first, upon the testimony of his grave that he was really dead. Those tender women could not have been mistaken, their eyes were too quick to suffer him to be buried alive, even if anyone had wished to do so. Of our Lord's actual death, we have many proofs connected with his burial. When Joseph of Arimathaea went to Pilate and begged the body, the Roman ruler would not give it up till he was certified of his death. The centurion, a man under authority, careful in all that he did, certified that Jesus was dead. The soldier who served under the centurion had by a very conclusive test established the fact of his death beyond all doubt, for with a spear he pierced his side, and forthwith there came out blood and water. Pilate, who would not have given up the body of a condemned person unless he was sure that execution had taken place, registered the death and commanded the body to be delivered to Joseph. Both Joseph of Arimathaea and Nicodemus and all the friends who aided in the interment were beyond all question convinced that he was dead. They handled the lifeless frame, they wrapped it in the bands of fine linen, they placed the spices about the sacred flesh which they loved so well: they were sadly assured that their Lord was dead.

Even his enemies were quite certain that they had slain him; they never had a suspicion that possibly a little life remained in him, and that it could be revived, for their stern hate allowed no doubt to remain upon that point; they knew even to the satisfaction of their mistrustful malice that Jesus of Nazareth had died. Even when in their anxiety they went to Pilate, it was not that they might obtain stronger proofs of death, but to prevent the disciples from stealing his dead body and giving out that he had risen from the dead.

Yes, Jesus died, literally and actually died, and his body of flesh and bones was really laid in Joseph's grave. It was no phantom that was crucified, as certain heretics dreamed of old. We have not to look to a spectral atonement or to a visionary sacrifice, though some in our own times would reduce redemption to something shadowy and unsubstantial. Jesus was a real man, and truly tasted the bitter pangs of death; and therefore he in very deed lay in the sepulcher, motionless as the rock out of which it was hewn, shrouded in his winding sheet. Remember as you think of your Lord's death that the day will come, unless the second advent should intervene, in which you and I shall lie low among the dead, as once our Master did. Soon to this heart there will be left no pulsing life, to this eye no glance of observation, to this tongue no voice, to this ear no sensibility of sound. We naturally start from this, yet must it be. We shall certainly mingle with the dust we tread upon and feed the worm. But as we gaze on Jesus' tomb and assure ourselves that our great Lord and Master died, each thought of dread is gone, and we no longer shudder: we feel that we can safely go where Christ has gone before.

Sitting down over against the sepulcher, after one has ruminated upon the wondrous fact that he who only has immortality was numbered with the dead, the next subject which suggests itself is *the testimony of the grave to his union with us*. He had his grave hard by the city, and not on some lone mountain peak where foot of man could never tread. His grave was where it could be seen; it was a family grave which Joseph had no doubt prepared for himself and his household. Jesus was laid in a family vault where another had expected to lie. Where was Moses buried? No man knows of his sepulcher unto this day. But where Jesus was buried was well known to his friends. He was not caught away in a chariot of fire, nor was it said of him that God took him, but he was laid in the grave, "as the manner of the Jews is to bury." Jesus found his grave among the men he had redeemed. Hard by the common place of execution there was a garden, and in that garden they laid him in a tomb which was meant for others; so that our Lord's sepulcher stands, as it were, among our homes and gardens, and is one tomb among many. Before me rises a picture. I see the cemetery, or sleeping place, of the saints, where each one rests on his lowly bed. They lie not alone, but like soldiers sleeping around their captain's pavilion, where he also spent the night, though he is up before them. The sepulcher of Jesus is the central grave of God's acre; it is empty now, but his saints lie buried all around that cave in the rock, gathered in ranks around their dear Redeemer's resting place. Surely it robs the grave of its ancient terror when we think that Jesus slept in one of the chambers of the great dormitory of the sons of men.

Very much might be said about the tomb in which Jesus lay. It was a *new* tomb, wherein no remains had been previously laid, and thus if he came forth from it there would be no suspicion that another had arisen, nor could it be imagined that he arose through touching some old prophet's bones, as he did who was laid in Elisha's grave. As he was born of a virgin mother, so was he buried in a virgin tomb, wherein never man had lain. It was a rocky tomb, and therefore nobody could dig into it by night or tunnel through the earth. It was a borrowed tomb; so poor was Jesus that he owed a grave to charity; but that tomb was spontaneously offered, so rich was he in the love of hearts which he had won. That tomb he returned to Joseph, honored unspeakably by his temporary sojourn therein. I know not whether Joseph ever used it for any of his house; but I see no reason why he should not have done so. Certainly, our Lord when he borrows always makes prompt repayment, and gives a bonus over: he filled Simon's boat with fish when he used it for a pulpit, and he sanctified the rocky cell wherein he had lodged, and left it perfumed for the next who should sleep therein.

We, too, expect, unless special circumstances should intervene, that these bodies of ours will lie in their narrow beds beneath the greensward, and slumber till the resurrection. Nor need we be afraid of the tomb, for Jesus has been there. Sitting over against his sepulcher we grow brave, and are ready, like knights of the holy sepulcher, to hurl defiance at death. At times we almost long for evening to undress that we may rest with God, in the chamber where "he giveth to his beloved sleep."

Now, note that our Lord's tomb was in a garden; for this is typically *the testimony of his grave to the hope of better things*. Just a little beyond the garden wall you would see a little knoll, of grim name and character, the Tyburn of Jerusalem, Golgotha, the place of a skull, and there stood the cross. That rising ground was given up to horror and barrenness; but around the actual tomb of our Savior there grew herbs and plants and flowers. A spiritual garden still blooms around his tomb; the wilderness and the solitary place are glad for him, and the desert rejoices and blossoms as the rose. He has made another paradise for us, and he himself is the sweetest flower therein. The first Adam sinned in a garden and spoiled our nature; the second Adam slept in a garden and restored our loss. The Savior buried in the earth has removed the curse from the soil; henceforth blessed is the ground for his sake. He died for us that we ourselves might become in heart and life fruitful gardens of the Lord. Let but his tomb, and all the facts which surround it, have due influence upon the minds of men, and this poor blighted earth shall again yield her increase: instead of the thorn shall come up the fir tree, and instead of the brier shall come up the myrtle tree, and it shall be to the Lord for a name.

Sitting over against the sepulcher perhaps the best thought of all is that now it is empty and *so bears testimony to our resurrection*. It must have made the two Marys weep, when before they left the grave they saw it filled with so beloved a treasure, so surely dead, they ought to have rejoiced to find it empty when they returned, but they knew not as yet the angel's message—"He is not here, for he is risen." Our Christ is not dead now; he ever lives to make intercession for us. He could not be held by the bands of death. There was nothing corruptible about him, and therefore his body has left the abode of decay to live in newness of life. The sepulcher is spoiled and the spoiler has gone up to glory, leaving captivity captive. As you sit over against the sepulcher, let your hearts be comforted concerning death, whose sting is gone forever. There shall be a resurrection. Be sure of this, for if the dead rise not then is Christ not risen; but the Lord is risen indeed, and his rising necessitates that all who are in him should rise as he has done.

Yet another thought comes to me: can I follow Christ as fully as these two women did? That is to say, can I still cling to him though to sense and reason his cause should seem dead and laid in a rocky sepulcher? Can I like Joseph and Magdalene be a disciple of a dead Christ? Could I follow him even at his lowest point? I want to apply this practically. Times have come upon the Christian church when truth seems to be fallen in the streets, and the kingdom of Christ is in apparent peril. Just now the Lord Jesus is betrayed by not a few of his professed ministers. He is being crucified afresh in the perpetual attacks of skepticism against his blessed gospel; and it may be things may wax worse and worse. This is not the first occasion when it has been so, for at various times in the history of the church of God his enemies have exulted, and cried out that the gospel of past ages was exploded, and might be reckoned as dead and buried. For one I mean to sit over against the very sepulcher of truth. I am a disciple of the old-fashioned doctrine as much when it is covered with obloquy and rebuke as when it shall again display its power, as it surely shall. Skeptics may seem to take truth and bind it, and scourge it, and crucify it, and say that it is dead, and they may endeavor to bury it in scorn, but the Lord has many a Joseph and a Nicodemus who will see honor done even to the body of truth, and will wrap the despised creed in sweet spices, and hide it away in their hearts. They may, perhaps, be half afraid that it is really dead, as the wise men assert, yet it is precious to their souls, and they will come forth right gladly to espouse its cause, and to confess that they are its disciples. We will sit down in sorrow but not in despair, and watch until the stone is rolled away, and Christ in his truth shall live again, and be openly triumphant. We shall see a divine interposition and shall cease to fear; while they who stand armed to prevent the resurrection of the grand old doctrine shall quake and become as dead men, because the gospel's everlasting life has been vindicated, and they are made to quail before the brightness of its glory.

This, then, is our first meditation: we admire that Jesus ever had a grave, and we sit in wonder over against the sepulcher.

II. Second, sitting here, *we rejoice in the honors of his burial.*

The burial of Christ was, under some aspects of it, the lowest step of his humiliation: he must not merely for a moment die, but he must be buried a while in the heart of the earth. On the other hand, under other aspects our Lord's burial was the first step of his glory: it was a turning point in his great career, as we shall hope to show you. Our Lord's body was given up by Pilate to Joseph, and he went with authority to receive it from those who were appointed to see him take it down. I yesterday had a glimpse at a work of art by one of our own Lambeth neighbors, exhibited by Mr. Doulton; it is a fine piece of work in terra-cotta, representing the taking down of Christ from the cross. I could have wished to have studied it more at leisure, but a mere glimpse has charmed me. The artist represents a Roman soldier at the top of the cross taking down the parchment upon which the accusation was written;

he is rolling it up to put it away forever. I thought of the taking away of the handwriting which was against him, even as he had taken away that which was against us. The Roman soldier by authority is thus represented as removing the charge which was once nailed over the ever-blessed head; there is no accusation against him now: he died, and the law is satisfied, it can no longer accuse the man who has endured its penalty. Another soldier is represented with a pair of pincers drawing out one of the big nails from the hands; the sacred body is free now, law has no further claims upon it, and withdraws its nails. A disciple, not a soldier, has mounted a ladder on the other side, and with a pair of scissors is cutting away the crown of thorns; and I think the artist did well to represent his doing so, for henceforth it is our delight to remove all shame from the name of Jesus, and to crown him in another fashion. Then the artist has represented certain of his disciples as gently taking hold of the body as it is gradually being unloosed by the soldiers, while Joseph of Arimathaea stands there with his long linen sheet ready to receive him. Jars of precious myrrh and spices are standing there, and the women ready to open the lids and to place the spices around the holy flesh. Every part of the design is significant and instructive, and the artist deserves great praise for it: it brought before my mind the descent from the cross with greater vividness than any painting I have ever seen. The nails are all extracted; he is held no longer to the cross; the body is taken down, no longer to be spit upon, and despised, and rejected, but tenderly handled by his friends; for all and everything that has to do with shame, and suffering, and paying of penalty is ended once for all.

What became of the cross of wood? You find in Scripture no further mention of it. The legends concerning it are all false upon the face of them. The cross is gone forever; neither gibbet, nor nail, nor spear, nor thorny crown can be found; there is no further use for them. Jesus our Lord has gone to his glory; for by his one sacrifice he has secured the salvation of his own.

But now as to his burial. Beloved, there were many honorable circumstances about it. Its first effect was *the development of timid minds*. Joseph of Arimathaea occupied a high post as an honorable counselor, but he was a secret disciple. Nicodemus, too, was a ruler of the Jews, and though he had spoken a word for the Master now and then, as probably Joseph had done (for we are told that he had not consented to their counsel and deed), yet he had never come out boldly till now. He came to Jesus by night aforetime, but he came by daylight now. At the worst estate of the Savior's cause, we should have thought that these two men would remain concealed, but they did not. Now that the case seemed desperate, they show their faith in Jesus and pluck up courage to honor their Lord. Lambs become lions when the Lamb is slain. Joseph went boldly in unto Pilate and begged the body of Jesus. For a dead Christ, he risks his position, and even his life, for he is asking the body of a reputed traitor, and may himself be put to death by Pilate; or else the members of the Sanhedrin may be enraged at him, and bind themselves with an oath that they will slay him for paying honor to the Nazarene, whom they called "that deceiver." Joseph can venture everything for Jesus, even though he knows him to be dead.

Equally brave is Nicodemus; for publicly at the foot of the cross he stands with his hundred pounds weight of spices, caring nothing for any who may report the deed. I cheerfully hope, dear brethren, that one result of the ferocious attacks made upon the gospel at this time will be that a great number of quiet and retiring spirits will be roused to energy and courage. Such works of evil might move the very stones to cry out. While, perhaps, some who have spoken well in other days and have usually done the battling may be downcast and quiet, these who have kept in the rear rank, and have only in secret followed Jesus, will be brought to the front, and we shall see men of substance and of position avowing their Lord. Joseph and Nicodemus both illustrate the dreadful truth that it is hard for them that have riches to enter into the kingdom of God; but they also show us that when they do enter they frequently excel. If they come last they remain to the last. If cowards when others are heroes, they can also be heroes when even apostles are cowards. Each man has his turn, and so while the fishermen-apostles were hiding away, the wealthy noncommittal brethren came to the front: though bred in luxury, they bore the brunt of the storm, and avowed the cause whose leader lay dead. Brave are the hearts which stand up for Jesus in his burial. "Sitting over against the sepulcher," we draw comfort from the sight of the friends who honored the Lord in his death.

I like to remember that the burial of the Lord *displayed the union of loving hearts.* The tomb became the meeting place of the old disciples and the new, of those who had long consorted with the Master, and those who had but newly avowed him. Magdalene and Mary had been with the Lord for years and had ministered to him of their substance; but Joseph of Arimathaea, as far as his public avowal of Christ is concerned, was, like Nicodemus, a new disciple: old and new followers united in the deed of love, and laid their Master in the tomb. A common sorrow and a common love unite us wondrously. When our great Master's cause is under a cloud and his name blasphemed, it is pleasant to see the young men battling with the foe and aiding their fathers in the stern struggle. Magdalene with her penitent love, and Mary with her deep

attachment to her Lord, join with the rabbi and the counselor who now begin
to prove that they intensely love the Man of Nazareth. That small society, that
little working meeting, which gathered around our Master's body, was a type
of the whole Christian church. When once aroused, believers forget all differ-
ences and degrees of spiritual condition, and each one is eager to do his part
to honor his Lord.

Mark, too, that the Savior's death *brought out abundant liberality*. The
spices, one hundred pounds in weight, and the fine linen, were furnished by
the men; and then the holy women prepared the liquid spices with which to
carry out what they might have called his great funeral, when they would
more completely wrap the body in odoriferous spices as the manner of the
Jews was to bury. There was much of honor intended by all that they
brought. A very thoughtful writer observes that the clothes in which our
Lord was wrapped are not called grave clothes but "linen cloth," and that the
emphasis would seem to be put upon their being linen; and he reminds us
that when we read of the garments of the priests in the Book of the Law we
find that every garment must be of linen. Our Lord's priesthood is, therefore,
suggested by the sole use of linen for his death robes. The Apostle and High
Priest of our profession in his tomb slept in pure white linen, even as now
today he represents himself to his servants as clothed with a garment down
to the foot. Even after death he acted as a priest, and poured out a libation of
blood and water; and it was, therefore, meet that in the grave he should still
wear priestly garments.

"He made his grave with the wicked"—there was his shame; "but with
the rich in his death"—there was his honor. He was put to death by rough sol-
diery, but he was laid in his grave by tender women. Persons of honorable
estate helped gently to receive, and reverentially to place in its position his
dear and sacred frame; and then, as if to do him honor, though they meant it
not, his tomb must not be left unsentineled, and Caesar lends his guards to
watch the couch of the Prince of peace. Like a king he slumbers, till as the
King of kings he wakes at daybreak.

To my mind it is very pleasant to see all this honor come to our Lord
when he is in his worst estate—dead and buried. Will we not also honor our
Lord when others despise him? Will we not cleave to him, come what may?
If the church were all but extirpated, if every voice should go over to the
enemy, if a great stone of philosophic reasoning were rolled at the door of
truth, and it should seem no longer possible for argument to remove it, yet
would we wait till the gospel should rise again to confound its foes. We will
not be afraid, but keep our position; we will stand still and see the salvation

of God, or "sitting over against the sepulcher," we will watch for the Lord's coming. Let the worst come to the worst, we would sooner serve Christ while he is conceived to be dead than all the philosophers that ever lived when in their prime. Even if fools should dance over the grave of Christianity, there shall remain at least a few who will weep over it, and brushing away their tears from their eyes expect to see it revive, and put forth all its ancient strength.

III. I must now pass to a third point. While sitting over against the sepulcher *we observe that his enemies were not at rest.*

They had their own way, but they were not content. They had taken the Savior, and with wicked hands they had crucified and slain him, but they were not satisfied. They were the most uneasy people in the world, though they had gained their point. It was their Sabbath day, and it was a high day, that Sabbath of Sabbaths, the Sabbath of the Passover. They kept a preparation for it and had been very careful not to go into the place called the pavement, lest they should defile themselves—sweet creatures! And now have they not gained all they wanted? They have killed Jesus and buried him: are they not happy? No: and what is more, their humiliation had begun—they were doomed to belie their own favorite profession. What was that profession? Their boast of rigid Sabbath keeping was its chief point, and they were perpetually charging our blessed Lord with Sabbath breaking, for healing the sick, and even because his disciples rubbed a few ears of wheat between their hands when they were hungry on the Sabbath day. Brethren, look at these men and laugh at their hypocrisy. It is the Sabbath day, and they come to Pilate, holding counsel on the Sabbath with a heathen! They tell him that they are afraid that Jesus' body will be spirited away, and he says, "Ye have a watch; go your way, make it as sure as you can"; and they go and seal the stone on the Sabbath. O you hypocritical Pharisees, here was an awful breaking of your Sabbath by your own selves! According to their superstitious tradition the rubbing ears of wheat between the hands was a kind of threshing, and therefore it was a breach of the law; surely, by the same reasoning, the burning of a candle to melt the wax must have been similar to the lighting of a furnace, and the melting of wax must have been a kind of foundry work, like that of the smith who pours metal into a mold; for in such a ridiculous fashion their rabbis interpreted the smallest acts. But they had to seal the stone and break their own absurd laws to satisfy their restless malice. One is pleased to see either Pharisees or Sadducees made to overturn their own professions and lay bare their hypocrisy. Modern-thought gentlemen will, before long, be forced to the same humiliation.

Next, they had to retract their own accusation against our Lord. They charged Jesus with having said, "Destroy this temple, and I will build it in three days," pretending that he referred to the temple upon Zion. Now they come to Pilate and tell him, "This deceiver said, 'After three days I will rise again.'" O you knaves, that is your new version, is it? You put the man to death for quite another rendering! Now you understand the dark saying? Yes, you deceivers, and you understood it before; but now you must eat your leek, and swallow your own words. Truly, he scorns the scorners, and pours contempt upon his enemies.

And now see how these kill-Christs betray their own fears. He is dead, but they are afraid of him! He is dead, but they cannot shake off the dread that he will vanquish them yet. They are full of agitation and alarm.

Nor was this all, they were to be made witnesses for God—to sign certificates of the death and resurrection of his Anointed. In order that there might be no doubt about the resurrection at all, there must be a seal, and *they* must go and set it; there must be a guard, and *they* must see it mustered. The disciples need not trouble about certifying that Jesus is in the grave, these Jews will do it, and set their own great seal to the evidence. These proud ones are sent to do drudges' work in Christ's kitchen, to wait upon a dead Christ, and to protect the body which they had slain. The lie which they told afterward crowned their shame: they bribed the soldiers to say that his disciples stole him away while they slept; and this was a transparent falsehood; for if the soldiers were asleep how could they know what was done? We cannot conceive of an instance in which men were more completely made to contradict and convict themselves. That Sabbath was a high day, but it was no Sabbath to them, nor would the overthrow of the gospel be any rest of soul to its opponents. If ever we should live to see the truth pushed into a corner, and the blessed cause of Christ fastened up as with rationalistic nails, and its very heart pierced by a critic's spear, yet, mark you, even in the darkest night that can ever try our faith, the adversaries of the gospel will still be in alarm lest it should rise again.

The old truth has a wonderful habit of leaping up from every fall as strong as ever. In Dr. Doddridge's days men had pretty nearly buried the gospel. Socinianism was taught in many if not most Dissenting pulpits, and the same was true of the Church of England: the liberal thinkers dreamed that they had won the victory and extinguished evangelical teaching; but their shouting came a little too soon. They said, "We shall hear no more of this miserable justification by faith, and regeneration by the Holy Ghost." They laid the gospel in a tomb cut out in the cold rock of Unitarianism, and they set the seal of their learning upon the great stone of doubt which shut in the gospel. There it was to lie forever; but God meant otherwise. There was a potboy [server of drinks in a tavern] over in Gloucester called George Whitefield, and there was a young student who had lately gone to Oxford called John Wesley, and these two passed by the grave of the gospel and beheld a strange sight, which they began to tell; and as they told it, the sods of unbelief and the stones of learned criticism began to move, and the truth which had been buried started up with Pentecostal power. Aha! you adversaries, how greatly had you deceived yourselves! Within a few months all over England the work of the devil and his ministers was broken to pieces, as when a tower is split by lightning, or the thick darkness scattered by the rising sun. The weight of ignorance and unbelief fled before the bright day of the gospel, though that gospel was for the most part proclaimed by unlettered men. The thing which has been is the thing which shall be.

History repeats itself. O generation of modern thinkers, you will have to eat your own words and disprove your own assertions. You will have to confute each other and yourselves, even as the Moabites and Elamites slew each other. It may even happen that your infidelities will work themselves out into practical evil of which you will be the victims. You may bring about a repetition of the French Revolution of 1789, with more than all its bloodshed, and who will wonder. You, some of you calling yourselves ministers of God, with your insinuations of doubt, your denials of future punishment, your insults of the gospel, your ingenious speeches against the Bible, are shaking the very foundation of society. I impeach you as the worst enemies of mankind. In effect you proclaim to men that they may sin as they like, for there is no hell, or if there be, it is but a little one: thus you publish a gospel of licentiousness, and you may one day rue the result. You may live to see a reign of terror of your own creating, but even if you do, the gospel of Jesus will come forth from all the filth you have heaped upon it, for the holy gospel will live as Christ lives, and its enemies shall never cease to be in fear. Your harsh speeches against those who preach the gospel, your bitterness and your sneers of contempt, all show that you know better than you say, and are afraid of the very Christ whom you kill. We who cleave to the glorious gospel will abide in peace, come what may, but you will not.

IV. And now our last thought is that while these enemies of Christ were in fear and trembling *we note that his followers were resting.*

It was the seventh day, and therefore they ceased from labor. The Marys waited, and Joseph and Nicodemus refrained from visiting the tomb; they obediently observed the Sabbath rest. I am not sure that they had faith enough to feel very happy, but they evidently did expect something, and anxiously awaited the third day. They had enough of the comfort of hope to remain quiet on the seventh day.

Now, beloved, sitting over against the sepulcher while Christ lies in it, my first thought about it is, *I will rest, for he rests.* What a wonderful stillness there was about our Lord in that rocky grave. He had been daily thronged by thousands: even when he ate bread they disturbed him. He scarcely could have a moment's stillness in life; but now how quiet is his bed! Not a sound is heard. The great stone shuts out all noise, and the body is at peace. Well, if he rests, I may. If for a while the Lord seems to suspend his energies, his servants may cry unto him, but they may not fret. He knows best when to sleep and when to wake.

As I see the Christ resting in the grave, my next thought is, *he has the power to come forth again.* Some few months ago, I tried to show you that when the disciples were alarmed because Jesus was asleep they were in error, for his sleep was the token of their security. When I see a captain on board ship pacing anxiously up and down the deck, I may fear that danger is suspected; but when the captain turns into his cabin, then I may be sure that all is right, and there is no reason why I should not turn in too. So if our blessed Lord should ever suffer his cause to droop, and if he should give no marvelous manifestations of his power, we need not doubt his power; let us keep our Sabbath, pray to him, and work for him, for these are duties of the holy day of rest; but do not let us fret and worry, for his time to work will come.

The rest of the Christian lies in believing in Christ under all circumstances. Go in for this, beloved. Believe in him in the manger, when his cause is young and weak. Believe in him in the streets, when the populace applaud him, for he deserves their loudest acclamations. Believe in him when they take him to the brow of the hill to cast him headlong, he is just as worthy as when they cry "hosanna." Believe in him when he is in an agony, and believe in him when he is on the cross; and if ever it should seem to you that his cause must die out, believe in him still. Christ's gospel in any circumstances deserves our fullest trust. That gospel which has saved your souls, that gospel which you have received, and which has been sealed upon your hearts by the Holy Ghost, stand fast in it, come what may, and through faith, peace and quiet shall pervade your souls.

Once more, it will be well if we can obtain peace by having fellowship with our Lord in his burial. Die with him, and be buried with him; there is nothing like it. I desire for my soul while she lives in the Lord that, as to the world and all its wisdom, I may be as a dead man. When accused of having no power of thought, and no originality of teaching, I am content to own the charge, for my soul desires to be dead to all but that which is revealed and taught by the Lord Jesus. I would lie in the rocky tomb of the everlasting truth, not creating thought, but giving myself up to God's thoughts. But, brethren, if we are ever to lie in that tomb, we must be wrapped about with the fine linen of holiness: these are the shrouds of a man who is dead to sin. All about us must be the spices, the myrrh, and aloes of preserving grace, that being dead with Christ we may see no corruption, but may show that death to be only another form of the new life which we have received in him. When the world goes by, let it know concerning our heart's desire and ambition, that they are all buried with Christ, and it is written on the memorial of our spiritual grave, "Here he lies"; as far as this world's sin and pleasure and self-seeking and wisdom are concerned, "Here he lies buried with his Master."

Know, you who are not converted, that the way of salvation is by believing in Christ, or trusting in him, and if you do so trust you shall never be confounded, world without end, for he that trusts Christ, and believes in him even as a little child, the same shall enter into his kingdom, and he that will follow him, even down to his grave, shall be with him in his glory, and shall see his triumphs forever and ever. Amen.

Mary Magdalene: A Handkerchief

Published on Thursday, October 5, 1905; delivered on Lord's Day evening, June 13, 1875, at the Metropolitan Tabernacle, Newington. No. 2956.

Jesus saith unto her, "Woman, why weepest thou? whom seekest thou?"
—JOHN 20:15

In the garden of Eden, immediately after the Fall, the sentence of sorrow, and of sorrow multiplied, fell upon the woman. In the garden where Christ had been buried, after his resurrection, the news of comfort—comfort rich and divine—came to a woman through the woman's promised Seed, the Lord Jesus Christ. If the sentence must fall heavily upon the woman, so must the comfort come most sweetly to her. I will not say that the resurrection reversed the curse of the Fall; but, at any rate, it took the sting out of it, lifted it up, and sanctified it. There was reason enough for the woman to weep after the sentence had been pronounced upon her; but there is no reason for her to weep now that Jesus Christ has fulfilled the promise which followed upon man's disobedience, namely, that the Seed of the woman should bruise the serpent's head.

Observe the wise method followed by the divine Consoler. In order to comfort Mary Magdalene, our Lord put a question to her. It is often the wisest way to relieve minds that are swollen through grief to allow them to find the natural end of their sorrow by asking them why they are weeping. We have to do this with ourselves sometimes; we inquire, "Why art thou cast down, O my soul? and why art thou disquieted within me?" The soul begins to ask for the reason of its grief, and often finds that it is insufficient to justify so bitter a sorrow; and perhaps it even discovers that the sources of its sorrow have been misunderstood, and that, if they had been rightly comprehended, they would have been sources of joy instead. He who would be wise in dealing with the daughters of grief must let them tell their own story; and, almost without a single sentence from you, their own story will be blessed by God to the relieving of their grief.

Moreover, it is always wise, before we attempt to comfort anyone, to know what is the peculiar form and fashion which grief has taken. The physician who, without investigation, should at once proceed to apply a remedy to his patient, might be giving the wrong medicine for the disease. He has to make his diagnosis of the malady, to see whence it came, what are its symptoms, and how it works, and then the physician adapts his medicine to the case. Sit down with your sorrow, my friend, and let us hear what ails you. What causes you to fret? What causes your soul to travail? Possibly, the sorrowing ones will themselves direct you to the right remedy for their malady, and so you shall be able to speak a word in season, and "a word spoken in due season, how good it is!" You are at present like a man groping in the dark, and you will be as one pouring vinegar upon niter if you do sing songs to a heavy heart, and you will make matters worse which you had hoped to make better unless you do find out the cause of the mourner's tears.

My one object, at this time, is to take this question of our Lord to Mary, and apply it to all who are sorrowing here; and although I shall keep to the text, and repeat the question, "Woman, why weepest, thou?" I shall hope that other sorrows besides [those of] the women here will find comfort from the words which the Holy Spirit will teach me to speak. I shall ask, first, *is it natural sorrow?* And, second, *is it spiritual sorrow?*

I. We will, first, inquire about that which is common to us all without exception: *is it natural sorrow?*

Is it sorrow which springs from our human nature, and is common to all who are born of woman, to whom sorrow comes as a portion of our heritage?

Well, my friend, what is the cause of your grief? What ails you? *Is it because you are bereaved?* Have you lost someone who was very dear to you? Then your grief is not unusual, and your weeping is not unpardonable, for Jesus wept as he stood at the grave of his friend Lazarus. But let not your weeping go beyond due bounds. Your tears are right enough so far, but they may be wrong if they go any further. There is a weeping of regret, and of a lacerated spirit, upon which God looks with pity; but there may come a weeping of rebelliousness upon which even our heavenly Father may feel that he must look with anger. "Why weepest thou?" Will you look into your heart, beloved, and see whether the cause of your grief is such as does fully justify it, or see whether you have carried it too far already? You have lost a child—a lovely child; but, my sister, you have not really lost your child. Call you that lost which is in Christ's keeping? Call you that babe lost which is up among the angels? If your child had been taken to be a prince in a palace, you would not have said that he was lost; inasmuch as he has been caught away to be with Jesus, say not that he is lost. You are the mother of one who can see the face of God, and thus says the Lord unto you, "Refrain thine eyes from weeping, for thy children shall come again from the land of their captivity."

Have you lost your husband? It is a heavy blow, and well may you weep; but, still, who took him from you? Was it not he who lent him to you? Bless the Lord that you have had all those years of comfort and joy, and say with Job, "The LORD gave, and the LORD hath taken away; blessed be the name of the LORD." The loss of your husband has made a great void in your life, but the Lord will fill that void. Do you know him? Then, he will be a Husband unto you, and a Father to your fatherless children. He has said, "Leave thy fatherless children, I will preserve them alive; and let thy widows trust in me." You are a widow; then, trust in the Lord. If you are a widow without faith in God, then yours is a sorrow indeed; but if the widow's sorrow shall drive her to trust in Christ as her Savior, if she shall look up, and in her deep sorrow trust herself with the great Helper of the helpless, she shall find her loss to be a gain.

"Woman, why weepest thou?" Whatever relative or friend you have lost, your God will be more to you than the loved one could ever be. The Well Beloved, the Lord Jesus Christ is better to us than all earthly friends; and when they are taken away from us, he more than fills the space which once they occupied; so that, if we have less of human love, we have more of the divine, and thus we are gainers rather than losers. Look forward to the resurrection and be comforted. Remember that the worm has not consumed the beauty forever, neither has the precious temple of the body been given up to everlasting will. If they fell asleep in Christ as surely as they were buried, they shall rise again in beauty, in the image of Jesus Christ; so let us not sorrow as those who are without hope. Brush away your tears; or, if they must fall, smile through them in sweet resignation to the divine will, and be still.

"Why weepest thou?" Is there another reason for your sorrow? *Do you weep because you are very poor?* There are some who do not know the sorrow of poverty, who will, perhaps, blame you; but I know that there are some of you who have a hard task to find a livelihood—a task at which a slave might be pitied. In this great city, how many toil till they wear themselves almost to skeletons, and even then scarcely find food enough to keep body and soul together! There are some of the choicest sons and daughters of the Lord who seem to be the lowest of all in the scale of this world's possessions, and their lot, from morning to night, is one of incessant drudgery. Were it not for these sweet Sabbaths, to live on earth would be to them altogether a bondage. But weep not, my poor sister; weep not, my poor brother; there is One who was poorer than you are, who will bear your burdens for you. Jesus Christ was poorer than poverty, because he had once been so exceedingly rich; and none are so poor as those who come down from wealth to poverty. You know that, though he was rich, yet, for our sakes, he became poor, that we, through his poverty, might become rich. Poor mourner, remember the promise to him that walks righteously, and speaks uprightly, "Bread shall be given him, his waters shall be sure." Recollect also how the Lord Jesus said to his disciples, "Consider the lilies of the field, how they grow; they toil not, neither do they spin; and yet I say unto you, that even Solomon in all his glory was not arrayed like one of these. Wherefore, if God so clothe the grass of the field, which today is, and tomorrow is cast into the oven, shall he not much more clothe you, O ye of little faith?" "Behold the fowls of the air; for they sow not, neither do they reap, nor gather into barns; yet your heavenly Father feedeth them." So will he not feed you also? Wipe away your tears; bend your back to the burden which God has laid upon you, "and be content with such things as ye have, for he hath said, 'I will never leave thee, nor forsake thee.'"

"Woman, why weepest thou?" Suppose that neither of these causes should account for your sorrow. *Have you a beloved sick one at home?* Yes, and you may well weep if that sickness has been long, and if it wears away the beauty from the cheek, and the brightness from the eye, and if it costs innumerable pains and anguish only to be understood by those who suffer it, and those who watch, hour by hour, by the sufferer. I can understand your weeping; and yet, beloved, your case is in Christ's hands, and you may safely leave your dear ones in his hands. He never sent a trial to any child of his unless it was so necessary that, to have withheld it would have been unkind. Accept it as the Lord's love token. Besides, remember that he can recover our loved ones if he deems it wise, or he can sustain them in their sickness if he does not see fit to recover them, and he can give them a joyful exit from this world, and an abundant entrance into his everlasting kingdom. So do not weep too much; but say, "It is the LORD; let him do what seemeth him good."

Possibly, however, the weeping may come to us because *we have sickness in our own bodies.* While we are sitting or standing here, some of us little know the amount of suffering that may be felt by the person who is sitting next to us. I have often wondered how some of my beloved hearers ever manage to get here at all; yet they are here, although full of pain. They find a sweet forgetfulness, at least for a little time, while the Word is being preached; and they cannot forgo the pleasure of mingling with the people of God, even though it costs them many a sharp pang. Yet I would urge even such sufferers to dry their tears; it may be that the dreaded disease of consumption is gradually wearing away the life; but, my sister, it is no ill thing just to swoon away into heaven, and gently to pass from this life to another and a brighter day. Perhaps you are suffering from some painful disease which is known to be fatal. Well, that is only another way of bringing a King's messenger to take you swiftly home. If you have no Christ, you may well weep if you have received your death wound, for after death comes judgment. This disease is a messenger sent to bid you prepare to meet your God. Suppose you were smitten down today, God has given you a timely warning. Take it, I pray you; and, instead of weeping over your sickness, may the Holy Spirit enable you to weep over your sin, and to trust in Christ as your Savior, for then all shall be well. If we have believed in Jesus, we need not weep, even though the dread archer may have lodged the fatal shaft quite near our heart. What is there to weep about?

When a Christian has received an intimation that he is soon to be with his Savior in glory, we may congratulate him that he is the sooner to be out of the strife and the sin, and to wear the crown of victory and glory forever, so we will not weep about that.

Perhaps I am addressing one who says, "My sorrow is neither bereavement, nor personal sickness, nor the sickness of friends, nor poverty; I sometimes think I could bear any or all of those trials; but I have been the victim of a treacherous friend; *I trusted and have been deceived.* I gave my heart's best affections and have been betrayed." You, too, dear friend, are not alone in that trial. There was One, better far than you, on whose cheek came the hot kiss from the betrayer's lips, so that Jesus said to Judas, "Betrayest thou the Son of man with a kiss?" Many have had so-called friends, who, in the time of testing, have been more cruel than avowed foes. They have been as the cunning fowler who spreads his net so warily that he may catch the little birds. Well, if your case is like that of the birds, fly away to Jesus; trust him, for he will never deceive you. If Jesus shall fill that vacancy in your heart, it will have been a blessed vacancy. A broken heart is best healed by a touch of the pierced hand of Jesus. Get you away to him, you Hannah, you woman of a sorrowful spirit; go you to the "Man of sorrows, and acquainted with grief," and he will find a balm for your spirit.

I cannot go further into these natural sorrows; they are so many, and the river of grief is so deep and rapid; but, whatsoever your sorrow may be, one piece of advice I have to give to every weeping one—find then the divine Comforter; and, whatever your griefs may be, they shall be assuaged.

II. Now I come to our main question, which is this: *is it spiritual sorrow?*

If so, is it sorrow for others, or sorrow for yourselves?

I will begin with the nobler form. "Woman, why weepest thou?" *Do you weep for others?* Are there some whom you love, and for whom you have often prayed, who remain in the gall of bitterness, and in the bonds of iniquity? This is a suitable subject for mourning. Weep not for those who have gone to be "forever with the Lord," for all is well with them; but weep for those who are living in sin—for the young man, in his unbridled lust, who has dishonored his father's name, for the daughter who, in her willfulness, has gone astray into the paths of transgression. Weep for the heart that will not break. Weep for the eyes that will not weep. Weep for the sinners who will not confess their sins, but are resolutely seeking their own damnation. Ah, my dear friends, when you are weeping like that, you are weeping as your Savior did when he wept over Jerusalem, and God will put your tears into his bottle. Be comforted, for those tears of yours are omens of good to the souls you pity; for, as surely as you groan and sigh and cry over these beloved ones, you are doing what you can to bring them the blessing, and I think that is a token that the blessing of God is on its way to them. You remember that it is written that "the power of the Lord was present to heal" on a certain occasion: why was it more present then than at any other time? Was it not because there were four men who were breaking up the roof to let down a sick one into the room where Christ was? Wherever there is real concern for souls, although it be only in four persons, there is about the ministry a power of an unusual kind. Go on, then, and still weep, but not hopelessly, not with the bitterness of despair. The Lord will see your tears, and will hear your prayers, and will grant your petition, even though you may not live to see it. Peradventure, when you are in heaven, your son, your husband, your sister, over whom you now are weeping, shall be brought to Christ.

Possibly, however, the sorrow for others relates to the church with which this mourner is connected. It is often my lot to meet with brethren and sisters coming from country towns who say to me, "What are we to do? The place of worship where we attend might almost as well be pulled down, for there is no life, no energy, no power there." Oh, it is wretched work indeed when that is the case! Many towns and villages would be all the better if the meeting house and the parish church, too, were utterly demobilized, because then they would feel that they had not any religious means at all, and would, perhaps, be stirred up to seek them. But now there is dead formalism in both places. There is nothing worse than sluggishness in the pastors and members of church. What is the use of a dead church? It is no use at all. The fact is, the better a church is, the sooner it rots when it is dead. The man who is very stout is the very worst person to keep in the house when once he is dead, and the church that seems to be most packed with divine truth is the most obnoxious to all when once the life goes out of it. Well, my dear friends, if you are sorrowing over the low condition of the church to which you belong, and the state of religion in general in the neighborhood where you live, I would not stay your tears, yet I would try to comfort you, and I would advise you to take the case to your Lord. He is the Head of the church, so carry that burden to him. Do not go about finding fault; do not try to sow dissension and dissatisfaction, or you will do hurt instead of good; but lay the matter before your Lord and Master, and give him no rest till once again he puts forth his almighty power and raises his church to life.

Now I must leave this point; but I think that it is a grand thing to sorrow and weep for others. We ought to make it a rule of our life to bear the sorrows of other people. If sinners will not repent, we cannot repent for them; if they will not believe, we cannot believe for them; true religion can never be a matter of sponsorship, but we can do this for sinners. We can say to the Lord, "O Lord, these sinners will not themselves feel their sin, but we feel it, it grieves us, and cuts us to the heart! O Lord, will you not give them repentance? Will you not cause these sinners to believe in you? We confess their iniquity before you, for we know the guiltiness of their hearts in rejecting you. We weep and mourn that they will not admire your beauty, and will not yield their hearts to you; but, dear Savior, *do* win their hearts in answer to our prayer. They are far away from God by their wicked works; bring them near by your precious blood." That is what I mean; and if you can do this, appropriating, as it were, the sins and sorrows of mankind to yourself, you will be showing your sympathy with them in the best possible way. Woman, if you weep thus for others, blessed are you among women.

But, now, "why weepest thou?" *Is it for yourself?* Are these spiritual sorrows on your own account? Are you a sorrowing child of God? Do you know yourself to be a Christian, and yet do you weep? Then, what is the cause of your grief? Do you miss your Lord's presence? If so, there is reason enough for your weeping; yet why should you weep? He is present even now; you have not seen him, but he has seen you, and is gazing upon you at this very moment. Beloved mourner, do not say, "I am out of fellowship with Christ, and I am afraid I cannot return to that blessed experience for months." Listen to this text: "Behold, I stand at the door, and knock: if any man hear my voice, and open the door,"—that is all—"I will come in to him, and will sup with him, and he with me." It was to the angel of the church of the Laodiceans, the lukewarm Laodiceans, that these words were written, and they are also written to you, my sister, and to you, my brother, if you have grown lukewarm. Be willing for Christ to come to you; and, before ever you are aware, your soul shall make you like the chariots of Amminadib. Do not imagine that restoration to communion with Christ need occupy a longer time than conversion, and conversion is often worked instantaneously. So you may be lifted up from the depths of despondency to the heights of sacred fellowship with your Lord before this present service closes. Be of good cheer, and let your joy be renewed this very hour.

But perhaps you say, "I weep because I have grieved my Lord." Those are blessed tears, although the offense which caused them is grievous. Well may we be grieved when Christ has been grieved by us; but, mourning soul, though he is rightly grieved with you, remember this gracious declaration, "He will not always chide: neither will he keep his anger forever"; and this comforting promise, "'For a small moment have I forsaken thee; but with great mercies will I gather thee. In a little wrath I hid my face from thee for a moment; but with everlasting kindness will I have mercy on these,' saith the Lord thy Redeemer." Only confess that you have transgressed against the Lord your Redeemer, and you may come back to him at once; no, even now he comes to meet with you, and he brings with him the basin and the towel, that he may wash your soiled feet, for he has washed you once in his blood, and now he will again wash your feet, and you shall be clean every whit, and shall walk with cleansed feet in renewed fellowship with your Lord.

Possibly, some of you say that your sorrow is that you are not as holy as you wish to be. Ah! that is a sorrow which I share with you, for I can say with the apostle Paul, "When I would do good, evil is present with me"; and though I hear of some who do not find that evil is present with them, I suspect that the reason is, because they do not know themselves as they really are, or they would find that it was so with them, at least at times. If I could, I would be without one sinful thought or word or deed or imagination or wish, and so would you; and because you cannot be so at present, you weep. It is well that such tears should fall, only do not let these tears dim your view of Christ. Do not let those longings prevent your knowing that you are perfect and complete in Christ Jesus. Do not let your struggles hinder you from believing that Christ has conquered sin for you, and that he will yet conquer sin in you. Do not let anything take away from you the full conviction that sin shall be altogether destroyed in you, and that Christ will present you to his Father "without spot, or wrinkle, or any such thing," "holy and unblamable and unreprovable in his sight."

Perhaps you say that your sorrow is because you can do so little for Christ. Ah! there again, I have sympathy with you; but do not fret about that. Those of us who have the largest opportunities are often those who most regret that we can so little avail ourselves of them. But I know some godly women who are confined to the house with the care of a numerous family, or, worse still, are confined to their bed, in constant pain, and one of their greatest griefs is that they can do so little for Christ. But, brother, sister, do you not know the rule of David, and the rule of David's Lord? They that abide by the stuff shall have the same portion as they who go out to the battle. You are like the soldiers who have to keep in the rear and guard the baggage; but when the King comes back, with all the active troops who have been doing the fighting, you will share the victory with them. You who are at home keeping the camp preserve many things which might be forgotten if we were all on active service. Be you comforted, then, if you are called to suffer or to be in obscurity; you shall be equal to the man and woman who are called to labor more prominently. Do what you can; I do not know that Christ himself ever praised anybody more than he did that woman of whom he said, "She hath done what she could." I daresay she wanted to do a great deal more, but she did what she could; and if you have done what you could, it is well.

"Ah!" says another, "but I am conscious of a great deal of weakness. What I do is done so badly. Even in prayer, I do not always prevail; my petitions often seem to come back to me unanswered." Well, dear friend, do not altogether regret your weakness, for there was one who said that when he was weak, he was strong. If you have many infirmities which make you weak, there is a way of glorying in infirmities because the power of Christ does rest upon you. Suppose that you are not only weak, but that you are weakness itself—that you are nothing and nobody; for when you have reached that point, the cause of your weeping will have vanished, because, where you end, there God begins; and when you have done with self, then Christ will be all in all to you, and you will lift up your voice in praise of him who has done such great things for you.

Many strange things happen to young Christians between the time of their conversion and their entrance into heaven. Their program of life is seldom carried out. The map which they make of the route is not according to the true geography of it. They reckon that, as soon as they have believed in Jesus, they will enter into sweet peace and rest, which is probably correct, but they also suppose that this peace and rest will always continue, and probably increase, that they will go to heaven, singing all the way, along pleasant roads and paths of peace, and that the light upon their way will get brighter and brighter, till it comes to the perfect day. They feel so happy, and they sing so sweetly, that they imagine it will always be with them just as it was in the first hours of their Christian experience. They are like persons who have, for the first time in their lives, come into the bright light of day, after having lived in a deep mine, or been immured in a dark dungeon. They ask what season of the year it is, and they are told that it is springtime, that the flowers have begun to bloom, but that there are more to follow. They hear the birds singing, but they are told that there are brighter days to come, that May is a fairer month than April, and June brighter still, and then will come the months of harvest, when the sickle shall be thrust in among the golden grain.

All this is very cheering, so this new beginner plans that, tomorrow, he will be out all day upon the green grass, or in the gardens admiring the bursting buds, and gathering for himself many a delightful garland of flowers; but, perhaps, when he gets up tomorrow morning, the heavens are all black with clouds, and a torrent of rain is falling. "Oh!" says he, "I never reckoned upon this." Then, perhaps, in June, there comes such a hurly-burly in the sky as he never thought of, flames of fire and loud thunders out of the heavens, and dreadful drenching showers intermixed with rattling hail. "Oh!" says he, "I never calculated upon this; I thought the months were to grow brighter and brighter, and that, at last, there would come the golden harvest." We tell him that these rains and storms all conduce to the very result which we promised him, and that they are by no means contrary to our statement. We were only giving him a brief outline of the year's history, and these things are by no means contrary to our outline, nor need he fear but that the month of harvest will come in due season. It is true, young Christian, that you will have a light upon your road, and that it will grow more and more bright unto the perfect day. It is true that the ways of wisdom "are ways of pleasantness, and all her paths are peace." Your highest conception of the joy to be found in Christ is not an exaggerated one. However much delight you may anticipate, you shall have all that, and you shall also have even more, as you are able to bear it; but intermittent times will come—strange times to you—in which your joy will seem to be dead, and your peace will be fearfully disturbed. Your soul will be "tossed with tempest, and not comforted." You will sorrowfully sit in sackcloth and ashes, and you will not go to the table of feasting, but to the house of mourning. There will you be made to drink the water of tears, and have your bread salted with grief. Be not surprised, then, when this comes to pass, as though some strange things had happened to you. Remember that we have told you of it; we, who have gone further on the road to heaven than you have gone, tell you that there will come dark times, and stormy times, and we bid you prepare for them.

Now I must turn to others in our assembly. "Woman, why weepest thou?"

Perhaps you say, "O sir, I dare not put myself down among the saints!" Well, then, will you put yourself down among the sinners? "Yes, I am a sinner," you reply; "yet I think—I hope—I am not altogether without some little faith in Christ. I sometimes feel myself inclined to love him; but, oftentimes, I am of another mind, averse to all that is good." Ah, my friend, I know you; and I have met with many like your class. I said once to one of your sort, "You say that you are not a Christian." "No," she said, "I fear I am not." "Then," I asked, "why do you go to the home of God on the Sabbath? Why don't you stop at home, or go where sinners go?" "Oh, no, sir!" she answered, "I could not do that; when I hear people blaspheme the name of Christ it cuts me to the quick; and I am never so happy as when I am with the people of God. I enjoy the hymns that they sing; and, while I am with them, my heart gets so warm that I feel as if I must praise the Lord. I think it is a great mercy that I cannot help blessing and praising God." "Well, then," I said, "I think that you must really have some faith in Christ, or you would not feel and act as you do."

I remember hearing of a minister, who wrote down these words, "I do not believe on the Lord Jesus Christ," and asked a person, who was full of doubt, to sign her name to that declaration, but she would not do that. She did believe in Christ though she did not think that she believed. I once offered a person who said she had no faith, a £5 note if she would give up her faith, but she said that she would not take a thousand worlds for it! Mrs. Much-Afraid and Mr. Despondency and Mr. Feeble-Mind and Mr. Ready-to-Halt—there are plenty of that family still living; and I know why you weep, good woman, for you also belong to that tribe. Well, then, if you cannot come to Christ as a saint, come to him as a sinner. If you have made a mistake, and have never trusted in Christ, do it now. If you really have not repented, and have not believed, and have not been renewed in heart, remember that it is still written, "Him that cometh to me I will in no wise cast out"; "and whosoever will, let him take the water of life freely." If the title deeds of your spiritual estate are not genuine, but forgeries, do not dispute the question with one who is wiser than yourself; but come straightaway to Jesus Christ empty handed, in the manner in which he bids all sinners come to him, and then I shall not have to ask, "Why weepest thou?"

But, last of all, is this person who is weeping a seeking sinner? Christ not only said to Mary Magdalene, "Why weepest thou?" but also, "Whom seekest thou?" for he knew that she was seeking *him*. I would give all I possess if I might always preach to weeping sinners who are seeking Christ. I sometimes think that I would like to be always weeping on account of sin, if I might be always sure that I was seeking Jesus. It is possible that there has come into this place someone who is seeking a Savior. Ah, weeping woman! Do you weep because sin burdens you? Do you weep because sweet sin has become bitter to you? Do you weep because the things wherein your soul once delighted have now become your torment and your grief? Then I rejoice over your tears, for they are precious in God's sight; they are more valuable than the finest diamonds in the world. Blessed is the soul that can repent of sin.

But, possibly, your weeping is because you are afraid of being rejected by Christ. Put every tear of that kind away, for there is no fear of one sinner who comes to Christ being rejected by him. As I reminded you just now, he has said, "Him that cometh to me I will in no wise cast out." Come, then, you burdened sinner; come, you heavily laden soul; and trust yourself with Jesus, and then he cannot—unless he can completely change, and that is impossible—he cannot reject you. Come and trust him even now, and you shall be saved this very hour.

But, perhaps, your weeping is for this reason; you say, "Alas! I have been aroused before this, and I thought that I would seek the Lord, and I did get some hope, and I fancied that I was relieved of sin; but I have gone back, and my last end has been worse than the first." Well may you weep if that is really the case, and I cannot forbid you to do so. But, my dear friend, if you came falsely once, that is only one more reason why you should come truly now. If you built on the sand once, and that house is gone, it is but another argument for building on the rock. If you were excited, and mistook a transient emotion for the work of the Spirit of God—if you put presumption in the place of faith, do not do so again; but come, just as you now are, and rest your weary soul on Christ's atoning sacrifice, and you shall find peace, immediate and permanent peace.

But, possibly, you weep because you say, "If I came to Christ I fear I should not hold on to him to the end." I know you would not by yourself, but I also know that he will hold you on if you will but come and trust him. It is not you who have to keep Christ; it is Christ who has to keep you. I should not wonder if your former failure arose from your having so much to do with it. So have nothing to do with it this time. If you are very weak, lean all the more heavily on your Beloved; no, if you are nothing, let Christ be all the more to you because of your nothingness. If you are black, give all the more praise to the blood that can make you whiter than snow. If you realize that you are lost, and fear that you will be found among the damned, flee the more eagerly to those bleeding wounds which give life, not merely to perishing sinners, but to sinners dead in trespasses and sins.

"Ah!" says one, "I think you have invited me, but I feel as though I could not come, and I weep because I cannot come for I do not properly understand the matter." Well, then, dry your tears, and listen while I tell you the story again, and we who believe in Jesus will pray the Holy Spirit to lead you to understand the truth. The Father, whom you have offended, does not ask you to do anything to make him pleased with you; he does not wish you to contribute either good works or right feelings in order to make an atonement for your sin. His dear Son, Jesus Christ, has made the only atonement for sin that can ever be made; what the Father bids you do is to accept of what his Son has done, and trust alone to that. Can you not do this? What more do you need, you doubting, sorrowing seekers, but that you trust in Jesus Christ, the Son of God, who was nailed to Calvary's cross, but is now risen from the dead, and gone back to his glory with the Father? We sometimes sing, in one of our hymns—

> What more can he say than to you he hath said,
> You who unto Jesus for refuge have fled?

And I say the same to you who are seeking Christ, "What more can he say to you?" What sort of a promise would you like him to make to you? Shall it be one like this, "Though your sins be as scarlet, they shall be as white as snow"? You say that you would like such a promise as that; well, there is that very one in the Bible. Or would this one suit you, "Let the wicked forsake his way, and the unrighteous man his thoughts: and let him return unto the LORD, and he will have mercy upon him; and to our God, for he will abundantly pardon"? Or would this one meet your case, "The blood of Jesus Christ his Son cleanseth us from all sin"? Surely this one must suit you, "Whosoever shall call on the name of the Lord shall be saved." Or this message, "If we confess our sins, he is faithful and just to forgive us our sins, and to cleanse us from all unrighteousness." Or this, "Seek ye the LORD while he may be found, call ye upon him while he is near." If these do not meet your case, I do not know what you would wish to have. My Lord, by his blessed Spirit, seems to have put the gospel into all sorts of lights to suit all sorts of eyes, and he tells us, his ministers, to labor for this end, to get you to look at Jesus Christ. I have tried to do this, and I beseech you not to be content with your weepings or your feelings or your Bible searchings; do not be content even with prayer. This way of salvation is "Believe on the Lord Jesus Christ"; so rest you in him; that is believing. Trust in him, depend upon him; that is another way of believing in him; and when you have done that, you are saved—saved the moment you believe in Jesus. The great work of salvation then commences in you, as the work of salvation for you is already complete, and you shall be saved from your sins, made new creatures, and made holy creatures, through the power of that blessed Spirit whom Jesus Christ bestows upon those who believe in him.

May God bless the words I have spoken to the comfort of some! I believe he will; I expect he will; I know he will; and he shall have the glory. Amen.

Mary, Mother of Mark: The Special Prayer Meeting

❧ঞ❧

Delivered on Lord's Day morning, July 20, 1875, at the Metropolitan Tabernacle, Newington. No. 1247.

> *When he had considered the thing, he came to the house of Mary the mother of John, whose surname was Mark; where many were gathered together praying.*—ACTS 12:12

It was a great wonder that the infant church of Christ was not destroyed. Truly, she was like a lone lamb in the midst of furious wolves, without either earthly power or prestige or patronage to protect her, yet, as though she wore a charmed life, she escaped from the hosts of her cruel foes. Had not this child been something more than others, it had been slain like the innocents at Bethlehem: but being heaven-born it escaped the fury of the destroyer.

It is worthwhile asking, however—with what weapons did this church protect herself? For *we* may very wisely use the same. She was preserved in her utmost danger from overwhelming destruction, what was her defense? Where found she shield and buckler? The answer is—in prayer: "many were gathered together praying." Whatever may be the danger of the times, and each age has its own peculiar hazard, we may rest in calm assurance that our defense is of God, and we may avail ourselves of that defense in the same manner as the early church did, namely, by abounding in prayer. However poisonous the viper, prayer can extract its sting; however fierce the lion, prayer can break its teeth; however terrible the fire, prayer can quench the violence of the flame.

But this is not all: the newborn church not only escaped, but it multiplied: from being as a grain of mustard seed, when it could all assemble in the upper room, it has now become a great tree; lo, it covers the nations, and the birds of the air in flocks find shelter in its branches. Whence this wondrous increase? What made it grow? Outward circumstances were unfavorable to its progress; upon what nourishment has it been fed? What means were taken with this tender shoot that has been so speedily developed? For, whatever means were used of old, we may wisely use them today also to strengthen which things remain and are ready to die, and to develop that which is hopeful in our midst. The answer is—the fact that on all occasions "many were gathered together praying." While praying, the Spirit of God came down upon them; while praying, the Spirit often separated this man and that for special work; while praying, their hearts grew warm with inward fire; while praying, their tongues were unloosed, and they went forth to speak to the people; and while praying, the Lord opened to them the treasures of his grace. By prayer they were protected, and by prayer they grew; and if our churches are to live and grow they must be watered from the selfsame source. "Let us pray," is one of the most needful watchwords which I can suggest to Christian men and women, for if we will but pray, prayer will fill up the pools in the valley of Baca, yes, and open to us all the channels of that river of God which is full of water, the streams whereof make glad the city of our God.

We have heard a great deal of talk in certain sections of the church about going back to primitive times, and they are introducing to us all sorts of superstitious inventions, under cover of the customs of the early church. The plea is cunningly chosen, for primitive practices have great weight with true Christians; but the weak point of the argument is that unfortunately what they call the early church is not early enough. If we must have the early church held up as a model, let us have the earliest church of all; if we are to have fathers, let us go back to apostolic fathers; and if we are to have ritual and rule and ceremonial modeled on strict precedent, let us go back to the original precedent recorded in the holy Scriptures. We who are called Baptists, have not the slightest objection to go back in everything to the apostolic habit and practice; we reverence the real primitive method, and desire to follow the customs of the true early church: and if we could see every ordinance restored to the exact mode in which it was practiced by the saints immediately after the ascension of our Lord, and during apostolic times, we would clap our hands with delight. 'Tis a consummation devoutly to be wished. To see the early church alive again would cause us unfeigned satisfaction. Especially upon this point would we imitate the early church: we would have it said of us—"Many were gathered together praying." May we have much prayer, much household prayer, much believing prayer, much prevalent prayer, and then we shall obtain great blessings from the Lord.

I. This morning my earnest desire is to stir up the church of Jesus Christ to increased prayerfulness, and I have taken this text as it furnishes me with one or two points of great interest and is full of

practical suggestions. The first is this: *let us notice the importance which the early church attributed to prayer,* and to prayer meetings.

Let this be *a lesson* to us. As soon as we begin to read in the Acts, and continually as we read on in that record, we note that meetings for prayer had become *a standing institution in the church.* We read nothing of masses, but we read much of prayer meetings. We hear nothing of church festivals, but we read often of meeting together for prayer. It is said that Peter considered the thing: I fancy that he considered it all around, and thought, "Where shall I go?" and he recollected that it was prayer meeting night down at John Mark's mother's house, and there would he go, because he felt that there he should meet with true brethren.

In those days they did things by plan and order, according to that text, "Let all things be done decently and in order," and I have no doubt that it had been duly arranged that the meeting should be held that evening at the house of John Mark's mother, and therefore Peter went there, and found, as he probably expected, that there was a prayer meeting going on. They were not met to hear a sermon. It is most proper that we should very frequently assemble for that purpose, but this was distinctly a meeting where "many were gathered together praying." Praying was the business on hand. I do not know that they even had an address, though some will come to the prayer meeting if the pastor is present to speak; but you see James, who is generally thought to have been pastor of the church at Jerusalem, was not there, for Peter said, "Go show these things to James," and most probably none of the apostles were there, because Peter added, "and to the brethren," and I suppose by that he meant the brethren of the apostolic college. The eminent speaking brethren seem to have been all away, and perhaps no one expounded or exhorted that night, nor was there any need, for they were all too much engrossed in the common intercession. The meeting was convened for praying, and this, I say, was a regular institution of the Christian church, and ought always to be kept up.

There should be meetings wholly devoted to prayer, and there is a serious flaw in the arrangements of a church when such gatherings are omitted or placed in a secondary position. These prayer meetings should be kept to their object, and their great attraction should be prayer itself. An address if you like, a few burning words to stir up prayer if you like, but if you cannot have them, do not look upon speech making as at all necessary. Let it be a standing ordinance in the church that at certain times and occasions many shall meet together to pray, and supplication shall be their sole object. The private Christian will read and hear and meditate, but none of these can be a substitute for prayer. The same truth holds good upon the larger scale. The church should listen to her teachers, and receive edification from gospel ordinances, but she must also pray; nothing can compensate for the neglect of devotion.

It appears, however, that while prayer meetings were a regular institution, the *prayer was sometimes made special*, for we read that prayer was made without ceasing of the church unto God "for him," that is, for Peter. It adds greatly to the interest, and not a little to the fervency, of prayer when there is some great object to pray for. The brethren would have prayed if Peter had been out of prison, but seeing that he was in prison, and likely to be put to death, it was announced that the prayer meeting would be specially to pray for Peter, that the Lord would deliver his servant, or give him grace to die triumphantly; and this special subject gave enthusiasm to the assembly. Yes, they prayed fervently, for I find the margin of the fifth verse runs thus, "Instant and earnest prayer was made of the church for him." They prized the man, for they saw what wonders God had worked by his ministry, and they could not let him die if prayer would save him. When they thought of Peter, and how his bleeding head might be exhibited to the populace on the morrow, they prayed heart and soul, and each succeeding speaker threw more and more fervency into his pleading. The united cry went up to heaven, "Lord, spare Peter"; I think I can hear their sobs and cries even now. God grant that our churches may often turn their regular prayer meetings into gatherings with a special object, for then they will become more real. Why not pray for a certain missionary or some chosen district or class of persons or order of agencies? We should do well to turn the grand artillery of supplication against some special point of the enemy's walls.

It is clear that these friends *fully believed that there was power in prayer*; for, Peter being in prison, they did not meet together to arrange a plan for getting him out. Some wise brother might have suggested the bribing of the guards, and another might have suggested something else; but they had done with planning, and took themselves to praying. I do not find that they met to petition Herod. It would have been of no avail to ask that monster to relent: they might as well request a wolf to release a lamb which he has seized. No, the petitions were to Herod's Lord and Master, to the great invisible God. It looked as if they could do nothing, but they felt they could do everything by prayer. They thought little of the fact that sixteen soldiers had him in charge. What are sixteen guards? If there had been sixteen thousand soldiers, these believing men and women would still have prayed Peter out. They believed in

God, that he would do wonders; they believed in prayer, that it had an influence with God, and that the Lord did listen to the believing petitions of his servants. They met together for prayer in no dubious mood. They knew what
they were at, and had no question as to the power which lay in supplication.
Oh, let it never be insinuated in the Christian church that prayer is a good thing
and a useful exercise to ourselves, but that it would be superstition to suppose
that it affects the mind of God. Those who say this have foolishly thought to
please us by allowing us their scientific toleration to go on with our devotions,
but do they think we are idiots, that we would continue asking for what we
knew we should not receive; that we would keep on praying if it would be of
no more use than whistling to the winds? They must think us devoid of reason if they imagine that we shall be able to keep up prayer as a pious exercise
if we once concede that it can have no result with God. As surely as any law
of nature can be ascertained and proved, we know both by observation and
experiment that God assuredly hears prayer; and, instead of its being a doubt-
ful agency, we maintain prayer to be the most potent and unfailing force
beneath the skies. We say in the proverb, "man proposes but God disposes,"
and here is the power of prayer, that it does not dally with the proposer but
goes at once to the Disposer, and deals with the First Cause. Prayer moves that
arm which moves all things else. O brethren, may we gather power in prayer
by having faith in it. Let us not say, "What can prayer do?" but, "What cannot
it do?" for all things are possible to him that believes. No wonder prayer meetings flag if faith in prayer be weak; and no wonder if conversions and revivals
are scarce where intercession is neglected.

This prayer in the early church we remark, in the next place, was *industri-
ously continued*. As soon as Herod had put Peter into prison, the church began
to pray. Herod took care that the guards should be sufficient in number to
keep good watch over his victim, but the saints of God set their watches too.
As in times of war, when two armies lie near each other, they both set their
sentries, so in this case Herod had his sentries of the night to keep the watch,
and the church had its pickets too. Prayer was made of the church without
ceasing; as soon as one little company were compelled to separate to go to
their daily labor, they were relieved by another company, and when some
were forced to take rest in sleep, others were ready to take up the blessed work
of supplication. Thus both sides were on the alert, and the guards were
changed both by day and by night. It was not hard to foresee which side would
win the victory, for truly "except the LORD keep the city, the watchman
waketh but in vain"; and, when, instead of helping to keep the castle, God
sends angels to open doors and gates, then we may be sure that the watchmen

will wake in vain, or fall into a dead slumber. Continually, therefore, the people of God pleaded at his mercy seat; relays of petitioners appeared before the throne. Some mercies are not given to us except in answer to importunate prayer. There are blessings which, like ripe fruit, drop into your hand the moment you touch the bough; but there are others which require you to shake the tree again and again, until you make it rock with the vehemence of your exercise, for then only will the fruit fall down. My brethren, we must cultivate importunity in prayer. While the sun is shining and when the sun has gone down, still should prayer be kept up and fed with fresh fuel, so that it burns fiercely, and flames on high like a beacon fire blazing toward heaven.

I would fain pause here a minute and urge my dear brethren to attach as much importance to prayer as the early church did. You cannot think too much of it. Believing prayer, dictated of the Spirit, and presented through Jesus Christ, is today the power of the church, and we cannot do without it. Some look at her active agencies, and prize them, but they suppose that prayer might be dispensed with. You have seen the threshing machine going along the country road from farm to farm: in front there is a huge, black engine which toils along the road, and then behind you see the machine which actually does the threshing. A novice might say, "I will hire the threshing machine, but I do not want your engine; that is an expensive affair which consumes coal and makes smoke; I do not require it. I will have the machine which actually does the work, but I do not want the engine." Such a remark would be absurd, for of what use would the machine be to you if the motive power were gone? Prayer in the church is the steam engine which makes the wheels revolve, and really does the work, and therefore we cannot do without it.

Suppose a foreman were employed by some great builder, and sent out to manage works at a distance. He has to pay the men their wages weekly, and he is very diligent in doing so; he neglects none of his duty toward the men, but he forgets to communicate with headquarters. He neither writes to his employer, nor goes to the bank for cash to go on with. Is this wise? When the next pay night comes round, I am afraid he will find that, however diligent he may have been toward the men, he will be in a queer position, for he will have no silver or gold to hand out, because he has forgotten to apply to headquarters. Now, brethren, the minister does, as it were, distribute the portions to the people, but if he does not apply to his Master to get them, he will have nothing to distribute. Never sunder the connection between your soul and God. Keep up a constant communication with heaven, or your communications with earth will be of little worth. To cease from prayer is to stop the vital stream upon which all your energy is dependent; you may go on preaching and teaching, and giving away tracts, and what you like, but nothing can possibly come of it when the power of almighty God has ceased to be with you.

Thus much on our first point. May the Holy Spirit use it and arouse the churches to unanimous, intense, importunate intercession.

II. Next we notice *the number assembled*, which is a rebuke to some here present.

The text says, *"Many* were gathered together praying." Somebody said the other day of prayer meetings, that two or three thousand people had no more power in prayer than two or three. I think that is a grave mistake in many ways; but clearly so in reference to each other; for have you never noticed that when many meet together praying, warmth of desire and glow of earnestness are greatly increased. Perhaps two or three might have been all dull, but out of a larger number someone at least is a warmhearted brother, and sets all the rest on a flame. Have you not observed how the requests of one will lead another on to ask for yet greater things? How one Christian brother suggests to another to increase his petition, and so the petitions grow by the mingling of heart with heart, and the communion of spirit with spirit? Besides, faith is a cumulative force. "According to thy faith so be it done unto thee" is true to one, to two, to twenty, to twenty thousand; and twenty thousand times the force will be the result of twenty thousand times the faith. Rest assured that while two or three have power with God in their measure, two or three hundred have still more. If great results are to come, they will be accompanied by the prayers of many; no, the brightest days of all will never come except by the unanimous prayer of the entire church, for as soon as Zion travails—not one or two in her midst, but the whole church travails—then shall she bring forth her children.

Therefore I do earnestly pray, brethren, to make the numbers gathered in prayer as great as they can be. Of course, if we come together listlessly, if each heart be cold and dead, there is only so much more coldness and deadness; but taking for granted that each one comes in the spirit of prayer, the gathering of numbers is like adding firebrand to firebrand, and piling on the burning coals, and we are likely to have a heat like that of coals of juniper, which have a most vehement flame.

Now this is *not a very common occurrence*, and why is it that so many prayer meetings are so very thin? I know some places in London where they talk about giving up the prayer meeting, where instead of two services during the week they have compassion on their poor, overworked minister, and only wish him to hold forth for a few minutes at a sort of mongrel service, half prayer meeting and half lecture. Poor dear things, they cannot manage to get out to worship more than once in the week, they are so much occupied. This is not in poor churches, but in respectable churches. Gentlemen who do not get home from the city and have their dinner till seven o'clock cannot be expected to go out to a prayer meeting; who would have the barbarity to suggest such a thing? They work so extremely hard all the day, so much harder than any of the working men, that they say, "I pray thee have me excused." Churches in the suburbs, as a general rule, have miserable prayer meetings, because of the unfortunate circumstances of the members who happen to be burdened with so much riches that they cannot meet for prayer as poor people do. Some of you who have your delightful villas are very careful of your health and never venture out into the evening air at prayer meetings, though I rather suspect that your parties and soirees are still kept up. I say not this with particular reference to anybody, except it happens to refer to him, and if it does refer to him the reference is very special.

After all, dear friends, this is a personal matter. It is of no use my standing here or your sitting there and complaining that so few come to the prayer meeting: how are we to increase the number? I would suggest to you a way of increasing it, namely, by coming yourself. You may be aware, perhaps, that one and one make two, and that another one will make three, so that by accretions of ones we shall gradually get up to thousands. The largest numbers are made up of units; so that the practical point of all is, if choice blessings are to be gained by numbers coming together for prayer, the way for me to increase the number is to go there myself, and if I can induce a friend to go also, so much the better.

I have a very high opinion of the early church, but I am not sure that quite so many would have been gathered together that night if it had not been that Peter was in prison. They said to one another, "Peter is in prison, and in danger of his life, let us go to the prayer meeting and plead for him." Did you ever know a minister who was often laid aside by illness and always found his people pray better when he was ill? Did it never strike you that one reason for his being afflicted was God's desire to stir the hearts of his people to intercede for him? Their prayers are better than his preaching; and so his Lord says to him, "I can do without you; I will put you on the bed of pain and make the people pray." Now I have an opinion that the best way for these people really to do good to their pastor is to pray that they may be kept in a right condition, and may not need his sickness as a stimulus to prayer. If churches become slack in prayer, those whom they most value may be laid aside, or even taken away by death, and then they will cry to God in the bitterness of their souls. Could not we do without such flogging? Some horses want to be reminded now and then with a little touch of the whip; if they did not need the lash they would not get it; and so it may be with us, that we need church trials to keep us up to the mark in prayer, and if we need them we shall have them; but if we are alive and earnest in prayer, it may be that Peter will not get into prison, and some other trying things will not happen besides.

III. The third thing in my text is *the place of assembly*. That we will dwell upon this morning as *a suggestion*.

"The house of Mary, the mother of John, whose surname was Mark." This was a prayer meeting held in a private house, and I want to urge upon my brethren here to consecrate their houses by frequently using them for prayer meetings. This would have an advantage about it: it would avoid all savor of superstition. There still lingers among people the notion that buildings may be consecrated and rendered holy. Well, it is so babyish an idea, that I should have hoped the manliness of this generation, let alone anything else, would have given up the notion. How can it be that inside four brick walls there should be more holiness than outside, or that prayer offered in some particular seat should be more acceptable than prayer offered anywhere else. Behold, this day, God hears prayer wherever there is a true heart.

> *Where'er we seek him, he is found,*
> *And every place is hallowed ground.*

Meetings for prayer, held at the house of the mother of Mark, at *your* mother's house, at your brother's house, at your own house, will do much to be a plain protest against the superstition which reverences holy places. There was a meetness in their meeting in this particular house, the house of Mark's mother, for that family stood in a very dear relationship to Peter. Do you know who Mark was, in reference to Peter? If you turn to 1 Peter 5, you will read, "Marcus, my son." Ah, I am sure Mark would pray for Peter, because Peter was his spiritual father. I should not wonder but what Mark and his mother were both converted on the day of Pentecost, when Peter preached that famous sermon. Anyhow, Mark was converted under Peter, and so both he and his mother often invited Peter to their house, and when he was imprisoned they had the special prayer meetings at their house, because they loved him greatly. There is sure to be prayer for the pastor in the house where the pastor has been blessed to the family. He need not be afraid but what his own sons and daughters in the faith will be sure to pray for him.

These meetings had a good effect upon Mrs. Mark's house. She, herself, no doubt, had a blessing, but her son Mark obtained peculiar favor of the

Lord. Naturally he was not all we should like him to have been, for though his uncle Barnabas was very fond of him, Paul, who was a very good judge, could not put up with his instability. But he obtained so great a blessing from the Lord that he became, according to the unanimous tradition of the church, the writer of the gospel of Mark. He might have been a very weak and useless Christian if it had not been that the prayer meetings at his mother's house warmed his heart, and he might never have used his graphic pen for the Lord had not the conversation of the good people who came to his house instructed him as to the facts, which he afterward recorded in the precious gospel which bears his name.

The house received a blessing, and so will you, too, if your house shall be every now and then opened for special prayer. I urge upon the followers of Jesus Christ to use their own houses more frequently than they now do for holy purposes. How largely might the Sunday schools in London be extended if all the better instructed gathered together Bible classes in their own houses and taught them during the Sabbath day; and what a multitude of prayers would go up to heaven if Christians who have suitable rooms would frequently call together their brethren and neighbors to offer prayer. Many an hour is wasted in idle talk, many an evening frittered away in foolish amusements, degrading to Christians, when the time might be occupied in exercises calculated to bring down untold blessings upon the family and upon the church.

Prayer meetings at private houses are very useful, because friends who would be afraid to pray before a large assembly, and others who if they did so would be very much restricted in language, are able to feel free and easy in a smaller company in a private house. Sometimes, too, the social element is consecrated by God to promote a greater warmth and fervor, so that prayer will often burn in the family when perhaps it might have declined in the public assembly. I never knew the little church of which I was pastor before I came here to be in such a happy condition as when the members took it into their heads to hold prayer meetings in their own houses. I have sometimes myself attended six or seven in an evening, running from one to another just to look in upon them, finding twelve in a kitchen, ten or a dozen in a parlor, two or three met together in a little chamber. We saw a great work of grace then; the biggest sinners in the parish felt the power of the gospel, the old saints warmed up and began to believe in young people being converted, and we were all alive by reason of the abundance of prayer.

Brethren, we must have the like abundance of prayer; do pray that we may have it. We have been distinguished as a church for prayerfulness, and I am jealous with a godly jealousy lest we should go back in any degree, and I do affectionately suggest to you with much earnestness of heart that we should try to increase the number of the places where many shall be met together praying. I do not know where the mother of John Mark is this morning, but I hope she will start a prayer meeting in her large room. She is well to do, I believe, because her brother Barnabas had land, and sold it, and I suppose she had property also; we will use her drawing room. If a poorer friend has a smaller and poorer room, we shall be glad of the loan of it, for it will be more suitable for persons of another class to go to. Perhaps they would not like to go to Mrs. Mark's drawing room, but they will come to your kitchen. All sorts will have an opportunity of praying when all sorts of chambers are dedicated to prayer.

IV. I have a little to say about *the time of this prayer meeting.*

It was held at dead of night. I suppose they prayed all through the night. They could say, "We have been waiting, we have been waiting, all the night long." After midnight the angel set Peter free. Peter went to the house, and they were not gone to bed, but many were met together praying. Now, as to the time for prayer meetings, let me say this. If it happens to be an inconvenient hour, and I should think the dead of night was rather inconvenient, nevertheless go. Better hold prayer meetings at twelve o'clock at night than not at all; better that we should be accused, as the Christians were of old, of holding secret conventicles under the shadow of night, than not meet together for prayer.

But there is another lesson. The dead of the night was chosen because it was the most suitable hour, since they could not safely meet in the day because of the Jews. It becomes those who appoint the times for prayer meetings to select as good an hour as they can, a quiet hour, a leisure hour, an hour suited to the habits of the people. Still let us remember that whatever hour is appointed, if we come together with true hearts, it will be an acceptable hour. Better still, it would be well if there could be meetings for prayer at all hours. Then every hour would be an acceptable hour, and if one happened to be unseasonable, another would be convenient, and all classes of believers could thus meet together at some time or other to pour out their hearts in prayer to God. O brethren, if your business will not let you meet in the middle of the day, meet in the middle of the night; if you cannot come together for prayer at the times that are generally appointed, then have prayer meetings at such times as will suit yourselves; but do let there be a unanimous resolve throughout the whole church of Christ, that much prayer shall be presented to the most High.

V. Notice, in the last place, the *success of the prayer meetings as an encouragement to us.*

They prayed, and they were heard at once. The answer came so speedily that they were themselves surprised. It has sometimes been said that they did not expect Peter to be set free, and that their astonishment was the result of unbelief. Perhaps so; but I doubt it, for you must remember that their prayer did set Peter free, and therefore it does not look as if it could have been unbelieving prayer. I trace their surprise to another cause. I think they expected that God would somehow or other deliver Peter, but they did not think he would deliver him in the dead of the night. They very likely had appointed in their own minds that something would happen next day, and so their surprise arose, not from the fact that Peter was free, so much as from his being out of the dungeon at that particular time, and in that particular manner, for I cannot judge that to have been an unbelieving prayer which really did win the day with the God of heaven.

Dear friends, the Lord Jesus waits to give us great boons in answer to prayer. He can send us surprises quite as great as those which astonished the assembly at midnight. We may pray for some sinner, and while we are yet praying we may hear him cry, "What must I do to be saved?" We may offer our prayers for the sleeping church, and while we pray it may be answered. True, the church sleeps still; she has had a smiting on the side of late, but has not yet girded herself and come out of the prison house of her coldness and conventionality; but if we continue in prayer we may see with astonishment the church rouse herself from sleep and come forth to liberty. We cannot tell what will happen, prayer operates in so many ways, but operate it will, and we shall assuredly have our reward.

I selected this topic just now for this reason. The American evangelists who have been so useful in this great city have gone from us, and the great assemblies which they gathered are no more. There must have been many converted: I cannot but believe that many thousands have the Lord Jesus Christ, and I have no sympathy whatever with the remarks of those who alarm that our friends have not touched the lowest class of society. I believe they have touched every class of society. At any rate their business was to preach the gospel to every creature, and they have done so with great impartiality and earnestness. If the poorest did not go, it was not because they were not welcome. But they did go; I am an eyewitness to it. I know that many who went nowhere before did attend the Bow and Camberwell Halls, and the fact that the congregation looked respectable by no means proves that they were not of the working classes; for what workingman is there among us but tries to dress as neatly as he can when he goes to a place of worship? There are plenty of friends here who work hard for their daily bread, but looking around they all seem by their dress to be well-to-do. No one has a right to judge that because a man does not come to worship in rags he cannot therefore belong to the lower portion of the working class, for it is not the habit of the working-men of London to go to places of worship in their everyday clothes or in rags. I saw with my own eyes that multitudes assembled there were of that class which did not habitually hear the gospel. I am sure that good was done, and I do not care who cavils. The practical point is—What is to be done now? We must keep up this work. And how? Not by those large assemblies, but by all the churches being revived all round, and the numbers in all the places of worship becoming more numerous, and at the same time becoming more prayerful.

Let us pray *now*. We want prayer to train the converts, to keep God's people warm now they are warm, and to make them yet more so. What wonders we have obtained in the tabernacle in answer to prayer. We began this work with a little handful of Christian men. I remember the first Monday night after I came to London; there was a slender audience on the Sabbath, but thank God there was almost as many at the prayer meeting as on the Sunday; and I thought, "This is all right; these people can pray." They did pray, and as we increased in prayer we increased in numbers. Sometimes, at prayer meetings, my heart was almost ready to break for joy because of the mighty supplication that was offered. We wanted to build this great house: we were poor enough, but we prayed for it, and prayer built it. Praying gave us everything we have. Praying brings us all manner of supplies, spiritual and temporal. Whatever I am in the church of God, this day I owe, under God's blessing, to your prayers. As long as your prayers sustain me, I shall not flag nor fail, but if your prayers be gone, then my power is gone, for the Spirit of God is gone, and what can I do? All through the church of God the true progress is in proportion to the prayer. I do not care about the talent of the speaker; I am glad if he has talent. I do not care about the wealth of the congregation, though I am glad if they have wealth. But I do care beyond everything for the deep, real, earnest prayer, the darting up of the souls of Christians to God, and the bringing down of the blessing upon men from God. And if this were the last word I had to address to this congregation, I would say to you, dear brethren, abound in prayer, multiply the petitions that you put up, and increase the fervor with which you present them to God.

When my venerable predecessor, Dr. Rippon, was growing old, this was one of the things everybody noticed about him, that he always prayed earnestly for his successors. He did not know who they might be, but his prayer was that God would bless the church and his successors in years to come, and I have heard old Christians say that our present prosperity might be traced to Dr. Rippon's prayers. Oh, let us pray. I believe we have had a revival very much in answer to the multitudinous fervent prayers that were put up here and elsewhere; and now that God is beginning to bless the church in answer to prayer, if she stays her hand she will be like that king of old, who had the arrows and the bow put into his hands, and shot once or twice, whereas, if he had shot many times, God would have destroyed Syria before him, and established his people. Take down your quivers full of desires, and grasp the mighty bow of faith. Now shoot again and again the arrow of the Lord's deliverance, and God will give us multitudes of converts all over London, and throughout the world. "'Prove me now herewith,' saith the LORD of hosts, 'and see if I do not open the windows of heaven and pour you out a blessing that ye shall not have room enough to receive it.'" God bless you, for Christ's sake.

Lydia: The First European Convert

❦

Intended for reading on Lord's Day, September 20, 1891; delivered at the Metropolitan Tabernacle, Newington. No. 2222.

And a certain woman named Lydia, a seller of purple, of the city of Thyatira, which worshiped God, heard us: whose heart the Lord opened, that she attended unto the things which were spoken of Paul.—ACTS 16:14

We may laudably exercise curiosity with regard to the first proclamation of the gospel in our own quarter of the globe. We are happy that history so accurately tells us, by the pen of Luke, when first the gospel was preached in Europe, and by whom, and who was the first convert brought by that preaching to the Savior's feet. I half envy Lydia that she should be the leader of the European band; yet I feel right glad that a woman led the vanguard, and that her household followed so closely in the rear.

God has made great use of women, and greatly honored them in the kingdom of our Lord and Savior Jesus Christ. Holy women ministered to our Lord when he was upon the earth, and since that time much sacred work has been done by their patient hands. Man and woman fell together; together they must rise. After the resurrection, it was a woman who was first commissioned to carry the glad tidings of the risen Christ; and in Europe, where woman was in future days to be set free from many of the trammels of the East, it seems fitting that a woman should be the first believer. Not only, however, was Lydia a sort of firstfruit for Europe, but she probably also became a witness in her own city of Thyatira, in Asia. We do not know how the gospel was introduced into that city; but we are informed of the existence of a church there by the message of the ascended Christ, through his servant John, to "the angel of the church in Thyatira." Very likely Lydia became the herald of the gospel in her native place. Let the women who know the truth proclaim it; for why should their influence be lost? "The Lord giveth the word; the women that publish the tidings are a great host." Woman can be as powerful for evil as for good: we see it in this very church of Thyatira, where the woman Jezebel, who called herself a prophetess, sought to seduce many from the truth. Seeing, then, that the devil employs women in his service, let those women whom God has called by his grace be doubly earnest in seeking to prevent or undo the mischief that others of their sex are working. If not called to public service, all have the home sphere wherein they can shed forth the aroma of a godly life and testimony.

If the gospel does not influence our homes, it is little likely to make headway among the community. God has made family piety to be, as it were, a sort of trademark on religion in Europe; for the very first convert brings with her all her family. Her household believed, and were baptized with her. You shall notice in Europe, though I do not mean to say that it is not the same anywhere else, that true godliness has always flourished in proportion as family religion has been observed. They hang a bell in a steeple, and they tell us that it is our duty to go every morning and every evening into the steeple house there to join in prayer; but we reply that our own house is better for many reasons; at any rate, it will not engender superstition for us to pray there. Gather your children together, and offer prayer and supplication to God in your own room.

"But there is no priest." Then there ought to be. Every man should be a priest in his own household; and, in the absence of a godly father, the mother should lead the devotions. Every house should be the house of God, and there should be a church in every house; and when this is the case, it will be the greatest barrier against priestcraft and the idolatry of holy places. Family prayer and the pulpit are the bulwarks of Protestantism. Depend upon it, when family piety goes down, the life of godliness will become very low. In Europe, at any rate, seeing that the Christian faith began with a converted household, we ought to seek after the conversion of all our families, and to maintain within our houses the good and holy practice of family worship.

Lydia, then, is the first European convert, and we will review her history so far as we have it in Holy Writ. Toward her conversion four things cooperated, upon which we will speak briefly. First, *the working of Providence*; second, *the working of Lydia herself*; third, *the working of Paul*; and fourth, *the working of the Holy Spirit*.

I. First, notice *the working of Providence*.

When I was in Amsterdam, I visited the works of a diamond cutter, where I saw many large wheels and much powerful machinery at work; and I must confess that it seemed very odd that all that great array of apparatus should be brought to bear upon a tiny bit of crystal, which looked like a fragment of glass. Was that diamond worth so much that a whole factory should be set to work to cut its facets, and cause it to sparkle? So the diamond cutter believed. Within that small space lay a gem which was thought worthy of all this care and labor. That diamond may be at this time glistening upon the finger or brow of royalty! Now when I look abroad upon Providence, it seems preposterous to believe that kingdoms, dynasties, and great events should all be cooperating and working together for the accomplishment of the divine purpose in the salvation of God's people. But they are so working. It might have seemed preposterous, but it was not so, that these great wheels should all be working for the cutting of a single diamond; and it is not preposterous, however it may seem so, to say that all the events of providence are being ordered by God to effect the salvation of his own people, the perfecting of the precious jewels which are to adorn the crown of Christ forever and ever.

In the case before us, the working of God's providence is seen, first of all, in bringing Paul to Philippi. Lydia is there. I do not know how long she had been there, nor exactly what brought her there; but there she is, selling her purple, her Turkey-red cloth. Paul must come there, too, but he does not want to come; he has not, indeed, had any desire to come there. He has a kind of prejudice hanging about him still, so that, though he is willing to preach to the gentiles, he scarcely likes to go out of Asia among those gentiles or the gentiles over in Europe. He wants to preach the word in Asia. Very singularly, the Spirit suffers him not, and he seems to have a cold hand laid on him to stop him when his heart is warmest. He is gagged; he cannot speak. "Then I will go into Bithynia," he says; but when he starts on the journey, he is distinctly told that there is no work for him to do there. He must not speak for his Master in that region, at least not yet: "the Spirit suffered him not." He feels himself to be a silenced man. What is he to do? He gets down to Troas on the verge of the sea, and there comes to him the vision of a man of Macedonia, who prayed him, saying, "Come over into Macedonia, and help us." He infers that he must go across to Macedonia. A ship is ready for him; he has a free course, a favorable passage, and he soon arrives at Philippi. God brings Paul to the spot where Lydia was, in this strange and singular manner.

But the working of Providence was quite as much manifested in bringing Lydia there; for Lydia was not originally at Philippi. She was a seller of purple, of Thyatira. Thyatira was a city famous for its dyers. They made a peculiar purple, which was much prized by the Romans. Lydia appears to have carried on this business. She was either a widow, or perhaps had had no husband, though she may have gathered a household of servants about her. She comes over to Philippi across the sea. I think I see them bringing the great rolls of red cloth up the hill, that she may sell at Philippi the cloth which she has made and dyed at Thyatira. Why does she come just at this season? Why does she come just when Paul is coming? Why does she come to Philippi? Why not to Neapolis? Why not press on to Athens? Why not sell her cloth over at Corinth?

Whatever reason she might have given for her choice, there was one cause, of which she was ignorant, which shaped her action, and brought her to Philippi at that time. God had a surprise in store for her. She and Paul have to meet. It does not matter what their will is; their wills shall be so moved and actuated by the providence of God that they shall cross each other's path, and Paul shall preach the gospel to Lydia. I think it never entered into Lydia's heart, when she left Thyatira with her purple bales, that she was going to find Jesus Christ over at Philippi; neither did Paul guess, when he saw, in a vision, a man of Macedonia, and heard him say, "Come over into Macedonia, and help us," that the first person he would have to help would not be a man of Macedonia at all, but a woman of Thyatira, and that the congregation he should preach to would be just a handful of women gathered by the side of the little stream that runs through Philippi. Neither Paul nor Lydia knew what God was about to do; but God knew. He understands the end from the beginning, and times his acts of providence to meet our deepest needs in the wisest way.

> His wisdom is sublime,
> His heart profoundly kind;
> God never is before his time,
> And never is behind.

What an odd thing it seemed that this woman should be a woman of Thyatira in Asia, and Paul must not go and preach in Asia; and yet, when he comes to Macedonia, the first person who hears him is a woman of Asia! Why, you and I would have said, "If the woman belongs to Thyatira, let her stop at home, and let Paul go there; that is the shortest cut." Not so. The woman of Thyatira must go to Philippi, and Paul must go to Philippi too. This is God's plan; and if we knew all the circumstances as God knows them, we should doubtless admire the wisdom of it. Perhaps the very peculiarity of the circumstances made Paul more alert to seize the opportunity at Philippi than he would have been had he gone on to Thyatira; perhaps the isolation of the strange city made Lydia yearn more after spiritual things. God can answer a dozen ends by one act.

One of our evangelists tells of a man who was converted in a small Irish town, and it was afterward discovered that he, and the preacher who led him to Christ, resided but a few hundred yards from each other in London. They had never met in this great city, where neighbors are strangers to each other; nor was it likely that they ever would have been brought into contact with one another here; for the man, who was a commercial traveler, was too careless ever to attend a place of worship in London. But to sell his goods he went to Ireland, where, also, went the evangelist to preach the gospel; and being somewhat at a loss to know what to do with his time, he no sooner saw the name of a preacher from London announced, than he determined to attend the service, and there he met with Christ. We can see how natural this was in the case of which we know all the particulars, and it was doubtless as well arranged in the case of Lydia and Paul.

Now I should not wonder tonight if there are a number of providences that have worked together to bring some of my hearers into their places at this time. What brought *you* to London, friend? It was not your intention to be in this city. Coming to London, what brought you to this part of it? What led you to be at this service? And why was it that you did not come on one of the Sundays when the preacher would have been here if he could, but could not be here by reason of his weakness? Because, it may be, that only from these lips can the word come to you, and only tonight, and you must come to this place. Perhaps there is someone who preaches the gospel much better in the town where you live; or, peradventure, you have had opportunities of hearing the same preachers near your own door, and you did not avail yourself of them; and yet God has brought you here. I wish we watched providences more. "Whoso is wise, and will observe these things, even they shall understand the lovingkindness of the LORD." If the Lord should meet with you, and convert you tonight, I will warrant you that you will be a believer in Providence, and say, "Yes, God guided my steps. He directed my path, and he brought me to the spot where Jesus met with me, and opened my heart that I might receive the gospel of his grace." Be of good courage, you ministers of the gospel! Providence is always working with you while you are working for God. I have often admired the language of Mahomet, when in the battle of Ohod he said to his followers, pointing to their foes, "Charge them! I can hear the wings of the angels as they hasten to our help." That was a delusion on his part, for he and his men were badly beaten; but it is no delusion in the case of the servants of Christ. We *can* hear the wings of the angels. We may hear the grinding of the great wheels of Providence as they revolve for the help of the preacher of the gospel. Everything is with us when we are with God. Who can be against us? The stars in their courses fight for the servants of God; and all things, great and small, shall bow before the feet of him who trod the waves of the Sea of Galilee, and still is Master of all things, and rules all things to the accomplishment of his divine purposes.

So much, then, for the working of Providence.

II. The next thing is, *the working of Lydia.*

God's intention is that Lydia shall be saved. Yet, you know, no woman was ever saved against her will. God makes us willing in the day of his power, and it is the way of his grace not to violate the will, but sweetly to overcome it. Never will there be anybody dragged to heaven by the ears: depend upon that. We shall go there with all our hearts and all our desires. What, then, was Lydia doing?

Having by God's grace been made willing, the first thing was that *she kept the Sabbath.* She was a proselyte, and she kept the seventh day. She was away from Thyatira, and nobody would know what she would do, yet she observed the Lord's Day carefully. She was abroad when she was at Philippi, but she had not left God behind her. I have known some English people, when they once reached the Continent, go rattling along, Sundays and weekdays, as if God did not live on the Continent, and as if at home they only observed the Sabbath because they happened to be in England, which is very probably the case with a good many. When they get away, they say, "When you are at Rome, you must do as Rome does"; and so they take their pleasure on God's day. It was not so with Lydia. There was no selling of purple that day; she regarded the Sabbath. Oh, I would to God that everyone would regard the Sabbath! May God grant that it may never be taken away from us! There is a plot now to make some of you work all the seven days of the week, and you will not get any more pay for seven days than you get for six. Stand out against it, and preserve your right to rest upon God's day. The observance of one day in seven as a day of rest materially helps toward the conversion of men, because then they are inclined to think. They have the opportunity to hear, and, if they choose to avail themselves of it, the probabilities are that God will bless the hearing, and they will be saved.

Now notice next that, not only did Lydia observe the Sabbath, but *she went up to the place of worship.* It was not a very fine place. I do not suppose there was any building. It may have been a little temporary oratory put up by the riverside; but very probably it was just on the bank of the river that they met together. It does not appear that there were any men, but only a few women. They only held a prayer meeting: "where prayer was wont to be made." But Lydia did not step away from the gathering. She might easily have excused herself after her long journey, and the wearying work of setting up a new establishment; but her heart was in this matter, and so she found it no drudgery to meet where prayer was offered. She did not say, "I can read a sermon at home," or, "I can read in the Book of the Law indoors." She wished to be where God's people were, however few, or however poor they might be. She did not go to the gorgeous heathen temple at Philippi, but she sought out the few faithful ones that met to worship the true God.

Now, dear friends, do the same. You that are not converted, still attend the means of grace, and do not go to a place simply because it is a fine building, and because there is a crowd, but go where they are truly worshiping God in spirit and in truth. If they should happen to be very few and very poor, yet go with them, for in so doing you are in the way of blessing. I think you will yet have to say, "Being in the way, God met with me." If it is what some call "only a prayer meeting," you will do well to go. Some of the best blessings that men have ever gained have been received at prayer meetings. If we would meet with God, let us seek him diligently, "not forsaking the assembling of ourselves together, as the manner of some is." Though you cannot save yourself or open your own heart, you can at least do what Lydia did: observe the Sabbath, and gather together with God's people.

Lydia, being there with the assembly, when Paul began to speak, we find that *she attended to the things that were spoken*, which is another thing that we can do. It is very ill when people come up to the house of God, and do not attend. I have never had to complain of people not attending in this house since the day I first preached in it; but I have been in places of worship where there seemed to be anything but attention. How can it be expected that there will be a blessing when the pew becomes a place to slumber in, or when the mind is active over the farm or in the kitchen or in the shop, forgetting altogether the gospel which is being preached to the outward ear? If you want a blessing, attend with all your might to the word that is preached; but of that we will speak more by and by.

So far we have spoken upon the working of Providence and the working of Lydia.

III. Now, next, *the working of Paul*; for this was necessary too.

In order to the conversion of men, it is necessary that the person who aims at their conversion should work as if it all depended upon him, though he knows that he cannot accomplish the work. We are to seek to win souls with as much earnestness and prudence and zeal, as if everything depended upon ourselves; and then we are to leave all with God, knowing that none but the Lord can save a single soul.

Now notice, Paul, wishing for converts, is *judicious in the choice of the place* where he will go to look after them. He goes to the spot where there should be a synagogue. He thinks that where people have a desire to pray, there he will find the kind of people who will be ready to hear the word. So he selects devout people, devout worshipers of the one God, that he may go and speak to them about Christ. It is sometimes our plain duty to publish the word from the housetop to the careless crowd; but I think you will generally find that more success comes when those, on whose hearts the Spirit of God has already begun to work, are sought out and instructed. When Christ sent out his disciples on their first journey, he told them, when they entered a town, to "inquire who in it is worthy; and there abide till ye go thence"; evidently showing that, even among those who do not know the truth, there are some whose hearts are prepared to receive it, who are of a devout spirit, and in that sense are worthy. These are the people who should first be sought after. In the same limited sense was Cornelius, to whom Peter was sent, worthy to hear the glad tidings of great joy. His reverent spirit was well pleasing to God; for we read, "Thy prayer is heard, and thine alms are had in remembrance in the sight of God." We must not, of course, think that these things give any claim to salvation; but rather that they are the expression of hearts prepared to receive the message of salvation, seeking the Lord, "if haply they might feel after him, and find him."

One of our greatest difficulties in these days is that so many have lost all reverence for authority of any kind, even God's: having risen against human despotism, they also foolishly try to break God's bands asunder. We are cast back on the infinite power of God when we come to deal with such people; but when we meet with others who are willing to listen and pray, we know that God has already begun to work. Now, dear worker, choose the person who is evidently pointed out to you by God's gracious providence. Choose judiciously, and try to speak with those with whom you may hopefully speak, and trust that God will bless the word.

When Paul goes down to the river, you notice that he is very *judicious as to his manner* of introducing his subject. He did not preach at all. He found only a few women; and to stand up and preach to them, as he did to the crowds at Corinth, or at Athens, might have seemed absurd; but we read this: "We sat down, and spake unto the women which resorted thither." He took his seat on the river's bank, where they were all sitting still, and at prayer, and he began just to have a talk. A sermon would have been out of place; but a talk was the right sort of thing. So he talked the gospel into them. Now be careful of the way in which you go to work with people; for much of the result must depend upon that. Some people can be preached right away from Christ; for the moment you begin to preach they say, "Oh, thank you, I do not want any of your sermon!" Perhaps you could slip a word in edgewise; just drop a seed in a crack; or leave a word with them, just one word. Say at once, "If you do not want any preaching, I do not want to preach to you: I am not so fond of preaching as all that; but I read a very curious story in the newspapers the other day!" And then tell the story, and wrap the gospel up in it. If they do not want pills, do not give them pills. Give them a bit of sugar. They will take the sugar, and when they get it, there will be a pill inside. I mention this, because we may miss opportunities of doing good through not being wide awake. "Be ye wise as serpents, and harmless as doves." Paul therefore just sits down, and has a friendly talk with the women who resorted thither.

But whether Paul preached, or whether Paul talked, it was all the same: he was *judicious as to the matter* of his discourse. He had but one subject, and that was Christ; the Christ who had met him on the way to Damascus, and changed his heart; the Christ who was able still to save; the Christ who bled upon the cross, to bring men to God, and cleanse them in his blood; the Christ in heaven, interceding for sinners; the Christ waiting to be gracious. Paul would not end his talk without saying, "Trust him: trust him. He that believeth in him hath everlasting life." So whether he preached or whether he talked, it was the same story of Jesus Christ, and him crucified. That is how Paul worked. He might have acted very differently. If his heart had not been all aflame for Jesus, he would very likely not have spoken at all, or if he had, it would have been a commonplace remark about the weather. He might have been eager to learn the method by which the beautiful purple dye was obtained, and not have remembered that gospel message, written by Isaiah long ago, which would come with special force to the hearts of his hearers: "Though your sins be as scarlet, they shall be as white as snow; though they be red like crimson, they shall be as wool." He might have been so interested in his inquiries about Thyatira as to forget to speak of the way to the city of light. A dozen subjects might have claimed attention, if his heart had not been set upon one object. He could have spoken of his journeys, and even of his plans, without actually preaching Christ to her.

He might have spoken about the gospel, as I fear we often do, and not have spoken the gospel itself. Some sermons which I have heard, though fault-lessly orthodox, have contained nothing that could convert anybody; for there has been nothing to touch the conscience or heart. Others, though very clever and profound, have had no possible bearing on the needs of the hearers; and so it was little wonder that they were without result.

But I am sure Paul's talk would aim straight at the center of the target: it was evidently addressed to the heart, for we are told that it was with the heart Lydia heard it. After all, it is not our most orderly discourses, nor our aptest illustrations, which bring people to Christ; but some little sentence which is slipped in unawares, or some burning word which comes straight out of our own heart's experience. There would be sure to be many such that day in that earnest simple talk by the riverside. Let us multiply such conversations, if we would win more Lydias for the church.

IV. But, now, fourth—and here is the main point—let us notice *the working of the Spirit of God.*

Providence brings Paul and Lydia together. Lydia comes there because she observes the Sabbath, and loves the place of worship. Paul comes there because he loves to win souls, and, like his Master, is on the watch for stray sheep. But it would have been a poor meeting for them if the Spirit of God had not been there also. So we next read of Lydia, "whose heart the Lord opened, that she attended unto the things which were spoken of Paul." It is not a wonder that the Lord can open a human heart; for he who made the lock knows well what key will fit it. What means he made use of in the case of Lydia, I do not know; but I will tell you what might have happened. Perhaps she had lost her husband; many a woman's heart has been opened by that great gash. The joy of her soul has been taken away, and she has turned to God. Perhaps her husband was spared to her; but she had lost a child. Oh, how many a babe has been sent here on purpose to entice its mother to the skies; a lamb taken away that the sheep might follow the Shepherd! Perhaps she had had bad trade; the price of purple may have fallen. She may have been half afraid she would fail in business. I have known such trouble to open some people's hearts. Perhaps she had had prosperity; possibly the purple had gone up in price. I have known some so impressed with God's temporal blessings that they have been ready to think of him, and to turn to him. I do not know; I cannot guess, and I have no right to guess what it was. But I know that God has very wonderful plows, with which he breaks up the hard soil of human hearts. When I have been through the Britannia Iron Works, at Bedford, I have wondered at the strange clod crushers, clod breakers, and plows, made there by the Messrs. Howard; and God has some marvelous machines in his providence for turning up the soil of our hearts. I cannot tell what he has done to you, dear friend, but I do trust that whatever has happened has been opening the soil, so that the good seed may drop in. It was the Spirit of God who did it, whatever the instrument may have been, and Lydia's heart was "opened."

Opened to what? To attend. "She attended unto the things which were spoken of Paul."

So, first, her heart was opened *to listen very intently.* She wanted to catch every word. She did as some of you do, put her hand to her ear, for fear she should not hear all that was spoken. There are many ways of listening. Some people listen with both their ears, allowing it to go in at one ear and out at the other; like that wit who, when he was being seriously spoken to, and yet seemed very inattentive, at length wearied the friend who was discoursing. "I am afraid it is not doing you much good," he said. "No," came the reply, "but I think it will do this gentleman some good," pointing to one who sat beside him, "for as it has gone in at this side it has gone out at the other." Oh, how I wish that you had only one ear, so that the truth you hear could never get out again after it had once got in! Well did the Lord speak through Isaiah the prophet unto the people, "Hearken *diligently* unto me, and eat ye that which is good." Many people can listen for an hour or two to a scientific lecture, or a political speech, without feeling in the least weary; they can even go to the theater, and sit there a whole evening without dreaming of being tired; yet they complain if the sermon is a minute beyond the appointed time. They seem to endure the preaching as a sort of penance, scarcely hearing the words, or, at least, never imagining that the message can have any application to their own case.

Lydia's heart was so opened "that she attended"; that is, she listened to the word of salvation until she began *to desire it.* It is always a pleasure to entertain guests who relish the food placed before them; and it is a great joy to preach to those who are eagerly hungering after the truth. But how heartbreaking a task it is to keep continually praising the pearl of great price to those who know not its value, nor desire its beauty! Daniel was a man "greatly beloved"; the Hebrew word there employed means "a man of desires." He was not one of your conceited, self-satisfied individuals. He longed and yearned for better things than he had yet attained, and hence was "greatly beloved." God loves people to thirst after him, and to desire to know his love and power. Let us explain the gospel as we may, if there is no desire in the heart, our plainest messages are lost. A man said, about something he wished to make clear, "Why, it is as plain as A B C!" "Yes," said a third party, "but the man you are talking to is D E F." So, some of our hearers seem to turn away from the Word of God. But when a person says, "I want to find salvation; I want to get Christ this very day; and I am going to listen with the determination that I will find out the way of salvation"; surely, if the things spoken are the same things that Paul spoke of, few in that condition will go out of the house without finding salvation. Lydia's heart was opened to attend to the gospel, that is, to desire it.

But, next, her heart was opened to understand it. It is wonderful how little even well-educated people sometimes understand of the gospel when it is preached in the simplest manner. One is constantly being astounded by the misapprehensions that persons have as to the way of salvation. But Lydia had grasped the truth. "Thanks be to God," she said, "I see it. Jesus Christ suffered in our stead; and we, by an act of faith, accept him as our Substitute, and we are saved thereby. I have it. I never saw it before. I read about a paschal lamb, and the sprinkling of the blood, and the passing over of the houses where the blood was sprinkled. I could not quite make it out. Now I see, if the blood be sprinkled upon me, God will pass over me, according to his word, 'When I see the blood, I will pass over you.'" She attended unto the things which were spoken of Paul, so as to understand them.

But more than that; her heart was so opened that she attended to the gospel so as to accept it. "Ah!" she said, "now I understand it, I will have it. Christ for me! Christ for me! That blessed Substitute for sinners! Is that all I have to do, simply to trust him? Then I will trust him. Sink or swim, I will cast myself upon him now." She did so there and then. There was no hesitating. She believed what Paul said; that Jesus was the Son of God, the appointed propitiation for sin, and that whosoever believed on him should then and there be justified; and she did believe in him, and she was justified; as you will be, my friend, if you will believe in him at this moment. You, too, shall have immediate salvation, my dear sister sitting yonder, if you will come, like this Lydia of old, and just take Christ to be yours, and trust him now. She attended unto the things which were spoken of Paul, so that she accepted Christ.

Having done that, she went further: her heart was so won, that she was, by the Spirit, led to obey the word, and avow her faith. Paul told her that the gospel was this—"He that believeth and is baptized shall be saved." He said to her, "My commission is, 'Go ye into all the world, and preach the gospel to every creature. He that believeth and is baptized shall be saved.'" Perhaps she said, "But why must I be baptized?" He said, "As a testimony of your obedience to Christ, whom you take to be your Master and your Lord; and as a type of your being one with him in his burial. You are to be buried in water as he was buried in the tomb of Joseph; and you are to be raised up out of the water even as he rose again from the dead. This act is to be a token and type to you of your oneness with him in his death and burial and resurrection." What did Lydia say? Did she say, "Well, I think I must wait a little while: the water is cold"? Did she say, "I think I must ask about it; I must consider it"? No, not at all. Paul tells her that this is Christ's ordinance, and she at once replies, "Here am I, Paul, let me be baptized, and my servants, too, and all that belong to my household, for they also believe in Jesus Christ. Let us have the baptism at once." There and then "she was baptized, and her household." She did at once obey the heavenly message, and she became a baptized believer. She was not ashamed to confess Christ. She had not known him long; but what she did know of him was so blessed and joyous to her soul, that she would have said, if she had known the hymn—

> *Through floods and flames, if Jesus lead,*
> *I'll follow where he goes;*
> *"Hinder me not," shall be my cry,*
> *Though earth and hell oppose.*

You can imagine her saying, "Did he go down into the Jordan, and say, 'Thus it becometh us to fulfill all righteousness'? Then I will go where he leads the way, and be obedient to him, and say to all the world, 'I, too, am a follower of the crucified Christ.'"

Now, last, after Lydia was baptized, *she became an enthusiastic Christian.* She said to Paul, "You must come home with me. I know you have not anywhere to go. Come along; and there is your friend Silas. I have plenty of room for him; and Timothy too; and Luke also. We can make room for the four of you among the purple bales, or somewhere; but, at any rate, I have house room for you four, and I have heart room for forty thousand of you. I wish I could take in the whole church of God." Dear good woman that she was, she felt that she could not do too much for the men who had been made a blessing to her; for she regarded what she did to them as done to their Lord and Master. They might have said, "No, really, we cannot trouble you. You have the household. You have all this business to look after." "Yes," she would answer, "I know that. It is very kind of you to excuse yourselves; but you must come." "No," Paul might urge, "my dear good woman, I am going to find out some tent makers, and make tents with them. We will find a lodging where we have been." "Ah!" she would say, "but I mean to have you. You must come to my home." "She constrained us." She would probably put it thus: "Now, I shall not think that you fully believe in me if you do not come home with me. Come, you baptized me, and by that very act you professed that you considered that I was a true believer. If you do really believe it, come and stay in my house as long as you like, and I will make you as comfortable as ever I can."

So at last Paul yields to her constraint, and goes to her home. How glad they would all be, and what praise to Christ would rise from that household! I hope that the generous spirit, which glowed in the heart of the first convert in Europe, will always continue among the converts of Europe till the last day. I trust that when they are called not merely to entertain God's ministers, but to help all God's people of every sort, they may be ready and willing to do it for Christ's sake; for love shall fill them with a holy hospitality, and an earnest desire to bless the children of God. Love one another, brothers and sisters, and do good to one another, as you have opportunity; for so will you be worthy followers of Lydia, the first European convert, whose heart the Lord opened.

The Lord open your hearts, for his name's sake! Amen.

T*h*e Women in Rome: Romans,
but Not Romanists

Delivered at the Metropolitan Tabernacle, Newington. No. 1113.

> *I commend unto you Phebe our sister, which is a servant of the church which is at Cenchrea: that ye receive her in the Lord, as becometh saints, and that ye assist her in whatsoever business she hath need of you: for she hath been a succorer of many, and of myself also.*
>
> *Greet Priscilla and Aquila my helpers in Christ Jesus: who have for my life laid down their own necks: unto whom not only I give thanks, but also all the churches of the gentiles. Likewise greet the church that is in their house. Salute my well-beloved Epaenetus, who is the firstfruits of Achaia unto Christ.*
>
> *Greet Mary, who bestowed much labor on us. Salute Andronicus and Junia, my kinsmen, and my fellow prisoners, who are of note among the apostles, who also were in Christ before me. Greet Amplias my beloved in the Lord. Salute Urbane, our helper in Christ, and Stachys my beloved. Salute Apelles approved in Christ. Salute them which are of Aristobulus' household. Salute Herodion my kinsman.*
>
> *Greet them that be of the household of Narcissus, which are in the Lord. Salute Tryphena and Tryphosa, who labor in the Lord. Salute the beloved Persis, which labored much in the Lord. Salute Rufus chosen in the Lord, and his mother and mine. Salute Asyncritus, Phlegon, Hermas, Patrobas, Hermes, and the brethren which are with them. Salute Philologus, and Julia, Nereus, and his sister, and Olympas, and all the saints which are with them. Salute one another with a holy kiss. The churches of Christ salute you.*
> —ROMANS 16:1–16

This chapter contains Paul's loving salutation to the various Christians dwelling at Rome. Remember that it is an inspired passage: although it consists of Christian courtesies addressed to different individuals, yet it was written by an apostle, and written not as an ordinary letter but as a part of the inspired volume. Therefore there must be valuable matter in it; and though, when we read it, it may appear to be uninstructive, there must be edifying matter beneath the surface, because all Scripture is given by inspiration, and is meant to benefit us in one way or another. It shows to us one thing, at any rate, that Paul was of a most affectionate disposition, and that God did not select as the apostle of the gentiles a man of a coarse, unfeeling, selfish turn of mind. His memory, as well as his heart, must have been in good condition to remember so large a number of names, and these were but a few of his many beloved brethren and spiritual children all over the world whom he mentions by name in his other epistles. His warm heart, I doubt not, quickened his memory, and secured to his remembrance the form, condition, history, character, and name of each one of his friends. He loved them too well to forget them. Christians should love one another, and should bear one another's names upon their hearts, even as the great High Priest wears the names of all his saints upon his jeweled breastplate. A Christian because of the love he bears to others is ever anxious to please by courtesy, and desires never to pain by rudeness. Grace makes the servant of God to be in the highest sense a true gentleman. If we learn nothing more from this passage than the duty of acting lovingly and courteously the one to the other, we shall be all the better for it, for there is none too much tender consideration and gentle speech among professors at this time.

I. Beyond this, our text is singularly full of instructive matter, as I shall hope to show you. Without preface, let us notice first, that *this passage illustrates remarkably the various relations of families to the church.*

Note in the third verse that the apostle says, "Greet Priscilla and Aquila my helpers in Christ Jesus." Here you have a household, in which both the father and the mother, or say the husband and the wife, were joined to the church of God. What a happy circumstance was this! Their influence upon the rest of the household must have been very powerful, for when two loving hearts pull together, they accomplish wonders. What different associations cluster around the names of "Priscilla and Aquila" from those which are awakened by the words "Ananias and Sapphira"! There we have a husband and a wife conspiring in hypocrisy, and here a wife and a husband united in sincere devotion. Thrice happy are those who are not only joined in marriage, but are one in the Lord Jesus Christ; such marriages are made in heaven. This couple appear to have been advanced Christians, for they became instructors of others; and not merely teachers of the ignorant, but teachers of those who already knew much of the gospel, for they instructed young Apollos, an eloquent man and mighty in the Scriptures. They taught him the way of God more perfectly, and therefore we may be sure were deep-taught Christians themselves. We must usually look for our spiritual fathers and nursing mothers to those households where husband and wife are walking in the fear of God; they are mutually helpful, and therefore grow in grace beyond others.

I do not know why Paul in this case wrote "Priscilla and Aquila," thus placing the wife first, for in the Acts we read of them as Aquila and Priscilla. I should not wonder but he put them in order according to quality rather than according to the rule of sex. He named Priscilla first because she was first in energy of character and attainments in grace. There is a precedence which, in Christ, is due to the woman when she becomes the leader in devotion, and manifests the stronger mind in the things of God. It is well when nature and grace both authorize our saying "Aquila and Priscilla," but it is not amiss when grace outruns nature and we hear of "Priscilla and Aquila." Whether the wife be first or second matters little if both be truly the servants of God. Dear husband, is your wife unconverted? Never fail to pray for her. Good sister, have you not yet seen the partner of your joys brought in to be a partaker in grace? Never bow your knee for yourself without mentioning that beloved name before the throne of mercy. Pray unceasingly that your life companions may be converted to God. Priscilla and Aquila were tent makers, and were thus of the same trade with the apostle, who for this reason lodged with them at Corinth; they had lived in Rome at one time, but had been obliged to leave owing to a decree of Claudius which banished the Jews from the imperial city. When that decree was no longer carried out, they seem to have gone back to Rome, which from the vast awnings used in the great public buildings must have afforded a fine sphere for the tent-makers' craft. It is very likely that their occupation of tent making necessitated their having a large room in which to carry on their work, and therefore they allowed the Christians to meet in it. Paul spoke of the church that was in their house.

It is a great privilege when a Christian family can accommodate the church of God. It is well when they judge that the parlor will be honored by being used for a prayer meeting, and consider that the best room in the house is none too good for the servants of God to meet in. Such a dwelling becomes like the house of Obededom, where the ark of God tarried and left a permanent blessing behind.

To pass on; in the seventh verse you have another family. "Salute Andronicus and Junia, my kinsmen, and my fellow prisoners, who are of note among the apostles, who also were in Christ before me." Now, if I understand this passage right, we have here a case of two men, perhaps they are both male names, Andronicus and Junius, or else a husband and wife or a brother and sister—

Andronicus and Junia; but at any rate they represent part of a household, and part of a very remarkable household too, for they were kinsmen of Paul, and they were converted to God before Paul was, which interesting fact slips out quite incidentally. I have wondered in my own mind whether the conversion of his relatives helped to irritate Paul into his murderous fury against the church of Christ, whether when he saw Andronicus and Junia his relatives, converted to what he thought to be the superstition of Nazareth—whether that excited in him the desperate animosity which he displayed toward the Lord Jesus Christ. I may leave that as a matter of question, but I feel certain that the prayers of his two relations followed the young persecutor, and that if you were to look deep into the reason for the conversion of Saul of Tarsus on his way to Damascus, you would find it at the mercy seat in the prayers of Andronicus and Junia, his kinsmen, who were in Christ before him.

This should act as a great encouragement for all of you who desire the salvation of your households. Perhaps you have a relative who is very much opposed to the gospel of Jesus Christ; for that very reason pray the more importunately for him! There is nonetheless hope for him because of his zealous opposition, the man is evidently in a thoughtful condition, and the grace of God is able to turn his ignorant zeal to good account when his heart has been enlightened and renewed. There is something to be made out of a man who has enough stuff in him to be opposed to the gospel; a good sword will make a good plowshare. Out of persecutors God can make apostles. Nowadays the world swarms with milksops of men who neither believe in the gospel, nor thoroughly disbelieve it; they are neither for nor against, neither true to God nor the devil. Such men of straw will never be worth their salt even if they should become converted. An out-and-out honest hater of the gospel is the man who with one touch of divine grace may be made into an equally sincere lover of the truth which once he despised. Pray on, pray hard, pray believingly for your relatives, and you may live to see them occupy the pulpit and preach the faith which now they strive to overturn. It is a happy and hopeful token for good to a family when a part of the household is joined to the church of God.

Passing on again, we meet with a third family in relation to the church, but in this case the master of the house was not a Christian—I suppose not, from the tenth verse, "Salute them which are of Aristobulus' household." Not "Salute Aristobulus," no, but they that are of his household. Why leave Aristobulus out? It is just possible that he was dead, but far more likely that he was unsaved. He was left out of the apostle's salutation because he had left himself out; he was no believer, and therefore there could be no Christian salutation sent to him. Alas for him, the kingdom of God was near to him, yes, in his house, and yet he was unblessed by it! Am I not speaking to a man in this condition? Where are you, Aristobulus? That is not your name, perhaps, but your character is the same as that of this unregenerate Roman, whose family knew the Lord. I might speak in God's name good words and comfortable words to your wife and to your children, but I could not so speak to you, Aristobulus! The Lord sends a message of grace to your dear child, to your beloved wife, but not to you; for you have not given your heart to him. I will pray for you, and I am happy to know that those of your household who love the Lord are interceding for you both day and night. It is a hopeful connection that you have with the church, though perhaps you do not care much about it. Yet be sure of this—the kingdom of God has come near unto you. This fact will involve dreadful responsibility, if it does not lead to your salvation, for if like Capernaum you are exalted to heaven by your privileges, it will be all the more dreadful to be thrust down to hell. It is a sad thing in a family when one is taken and another left. Oh, think you how wretched will be your condition if you continue in unbelief, for when your child is in heaven and your wife is in heaven, and you see your mother who is there already, and you yourself are cast far off into hell, you will remember that you were called but refused, were bidden but would not come. You shut your eyes to the light and would not see; you rejected Christ and perished willfully, a suicide to your own soul.

Another instance of this, and I think a worse one, is to be seen further on in our text where the apostle speaks of the "household of Narcissus," in the eleventh verse: "Greet them that be of the household of Narcissus, which are in the Lord." Now I fancy that Narcissus was the master of the house, and that the converts in the house were his servants or his slaves. There was a Narcissus in the days of Nero, who was put to death by Nero's successor. He was Nero's favorite, and when I have said that, you may conclude that he was a man of no very commendable character. It is said of him that he was extremely rich, and that he was as bad as he was rich. Yet while the halls of the house of Narcissus echoed to blasphemous songs, and while luxurious gluttony, mingled with unbridled licentiousness, made his mansion a very hell, there was a saving salt in the servants' hall and the slaves' dormitory. Perhaps under the stairs, in the little place where the slave crept in to sleep, prayer was made unto the living God, and when the master little dreamed of it, the servants about his house sang hymns in praise of one Jesus Christ, the anointed Savior, whom they adored as the Son of God. Wonderful are the ways of electing love, which passes by the rich and great to have respect unto the man of low degree.

It may be there is some bad master within reach of my voice; he is himself utterly irreligious, but yet in his house there are those who wait upon the

Lord in prayer. He who blacks your shoes may be one of the beloved of the Lord, while you who wear them may be without God and without hope in the world. The little maid in your house fears the Lord, though you are forgetful of his praises; an angel received unawares waits upon you at table. There was a good man some years ago who used to sit up for a certain king of ours of wretched memory—let his name rot! This king was called a gentleman, but other titles might better describe him. While his master would be rioting, this man was communing with God, and reading Boston's *Crook in the Lot,* or some such blessed book, to while away the weary hours. There are still at this day in the halls of the great, and wicked, and in the abodes of transgressors of all classes, God's hidden ones, who are the salt of the earth, and cry unto God day and night against the iniquity of their masters. There shall be an inquisition concerning all this; the godly shall not always be forgotten, the golden nuggets shall not always lie hidden in the dust. Think you, O masters, how will it fare with you when your humblest menials shall be crowned with glory and you yourselves shall be driven into the blackness of darkness forever? Seek ye also the Lord, ye great ones, and he will be found of you.

We cannot afford to stay with Narcissus. Let us turn to the twelfth verse, and you have another instance of a family in connection with Christ's people: "Salute Tryphena and Tryphosa, who labor in the Lord"—I suppose two sisters, the names sound very like it. Where were their brothers? Where was their father? Where was their mother? "Tryphena and Tryphosa," how often have I seen them in the church, two humble, earnest, faithful women, the lone ones of the family, and all the rest far off from God! O brother, let not your sister go to heaven alone. Father, if your daughters be children of God, do not yourself remain his enemy. Let the examples of your godly children help you, O parents, to be yourselves decided for the Redeemer! Hail to you, you gracious women who keep each other company on the road to heaven! The Lord make you a comfort to one another. May you shine both here and hereafter like twin stars, shedding a gentle radiance of holiness on all around. There is work for you in your heavenly Father's house, and though you may not be called to public preaching, yet, in spheres appropriate, you may with much acceptance "labor in the Lord."

Further down, in the fifteenth verse, we have a brother and his sister, "Nereus, and his sister." It is pleasant to see the stronger and weaker sex thus associated. "They grew in beauty side by side" in the field of nature, and now they bloom together in the garden of grace. It is a sweet relationship, that of a godly brother and sister; they are as the rose and the lily in the same posy; but had they no other relatives? Were there no others remaining of their kindred? Had they no trouble in spirit concerning others dear to them? Depend upon it, they often prayed together, and sighed because their relatives were not in Christ, for concerning all the rest of the family the record is blank. God hear your prayers, my dear friends, when you, like Nereus and his sister, unite in brotherly prayer and sisterly intercession.

One other very beautiful instance of a family connection with the church is in the thirteenth verse: "Salute Rufus chosen in the Lord, and his mother and mine." Now, this is a case of a mother and her son. I would not wish to say anything that is far-fetched, but I think there is no vain conjecture in supposing that this good woman was the wife of Simon the Cyrenian, who carried the cross of Christ. You will remember he is said by Mark to be the father of Alexander and Rufus, two persons who evidently were well known in the church of God at that time. And here we have familiar mention of Rufus and his mother. Whether she was the wife of Simon or not, she seems to have been a kind, good, lovable soul, one of those dear matrons who are at once an ornament and a comfort to the Christian church; and such an excellent woman was she that Paul when he calls her the mother of Rufus adds, "and mine"—she had been like a mother to him. I do not wonder that such choice mothers have choice sons—"chosen in the Lord." If those whom we deeply love carry their religion about with them set in a frame of affectionate cheerfulness, it is hard to resist the charms of their lovely piety. When a godly woman is a tender mother, it is no wonder if her sons, Rufus and Alexander, become believers in Jesus Christ too, for their mother's love and example draw them toward Jesus.

There is a legend connected with Rufus and Alexander; I have never read it, but I have seen it set forth in glowing colors by an artist in a cathedral in Belgium. I saw a series of paintings which represented Christ bearing his cross through the streets of Jerusalem, and among the crowd the artist has placed a countryman looking on, and carrying with him his mattock and spade, as if he had just come into the town from laboring in the fields. In the next picture this countryman is evidently moved to tears by seeing the cruelties practiced upon the Redeemer, and he shows his sympathy so plainly that the cruel persecutors of our Lord who are watching the spectators observe it, and gather angrily around him. The countryman's two boys are there too, Alexander and Rufus; Rufus is the boy with the red head; he is ardent and sanguine, bold and outspoken, and you can see that one of the rough men has just been cuffing him about the head for showing sympathy with the poor cross-bearing Savior. The next picture represents the father taken and compelled to bear the cross, while Alexander holds his father's pick, and Rufus is carrying his father's spade, and they are going along close by the Lord Jesus, pitying him greatly. If they cannot bear the cross, they will at least help their father by carrying his tools.

Of course it is but a legend, but who marvels if Alexander and Rufus saw their father carry Christ's cross so well, that they, too, should afterward count it their glory to be followers of the crucified One, so that Paul should say when he wrote down the name of Rufus, that he was a choice man, for so we may translate of the passage, "chosen in the Lord," or, "the choice one of the Lord"! He was a distinguished Christian, with great depth of Christian experience, and in all respects a fit descendant of a remarkable father and mother.

Thus have we observed the different ways in which families come in contact with Christ, and I pray God that every family here may make up a part of the whole family in heaven and earth, which is named by the name of Jesus. May all your sons and your daughters, your brethren and your sisters, your servants and kinsfolk, but chiefly yourselves, take up the cross of Jesus, and be saved in the Lord with an everlasting salvation.

II. The interesting passage before us shows *what are points of interest among Christians.*

Now, among worldly people points of interest are very many and characteristic. In any worldly community one very important point of interest is, how much is a man worth? That is an important point with Christians, too, in the right sense, but the worldly man means by that, "How much money has the man scraped into his own till?" He may have gained his pelf in the worst way in the world, but nobody takes account of that, the one all-important question among mammonites is, "What is his balance at the bankers?" Now Paul does not in his salutation make a single reference to any one on account of his wealth or poverty. He does not say, "To Philologus, our brother, who has £10,000 a year, and Julia, our sister, who keeps a carriage and pair"—nothing of the sort. He makes no account of position or property, except so far as those may be implied in the service which each person rendered to the cause of God. Neither is there any allusion made to their holding important offices under government, or being what is called exceedingly respectable people or persons of good family. The points of interest with Paul, as a Christian, were very different from those.

The first matter of which he made honorable mention was their service for the church. Phebe, in the first verse, is "a servant of the church, which is at Cenchrea. She hath been a succorer of many, and of myself also." It is a distinction and honor among Christians to be allowed to serve, and the most menial employment for the church of God is the most honorable. Every man who seeks honor after God's fashion seeks it by being abased, by undertaking that ministry which will involve the most self-denial, and will secure the greatest reproach. Foremost in the ranks of the divine peerage are the martyrs, because they were the most despised; they suffered most, and they have the most of honor. So Phebe shall have her name inscribed in this golden book of Christ's nobility, because she is the servant of the church, and because, in being such, she succored the poor and needy. I doubt not she was a nurse among the poorer Christians, or as some call them, a deaconess, for, in the olden time, it was so, that the elder women who had need were maintained by the church, and in return occupied themselves with the nursing of sick believers; and it were well if such were the case again, and if the old office could be revived.

Another special point for remark among Christians is their labor. Kindly refer to your Bibles, and read the sixth verse: "Greet Mary, who bestowed much labor on us." This is the sixth Mary mentioned in the Bible. She appears to have been one who laid herself out to help the minister. "She bestowed much labor *on us*," says the apostle, or, "on me"—she was one of those useful women who took personal care of the preacher, because she believed the life of God's servant to be precious, and that he should be cared for in his many labors and perils. What she did for Paul and his fellow laborers we are not told, but it was something which cost her effort, amounting to "much labor." She loved much and therefore toiled much. She was "always abounding in the work of the Lord." Sister Mary, imitate your namesake.

Then follow the two good women, Tryphena and Tryphosa, of whom it is said, "who labor in the Lord," and Persis, of whom it is written she "labored *much* in the Lord." I do not suppose Tryphena and Tryphosa were angry because the apostle made this distinction, but it is certainly a very plain and explicit one; the first two "labored," but Persis "labored much." So there are distinctions and degrees in honor among believers, and these are graduated by the scale of service done. It is an honor to labor for Christ; it is a still greater honor to labor much. If, then, any, in joining the Christian church, desire place or position, honor or respect, the way to it is this—labor, and labor much. Persis had probably been a slave, and was of a strange race from the far-off land of Persia, but she was so excellent in disposition that she is called "the beloved Persis," and for her indefatigable industry she receives signal mention. Among believers the rewards of affectionate respect are distributed according to the self-denying service which is rendered to Christ and to his cause. May all of us be helped to labor much, by the power of the Holy Spirit.

At the same time, another point of interest is *character*, for as I have already said, Rufus in the thirteenth verse is said to be "chosen in the Lord," which cannot allude to his election, since all the rest were chosen too, but must mean that he was a choice man in the Lord, a man of peculiarly sweet spirit, a devout man, a man who walked with God, a man well instructed in the things of God, and a man whose practice was equal to his knowledge. "Salute" him, says the apostle. He who would be noted in the church of God must have real character: there must be holiness unto the Lord, there must be faith; a man must have it said of him, "he is full of faith and of the Holy Ghost." This shall get him commemoration, but nothing else will do it. Apelles is described as "approved in Christ," a tried, proved, and experienced believer. Christians value those who have been tested and found faithful; tried saints are had in honor among us.

Character, you see, is the one noteworthy point in the society of the church, and nothing else. Yes, there is one thing else. I find one person here noted in the church as a person around whom great interest centered, because of the time of his conversion. It is in the fifth verse: "Salute my well-beloved Epaenetus, who is the firstfruits of Achaia unto Christ." You know what that means. When Paul began to preach in Achaia, Epaenetus was one of his first converts, and while every minister feels a peculiar attachment to all his converts, he has the tenderest memory of the first ones. What parent does not prize above all others his first child? I can speak from experience. I remember well the first woman who professed to be brought to Christ when I began to preach the gospel. I have the house in my mind's eye at this moment, and though I cannot say that it was a picturesque cottage, yet it will always interest me. Great was the joy I felt when I heard that peasant's story of repentance and of faith. She died, and went to heaven a short time after her conversion, being taken away by consumption, but the remembrance of her gave me more comfort than I have ordinarily received by the recollection of twenty or even a hundred converts since then. She was a precious seal set upon my ministry to begin with, and to encourage my infant faith. Some of you were the firstfruits of my ministry in London, in Park Street, and very precious people you were. How gladly would I see some of you in this tabernacle become the firstfruits of this present year; there would be something very interesting about you, for it would encourage us all through the year. If you are brought to seek the Lord just now, I shall always view you with love, and think of you as I read this chapter so full of names. I shall be as thankful for those born to God tonight as for those regenerated at any other time, for my heart is earnestly going out after you.

So I have shown you that there are points of interest about individual persons in the church of God, and what they are.

III. But as time has fled, though I have much to say I must close with the third point, which is this. This long passage *reveals the general love which exists* (must I say which ought to exist?) *in the church of God*.

For, first, the whole passage shows the love of the apostle toward the saints and brethren at Rome. He would not have taken the trouble to write all this to them if he had not really loved them. And it shows that there were Christians in those days who were full of love to each other. Their salutation, the holy kiss, marked their fervor of love, for they were by no means a people given to use outward signs unless they had something to express thereby. Oh, that Christian love reigned among all Christians now to a greater extent! "Ah!" says one, "there is very little of it." I know you, my friend, very well indeed; you are the man who is forever grumbling at others for want of love, when the truth is that you are destitute of it yourself. I always find that those who say there is no love among Christians now, judge by what they see at home in their own hearts, for those who love Christians believe that Christians also love one another; and you shall find the man of loving heart, though he will say, "I wish there were more love," will never be the man to say that there is none. Brethren, it is a lie that there is no love among Christians: we love each other still, and we will show it by the grace of God even more, if the Spirit of God shall help us.

Note according to this passage the early Christians were accustomed to show their love to one another by practical help; for in the second verse Paul says of Phebe, "Receive her in the Lord, as becometh saints, and assist her in whatever business she hath need of you, for she hath been a succorer of many, and of myself also." I do not think that the apostle alluded to any church business, but to her own business, whatever that may have been; she may have had monies to gather in, or some complaint to make at headquarters of an exacting tax gatherer. I do not know what it was; and it is quite as well that Paul did not tell us. It is no part of an apostle's commission to tell us other people's business; but whatever business it was, if any Christian in Rome could help her, he was to do so. And so if we can help our Christian brethren in any way or shape, "as much as lieth in us" we are to endeavor to do it. Our love must not lie in words alone or it will be unsubstantial as the air. Mark you, you are not called upon to become sureties for your brethren, or to put your name on the back of bills for them; do that for nobody, for you have an express word in

Scripture against it—"He that hateth suretyship is sure," says Solomon, and "he that is a surety shall smart for it." I could wish that some brethren had been wise enough to have recollected the teaching of Scripture upon that point, for it might have saved them a sea of troubles. But for your fellow Christians, do anything that is lawful for you to do, do it for one another out of love to your common Lord, bearing one another's burdens, and so fulfilling the law of Christ.

We are bound to show our love to each other, even when it involves great sacrifices; for in the fourth verse the apostle says of Priscilla and Aquila that for his life "they laid down their own necks." They went into great peril to save the apostle. Such love exists in our churches still. This is denied, but I know it is so. I know Christians who could say honestly that if their minister's life could be spared, they would be willing to die in his stead. It has been said by some here, and I have heard it, and have felt that they who said it meant what they said. I know the prayer has gone up from some lips here that they might sooner die than I should. When your pastor has been in danger, many of you have lovingly declared that if your life could stand for his life, it should be freely rendered before God. Christians love each other still, and they make sacrifices for one another still. I speak this to the honor of many of you, that your love to your pastor has not been in word only, but in deed and in truth; and for this may the Lord reward you.

Christian love in those days had an intense respect for those who had suffered for Christ. Read the seventh verse. Paul says that Andronicus and Junia were his fellow prisoners, and he speaks of them with special unction because of that. No one was thought more of among the early Christians than the prisoner for Christ, the martyr, or the almost martyr. Why, there was even too much made of such sufferers, so that while Christians were in prison, expecting to be martyred, they received attentions which showed almost too great a reverence for their persons. Now, brethren, whenever any man in these times is laughed at for following Christ fully, or ridiculed for bearing an honest testimony for the truth, do not be ashamed of him and turn your backs upon him. Such a man may not expect you to give him double honor, but he may claim that you shall stand shoulder to shoulder with him, and not be ashamed of the reproach which he is called to bear for Christ his Lord.

So was it with the church in the olden time, the men who went first in suffering were also first in their love and esteem. They never failed to own that they were brothers to the man who was doomed to die; on the contrary, the Christians of the apostolic times used to do what our Protestant forefathers did in England. The young Christian people of the church, when there was a martyr to be put to death, would go and stand with tears in their eyes to see him die, and what think you for? To learn the way! One of them said when his father asked him why he stole out to see his pastor burned, "Father, I did it that I might learn the way"; and he did learn it so well that when his turn came he burned as well, and triumphed in God as gloriously as his minister had done. Learn the way, young man, to bear reproach. Look at those who have been lampooned and satirized, and say, "Well, I will learn how to take my turn when my turn comes, but as God helps me, I will speak for the truth faithfully and boldly."

Again, that love always honored workers. For Paul says, "Mary, who bestowed much labor on us"; and he speaks of the laborers over and over again, with intense affection. We ought to love much those who do much for Christ, whether they are Christian men or women. Alas, I know some who, if anybody does a little more than another, straightaway begin to pick holes in his coat. "Mr. So-and-So is very earnest, but—ah—yes! And Mrs. So-and-So, yes—God blesses her, but—but—yes." For want of anything definite to say, they shrug their shoulders and insinuate. This is the reverse of the spirit of Paul, for he recognized holy industry and praised it. Dear friend, do not become a faultfinder; it is as bad a trade as a pickpocket's. Till you can do better, hold your tongue! Did you ever know a man or woman whom God blessed that was perfect? If God were to work by perfect instruments, the instruments would earn a part of the glory. Take it for granted that we are all imperfect; but when you have taken that for granted, love those who serve God well, and never allow anybody to speak against them in your hearing. Silence cavilers at once by saying, "God honors them; and whom God honors, I dare not despise!" We cannot be wrong in putting our honor where God is pleased to place his.

Still, Christian love in Paul's days—though it loved all the saints—had its specialties. Read down the chapter, and you will find Paul saying, "my well-beloved Epaenetus," "Amplias my beloved in the Lord," "Stachys my beloved." All these were persons whom he especially esteemed. There were some whom he liked better than others, and you must not blame yourself if you judge some Christians to be better than others, and if you therefore love them better; for even the Lord himself had a disciple whom he loved more than the rest. I desire to love all the Lord's people, but there are some of them whom I can love best while I know the least about them, and feel the most comfort in them when I have not seen them for a month or so. There are Christian people whom you could live with in heaven comfortably enough, but it is a severe trial to bear with them on earth, although you feel that they are good people, and since God puts up with them, so ought you. Since there are such peculiar people, do not be always getting in their way to irritate them—leave them alone, and seek peace by keeping out of their way. Brethren, let us love one another; by all means let us love one another, for love is of God. But let us all try to be lovable, so as to make this duty as easy as possible to our brethren.

Once more, love among Christians in those early days was wont to respect seniority in spiritual life; for Paul speaks of some who were in Christ before himself. Among us I hope there always will be profound esteem for those who have been longest in Christ, for those who have stood the test of years, for our aged members, the elders and the matrons among us. Reverence to old age is but a natural duty, but reverence to advanced Christians is a privilege as well. Let it always be so among us.

And the last word is this: love to all Christians should make us recollect even the most obscure and mean members of the church. When the apostle Paul wrote, "Salute Asyncritus, Phlegon, Hermas," why, many of us say, "whoever were these good people?" And when he goes on to mention, "Patrobas, Hermes," we ask, "And who were they? What did these men attempt or perform? Is that all? Philologus, who was he? And who was Olympas? We know next to nothing about those good people." They were like the most of us, commonplace individuals; but they loved the Lord, and therefore as Paul recollected their names he sent them a message of love which has become embalmed in the holy Scriptures. Do not let us think of the distinguished Christians exclusively so as to forget the rank and file of the Lord's army. Do not let the eye rest exclusively upon the front rank, but let us love all whom Christ loves; let us value all Christ's servants. It is better to be God's dog than to be the devil's darling. It were better to be the meanest Christian than to be the greatest sinner. If Christ is in them, and they are in Christ, and you are a Christian, let your heart go out toward them.

And now, finally, may grace, mercy, and peace be with all them that love our Lord Jesus Christ; and may we labor to promote unity and love among his people. The God of peace shall bruise Satan under our feet shortly. May we therefore in patience possess our souls. Oh, that those who are not yet numbered among the people of the Lord may be brought in through faith in Jesus Christ to his glory! Amen.

Index to Key Scriptures